FROM THE THIRTIES
TO THE EIGHTIES

INTRODUCTION BY

E. NELSON BRIDWELL

EDITOR, DC COMICS INC.

CROWN PUBLISHERS, INC., NEW YORK

Published by Crown Publishers, Inc., One Park Avenue, New York, New York 10016
and simultaneously in Canada by General Publishing Company Limited
SUPERMAN, the SUPERMAN Character, S in Shield Device are trademarks of DC
Comics Inc.
Manufactured in the United States of America.

Library of Congress Cataloging in Publication Data

Superman (Comic strip)
    Superman, from the thirties to the eighties.

    Rev. ed. of: Superman, from the thirties to the seventies. 1971.
    Bibliography: p.
    I. Title.
PN6728.S9   1983   741.5′973   83-10086

ISBN: 0-517-55100-4
10 9 8 7 6 5 4 3 2 1
First Edition

CONTENTS

FOREWORD

He's better known than the president of the United States, more familiar to school children than Abraham Lincoln. And although only a handful of people ever achieve international acclaim, he not only is hailed the world over but also retains honorary citizenship in every country on our globe. And yet this hero, this champion of justice whose earnestness and passion for right irradiate his entire being, is not an ordinary human nor even an extraordinary one. Instead he is Superman, a fictional character who lives so vividly in our imaginations that we suspend our incredulity and believe for the reading and rereading of a comic book, while his voice still echoes in our radios, until the credits roll on our television sets or the lights come on again in a movie house that he is flesh and blood.

Superman was the first of the superheroes—and now they number close to two thousand—ever to see print. His fabulous success spawned an entire industry, and yet every comic book fan knew and knows that he is not only the first but also the best. It is a given that without Superman there would be no other costumed superpowered heroes. Who else has his enthralling range of powers? And who else so purely embodies male consciousness at its highest, most protective, most intensely spiritual peak? Superman is the sun-god, flooding us with the warmth of his being, assuring us that he shall extract from a chaotic world fairness, stability, sanity, and the hope of a more just future.

He has been called the Action Ace, the Man of Steel, and also the Man of Tomorrow. As the decades roll back into history, the last epithet feels more and more appropriate. Superman is a masterwork of dream fulfillment, the indelible fusion of myth and desire. Even as an infant he began his perilous solo journey that was followed by years of training and self-mastery that led eventually to his unassailable leadership. Like Moses, like Odysseus, like every abandoned baby of heroic myth, he was cast afloat by his parents only to survive and become a savior himself. Yet the intricate beauty of Superman is not simply that he is everything heroic we might desire to be, but also everything we are. Superman is equal parts Clark Kent: Clark, the bumbling, awkward social failure; Clark, the sincere, hardworking, most loyal of all friends. How we wish that someone (Lois?) might see through our imperfect exteriors to the secret, special person below.

That Superman only grows in popularity is no surprise. He combines our most basic primal dreams, like the power to fly, with our everyday, every-person wishes—to be loved for our true selves. It also is not surprising that two teenagers (in that strangely potent limbo before over-consciousness deprives us of our ability to dream "ridiculous" dreams or wish "immature" wishes) should have created this first god of a new mythology: definitely American, not borrowed, wholly our own.

Jerry Siegel and Joe Shuster were two boys in Cleveland who clung to their vision of Superman until finally, when both were young men in their twenties, it became reality. Jerry and Joe, we thank you not just for your dream but for your fortitude. You not only gave this country its own mythic heritage but also shared with all of us who have loved Superman the joy and power of imagination.

Jenette Kahn

President and Publisher,
DC Comics Inc.

8

INTRODUCTION

by E. Nelson Bridwell

In the ninth year of the Great Depression, the streets of America were still lined with the jobless, the homeless, and the hungry. In Europe, Adolf Hitler took over Austria, and though Chamberlain assured us there would be "peace in our time," visions of Der Führer's jackbooted soldiers were hardly encouraging.

It was a time when Hollywood musicals helped take the public's mind off the grim realities of life. A time when heroes were sought—and found—in radio, movies, comic strips, pulps, comic books.

It was 1938, and the greatest of heroes was about to make his debut.

But the story actually begins several years earlier, with two young pals growing up in Cleveland, Ohio, reading the science-fiction magazines of the day and trying to create their own stories. Jerry Siegel wanted to be a writer, while Joseph Shuster had artistic aspirations. They created their own fanzine, called *Science Fiction*, and the January 1933 issue contained a short story called "Reign of the Superman." Jerry wrote it while Joe did the accompanying illustrations.

The character was a man who gained fantastic mental powers but misused them. He had only one power the later Superman would possess: telescopic vision. He could see from Earth what was happening on Mars!

The story was written in 1932, and in the following year, Jerry thought of turning it into a comic strip. The idea never succeeded. It needed more thought.

One hot July night in 1934, Jerry lay in bed, unable to sleep, and began to think of doing a different kind of Superman—one clad in a colorful, tight-fitting costume, like those depicted by Frank R. Paul and other sci-fi illustrators. One with a secret identity—as a mild-mannered reporter. Idea after idea came. With the dawn, Jerry didn't wait for breakfast before hurrying over to Joe's house to tell him of the new concept.

Together, they designed the costume, and Joe drew up strips from Jerry's scripts. All they had to do was sell them.

Publisher after publisher turned them down. Some were interested but wanted to change the character or do a limited story.

At the time, most comic books were simply collections of newspaper strips. Then, in 1935, Malcolm Wheeler-Nicholson began publishing all-new comic books, beginning with *New Fun Comics* (later *More Fun*) and *New Comics* (later *New Adventure Comics*, then *Adventure Comics*). He was interested in using Superman, but Siegel and Shuster were dubious about his company at the time so turned him down. However, they did agree to create new features for him. "Federal Men," "Doctor Occult," "Radio Squad," "Henri Duval"—they churned them out but pinned their main hopes on the still unsold Superman.

An interesting digression was in the January 1937 issue of *New Adventure Comics*. The "Federal Men" strip speculated on crime-fighting in the future space age. Jerry gave the space detective in the story a name derived from his: Jor-L. He would later give the same name (since altered to Jor-El) to Superman's father!

Meanwhile, Wheeler-Nicholson sold out to Harry Donenfeld, who proceeded to publish the first all-new comic book with a theme: *Detective Comics*. Siegel and Shuster created two new features for it: "Slam Bradley" and "Spy." The success of this mag caused Donenfeld to follow it up the next year with *Action Comics*. He only needed a lead feature.

He called M. C. Gaines, father of the comic book, who was then working at the McClure Syndicate. A strip had been called to Gaines's attention by Sheldon Mayer, and this Gaines recommended to Donenfeld. It was "Superman"!

And so the publishing company whose offer they had once rejected did eventually publish the Man of Steel. The outfit's name became DC for *Detective Comics*.

Superman made his debut on the cover of *Action Comics #1*, cover-dated June 1938. It was a textbook example of the virtues of perseverance; it took *four years* from Siegel and Shuster's creation of the character to Superman's first appearance in print!

Audience response was immediate! *Action Comics* meant plenty of action on the newsstands. The book was a hit, but no one was really sure why until a survey showed it was Superman who was selling the magazine. Within a year, Superman earned his own book, which met with equally wild success.

What was the appeal? Superman's exploits held something for everyone. There was his science-fiction background and his ancestry on the planet Krypton. There was high adventure in his incredible feats of strength and daring, each one topping the last. There was a maddening romantic triangle, wherein Clark Kent, reporter for the Daily Planet, fell in love with coworker Lois Lane, who, it seemed, had eyes only for Clark's secret identity as Superman! How perplexing! Clark was his own competition for Lois's affections, his own chief rival.

Further, Clark had an "Everyman" quality. He was easy to relate to and brought the lofty Superman down to Earth. Clark's presence assured the reader that every man had a Superman locked inside him.

Superman's popularity rose and was by no means confined to comic books. The same year *Superman Comics #1* reached the stands, a daily newspaper strip featuring the Man of Steel was launched as well. Then, in 1940, the radio waves rang with the now legendary words:

> *Faster than a speeding bullet!*
> *More powerful than a locomotive!*
> *Able to leap tall buildings at a single bound!*
> *Look! Up in the sky!*
> *It's a bird!*
> *It's a plane!*
> *IT'S SUPERMAN!*

Yes, it's Superman. Strange visitor from another planet, who came to Earth with powers and abilities far beyond those of mortal men. Superman, who can change the course of mighty rivers, bend steel in his bare hands, and who, disguised as Clark Kent, mild-mannered reporter for a great metropolitan newspaper, fights a never-ending battle for truth, justice, and the American way!

The Mutual Network began broadcasting *The Adventures of Superman* for fifteen minutes every weekday. In order to distinguish Clark Kent from his mighty alter ego, it was intended to have the two sides of the same character played by different actors. However, a fellow named Clayton Collyer proved equal to the necessary voice change, doing Clark as a tenor and Superman as a baritone. He would demonstrate this change to a radio audience by dropping his voice in midsentence:

> "This is a job
> for
> SUPERMAN!"

By this time, Superman had begun to change. He was conceived as a man who could leap great distances. Not long afterward, though, he was literally flying. His strength increased and so did his speed. Once only able to outrace a train, he finally, in the late forties, began traveling through time by exceeding the speed of light! And his invulnerability grew, too. "Nothing less than a bursting shell could penetrate his skin" in 1939; by World War II he was shrugging off bursting shells as if they were bursting soap bubbles. At the end of the war, he was surviving atomic blasts!

The early Superman had no supersenses. In one story, he had to crash through a roof to find the man he suspected was in that certain house. The invention of X-ray vision proved to be a great roof-saver.

The account of Superman's origin depicted him as simply more advanced than Earthmen, but this, too, was soon altered, and it was later explained that Earth's size and gravity were far less than that of Krypton; hence, on Earth, a Kryptonian could do fantastic things. He could lift weights and make incredible leaps. Even after Superman began to fly, this same explanation was given.

Superman, like most heroes of the late thirties, had an extra reason for keeping his identity a secret. He was wanted by the police for taking the law into his own hands! Before long, however, he stopped dealing out justice himself and started working *with* the police. After all, the world's greatest hero couldn't be an outlaw!

Between 1941 and 1943, Paramount brought out seventeen animated cartoons of the Man of Tomorrow, with Clayton "Bud" Collyer again doing the voice in the first half dozen. And in 1942, Superman made his first appearance between hardcovers, in a novel by George Lowther entitled (what else?) *Superman*.

Jimmy, the office boy, who got his first byline in the Archer tale reprinted in this book, was seized upon by the radio writers who wanted a boy their audience could identify with. So Jimmy Olsen, cub reporter, became a feature of the show. Jimmy was featured a good deal more there and in the newspaper strip than in comic books in the early forties.

It wasn't long before the comics spun off Superman in another direction. In the January-February issue of *More Fun Comics*, a new feature began its lengthy run: *Superboy*, relating the adventures of Superman when he was a boy. This series went into the details of our hero's youth, his boyhood in the all-American town of Smallville, and his relationship with his foster parents, Jonathan and Martha Kent. (Actually, the Kents appeared so seldom in early stories that it wasn't until Superboy got his own magazine that they acquired first names!)

It stood to reason that pitting the nearly omnipotent Superman against the garden-variety burglar, hijacker, and bank robber would soon grow tiresome, if not actually seem downright unfair. The odds needed to be made more even! Superman had to fight someone who ranked in his class, someone who could at least give our hero a healthy workout!

It was only natural, then, that the first superhero should encounter supervillains! The first was the Ultra-Humanite, whose awesome brain outlived his body by being transplanted into the skull of a beautiful actress. But he disappeared when Luthor came on the scene—the criminal scientist who was to become Superman's archenemy. Though sporting a crop of red hair at first, Luthor later became bald and bore a striking resemblance to the original appearance of the Ultra-Humanite. Luthor finally got a first name in 1960 in a story reprinted in this book entitled "How Luthor met Superboy." He has since been Lex (short for Alexis).

Other villains followed: The Prankster, The Toyman, The Puzzler, and Mr. Mxyztplk (or Mxyzptlk as it was later spelled) among them. Mxyztplk's first encounter with Superman is included in this volume.

The radio show gave Superman another nemesis: Kryptonite. (There is evidence that Siegel and Shuster created it for an unpublished Superman comic-book story in which Lois was to learn Superman's identity!)

It began innocuously enough. It was time for Bud Collyer to take a two-week vacation. But Collyer's distinctive voices were vital to the show. How could they go on the air without either Superman or Clark Kent in evidence?

The writers racked their brains for the answer and came up with Kryptonite. This substance was the debris of Superman's home planet, changed by that world's explosion into a radioactive element that could weaken, or kill, only a native of Krypton.

The plot called for the villains to discover the Kryptonite and hold Superman captive with it. For two weeks, Superman's dialogue was comprised entirely of the moans and groans of another actor, portraying him suffering from the effects of the deadly debris!

But before Kryptonite reached the comics, Superman had returned to the silver screen in two Columbia serials: *Superman* (1948) and *Atom Man vs. Superman* (1950). This latter picture was the first to feature Luthor as the villain. Later came a feature film, *Superman and the Mole Men* (1952).

In 1949, Superboy had his own comic book. In 1954, Jimmy Olsen became the star of his own magazine.

Radio was giving way to television, and a new series of *The Adventures of Superman* began on TV starring George Reeves. Some scripts gave Superman odd powers that he had nowhere else, including the ability to walk through walls and split into two Supermen!

For a time in 1949–50, Clark Kent and Lois Lane were married, but only in the newspaper strip. Eventually, the writer ran out of ideas and resorted to an out as old as *Alice in Wonderland*—he decided the whole marriage had been a dream!

Change swept through the series in the fifties. Superboy got a girl friend, who, like Lois Lane, attempted unsuccessfully to penetrate his disguise. This young lady was Lana Lang, who eventually entered the Superman scene as a rival to Lois, after the latter had won her own magazine in 1958.

Lois began to suspect that Clark was Superman in a tale reprinted herein. It may surprise the sophisticate of today that she took so long to penetrate the simple disguise of a pair of glasses. But in a day when people accepted the chestnut about the girl whose attractions are never noticed until she is seen without her glasses, Superman's camouflage worked.

Red Kryptonite came along in the late fifties. It was unlike Green K in that its effects were temporary, but they were also weird and unpredictable. The substance might change Superman into a giant, a madman, or a huge serpent.

Brainiac was also introduced in the fifties. He was a space-villain who had shrunk a city of Krypton—Kandor—and placed it in a bottle before the planet exploded. How Superman rescued the city is told in another story in this collection. For many years, Kandor was kept in Superman's Fortress of Solitude.

The Fortress was another innovation of the time. In the forties Superman had had a secret hideaway in the mountains near Metropolis. But in the fifties, Luthor discovered the Man of Steel's secret workshop. Beginning in 1958, Superman was shown with a secret Fortress of Solitude in the Arctic.

Superboy had a superdog now—Krypto. But the greatest addition to the Superman family in the fifties was Superman's cousin, Supergirl. She had been born on a fragment of Krypton that contained a complete city—preserved, it was explained, under a bubble of air (later changed to a plastic dome, so the air could be believably kept in place). When Kryptonite wiped out the inhabitants, Supergirl's parents sent her to Earth.

Bizarro, Superman's imperfect double, was also introduced at this time. Initially a tragic figure in the Frankenstein monster mold, in the sixties he changed into a comedic figure. In one story, Bizarro adopted a Clark Kent disguise on his Bizarro World but didn't fool anyone— mainly because he forgot to take off his medallion which read "Bizarro #1."

The sixties brought a rainbow of Kryptonites—Blue, White, Gold, and

Jewel—most of which affected something or someone other than Superman. Only Gold K could affect the Man of Might, but it never did—because if that happened, he would lose all his powers, permanently!

Then there was Superman on Broadway. *It's a Bird . . . It's a Plane . . . It's Superman!* was a musical written by David Newman and Robert Benton, with music by Charles Strouse and lyrics by Lee Adams. Not much of the comics' cast appeared in this play; aside from Superman, the only familiar names were Lois Lane and Perry White. But it had its moments, as when Linda Lavin (playing a girl named Sydney) sang "You've Got Possibilities" to Clark Kent. As she sang "Underneath, there's something there," she toyed with his shirt buttons, while Clark (Bob Holiday) nearly panicked at the thought that she might find what was there—his Superman suit!

And Superman returned to TV in a new form—a new series of animated cartoons for the home screen. Bud Collyer was back doing the voice; thus he had been Superman for radio, movies, and TV.

The seventies made their own mark on the Superman magazines. The *Daily Planet* was bought, lock, stock, and linotype, by a conglomerate, the Galaxy Broadcasting System, part of Galaxy Communications. The owner of Galaxy, Morgan Edge, switched Clark from his beat at the *Planet* to a job as anchorman on TV's "WGBS Six O'clock News." (Clark later began dividing his time between the *Planet* and WGBS.)

An end was called to Kryptonite proliferation as well. Radiation from an explosion at a Kryptonite-fueled reactor turned all Earth's Kryptonite to iron. It was a try at making the stories seem less gimmicky by de-emphasizing the glowing substance. This worked for a time, until it was decided that there was still plenty of Kryptonite floating out in space. By the time the seventies closed, the deadly element returned to plague the Action Ace, though not nearly as much as before.

Further, it was decided that an entire city in a bottle full of Kryptonian survivors detracted from Superman's status, since they all had his powers when they left the city, so the residents of Kandor were finally restored to full size on a far-off planet in another dimension.

The decade also saw the release of *Superman, The Movie*, a full-length live-action feature, boasting the talents of Christopher Reeve in the dual role of Clark and Superman; Marlon Brando as his father, Jor-El; Susannah York as his mother, Lara; Gene Hackman as his archenemy, Luthor; and Margot Kidder as Lois Lane. Jackie Cooper played Clark's cigar-puffing *Planet* boss, Perry White, and Glenn Ford portrayed Clark's foster father, Jonathan Kent.

Two new characters were created for this movie as well. Otis, Luthor's bumbling assistant, was played by Ned Beatty, and Eve Teschmacher, Luthor's sultry girl friend, was played by Valerie Perrine.

Kirk Alyn, who played Superman in the forties serials, and Noel Neill, who portrayed Lois Lane in those films and later on the fifties TV show, were enlisted to play Lois Lane's parents in a special cameo appearance.

Krypton, often depicted in the comics as an ideal, futuristic planet of scientific wonder, was displayed in the movie as a cold, crystalline tundra, as though that world's civilization was built on an iceberg. This motif was later repeated when Superman's Fortress of Solitude was shown.

The eighties dawned, bringing two sequels to that film. *Superman II* pitted our hero against three refugees from the Phantom Zone, the nether dimension where Kryptonian criminals were exiled. On Earth, the escapees—Zod, Non, and Ursa—gained all of the powers of Superman. *Superman III* depicts, among other things, Richard Pryor as Gus Gorman, a computer wizard who finds a way to synthesize a pseudo-Kryptonite.

In the comics, Superman's greatest foes, Luthor and Brainiac, were strengthened and streamlined, making them even more dangerous, if that's possible. Also, Superman's boyhood sweetheart, Lana Lang, reentered his life. She now works as Clark's coanchor at GBS, making Lois and Lana as much competitors as ever. This time, however, their feud stems from the rivalry of print and electronic journalism.

Lois, herself, has felt the changes brought by time. She has decided to break off her long standing relationship with Superman, a relationship she found as frustrating as it was eventful. Instead, Lois has (as of this writing) chosen to assert her independence, and quite a number of her adventures depict Lois on her own, going on assignment and getting herself in and out of trouble without help from her former boyfriend.

Today, Superman's adventures are featured in his own magazine, *Superman*, as well as *Action Comics*, which has run uninterrupted since its inception in 1938. He joins forces with Batman and other costumed characters regularly in *World's Finest Comics* and *DC Comics Presents* and appears as a charter member of the *Justice League of America*. Both Superboy and Supergirl star in their own magazines as well.

And that's not all. Of course, the eighties are a young decade, and there are plenty of challenges ahead for the Man of Steel. No one can say for certain what the future holds for Superman, but the best part of the future is getting there.

With that in mind, enjoy the stories reprinted in this volume. Everyone have their capes fastened tight? Then, let's go . . .

17

As the lad grew older, he learned to his delight that he could hurdle skyscrapers . . .

. . . LEAP AN EIGHTH OF A MILE . . .

. . . RAISE TREMENDOUS WEIGHTS . . .

. . . RUN FASTER THAN A STREAMLINE TRAIN --

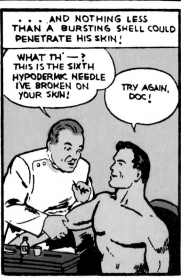

. . . . AND NOTHING LESS THAN A BURSTING SHELL COULD PENETRATE HIS SKIN!

WHAT TH' —? THIS IS THE SIXTH HYPODERMIC NEEDLE I'VE BROKEN ON YOUR SKIN!

TRY AGAIN, DOC!

THE PASSING AWAY OF HIS FOSTER-PARENTS GREATLY GRIEVED CLARK KENT. BUT IT STRENGTHENED A DETERMINATION THAT HAD BEEN GROWING IN HIS MIND.

CLARK DECIDED HE MUST TURN HIS TITANIC STRENGTH INTO CHANNELS THAT WOULD BENEFIT MANKIND

•

AND SO WAS CREATED--

SUPERMAN

CHAMPION OF THE OPPRESSED, THE PHYSICAL MARVEL WHO HAD SWORN TO DEVOTE HIS EXISTENCE TO HELPING THOSE IN NEED!

OUTER WAITING-ROOM OF THE *DAILY STAR* . . .

YOU MAY SEE THE EDITOR NOW. BUT IF YOU ASK ME YOU'RE WASTING YOUR TIME.

THERE'S NOTHING LIKE TRYING!

I KNOW I HAVEN'T HAD ANY EXPERIENCE, SIR, BUT STILL, I THINK I'D MAKE A GOOD REPORTER.

SORRY, FELLA! CAN'T USE YOU!

IN AN ALLEY, CLARK REMOVES HIS STREET-CLOTHES, REVEALING HIMSELF CLAD IN THE *SUPERMAN* COSTUME . . .

IF I GET NEWS DISPATCHES PROMPTLY, I'LL BE IN A BETTER POSITION TO HELP PEOPLE. I'VE GOT TO GET THAT JOB!

SUPERMAN LAUNCHES HIMSELF UP ALONG THE SIDE OF THE BUILDING IN A GREAT LEAP!

WITHIN THE EDITOR'S OFFICE . . .

WHAT'S THAT? A MOB ATTACKING THE COUNTY JAIL? *COVER THAT STORY!*

HM·M! SOUNDS LIKE MY BIG CHANCE TO IMPRESS THE EDITOR!

HERE'S HOPING I GET THERE ON TIME!

THAT VERY MOMENT . . . BEFORE THE COUNTY JAIL . . .

GET 'IM!

LYNCH TH' DIRTY DOG!

JAIL

A FEW MOMENTS LATER...

LEMME GO! I AIN'T GUILTY I TELL YA!

THAT'S RIGHT, SIMS! BEG FOR MERCY!

BUT IT WON'T DO YOU ANY GOOD!

DON'T DO THIS TO ME! PLEASE — PLEASE!

HANGIN'S TOO GOOD FER YOU!

JUST AS THE LYNCHING IS ABOUT TO BEGIN ... DOWN HURTLES A FANTASTIC FIGURE

GO ON! SCATTER!

WHAT IN--?

THIS PRISONER'S FATE WILL BE DECIDED IN A COURT OF JUSTICE.—RETURN TO YOUR HOMES!

RUSH HIM!

YOU'RE BEGGING FOR IT!

THE CROWD IS ASTOUNDED TO FIND ITSELF SWEPT BACK BY THE LONE FIGURE . . .

I DON'T KNOW HOW YOU DID IT, BUT YOU'VE MY THANKS! WHO ARE YOU?

A REPORTER. — LET'S GET THE PRISONER BACK IN HIS CELL.

YA SAVED MY LIFE . . . AN' I'M NOT FORGETTIN' IT. I'LL LET YA IN ON A RED-HOT STORY!

LET'S HAVE IT!

I'M BEIN' HELD FOR TH' MURDER OF JACK KENNEDY. BUT I DIDN'T DO IT... AND NEITHER DID EVELYN CURRY, TH' GIRL WHO'S BEIN' ELECTROCUTED TO-NIGHT FOR IT!

WHO IS THE MURDERER?

BEA CARROLL... SINGER AT THE HILOW NIGHT CLUB-- SHE RUBBED HIM OUT FOR TWO-TIMING HER, THEN FRAMED EVELYN!

THANKS FOR THE INFORMATION!

THAT'S ALL I KNOW ABOUT THE ATTEMPTED LYNCHING. WELL, DO I GET THE JOB NOW?

YOU'RE O.K., KENT! REPORT TO WORK TOMORROW!

CLARK DROPS IN ON THE HILOW CLUB.

SHE'LL BE ON ANY SECOND!

AS BEA SINGS HER NUMBER, SHE DOES NOT REALIZE SHE IS BEING CLOSELY OBSERVED BY THE GREATEST EXPONENT OF JUSTICE THE WORLD HAS EVER KNOWN.

LATER-- WHEN SHE ENTERS HER DRESSING-ROOM...

SAY! WHAT ARE YOU DOING IN MY ROOM?

WAITING FOR YOU, NATURALLY!

I THOUGHT YOU MIGHT BE INTERESTED IN LEARNING I KNOW THAT YOU KILLED JACK KENNEDY!

WHAT KIND OF NUT ARE YOU, ANYWAY? -- GET OUT OF HERE BEFORE I CALL THE MANAGER!

28

A TIRELESS FIGURE RACES THRU THE NIGHT SECONDS COUNT.. DELAY MEANS FORFEIT OF AN INNOCENT LIFE

THE GOVERNOR'S ESTATE FINALLY IS REACHED

MAKE YOURSELF COMFORTABLE! I HAVEN'T TIME TO ATTEND TO IT

WHAT DO YOU MEAN BY KNOCKING THIS HOUR OF THE NIGHT?

I MUST SEE THE GOVERNOR. IT'S A MATTER OF LIFE AND DEATH!

SEE HIM IN THE MORNING!

I'LL SEE HIM NOW!

THIS IS ILLEGAL ENTRY! I'LL HAVE YOU ARRESTED!

ANSWER MY QUESTION! ARE YOU GOING TO TAKE ME TO THE GOVERNOR?

NO! I WON'T!

THEN I'LL TAKE YOU TO HIM!

HELP! HELP!

YES, THIS IS THE GOVERNOR'S SLEEPING ROOM. — DON'T THINK YOU'RE GOING TO GET AWAY WITH THIS OUTRAGE!

IT'S LOCKED!

YES! AND MADE OF STEEL! TRY AND KNOCK THIS DOOR DOWN!

IT WAS YOUR IDEA!

WHAT'S THE MEANING OF THIS?

EVELYN CURRY IS TO BE ELECTROCUTED IN 15 MINUTES FOR MURDER. I HAVE PROOF HERE OF HER INNOCENCE — A SIGNED CONFESSION!

BELIEVING THE GOVERNOR MENACED BY A MADMAN, THE BUTLER PRODUCES A CONCEALED WEAPON!

REACH FOR THE CEILING, QUICK!

PUT THAT TOY AWAY!

I WARN YOU! TAKE ANOTHER STEP AND I SHOOT!

THE DAILY STAR OFFICE IS REACHED...

YOU WANTED TO SEE ME?

YES, BE SEATED

34

DID YOU EVER HEAR OF SUPERMAN?

WHAT!

EDITOR

35

REPORTS HAVE BEEN STREAMING IN THAT A FELLOW WITH GIGANTIC STRENGTH NAMED SUPERMAN ACTUALLY EXISTS. IM MAKING IT YOUR STEADY ASSIGNMENT TO COVER THESE REPORTS. THINK YOU CAN HANDLE IT, KENT?

LISTEN, CHIEF, IF I CAN'T FIND OUT ANYTHING ABOUT THIS SUPERMAN NO ONE CAN!

36

HURRY, KENT-- A PHONED TIP... WIFE-BEATING AT 211 COURT AVE!

IM ON MY WAY!

37

AT 211 COURT AVE. --

38

HOLD IT!

WHAT D'YOU WANT?

DON'T GET TOUGH!

TOUGH IS PUTTING MILDLY THE TREATMENT YOUR GOING TO GET!

39

YOU'RE NOT FIGHTING A WOMAN, NOW!

40

I SAID RUN ALONG, I'M CUTTIN' IN!

BUT THIS IS NOT A ROBBER'S DANCE

TRYIN' T'GET FLIP? MOVE QUICK IF Y'KNOW WHAT'S GOOD FOR YA!

CLARK! ARE YOU GOING TO STAND FOR THIS?

RELUCTANTLY, KENT ADHERES TO HIS ROLE OF A WEAKLING.

BE REASONABLE, LOIS. DANCE WITH THE FELLOW AND THEN WE'LL LEAVE RIGHT AWAY

YOU CAN STAY AND DANCE WITH HIM IF YOU WISH BUT I'M LEAVING NOW!

YEAH? YOU'LL DANCE WITH ME AND LIKE IT!

WHY, YOU—!

GOOD FOR YOU, LOIS!

LOIS—DON'T!

FIGHT... YOU WEAK-LIVERED POLE-CAT!

REALLY— I HAVE NO DESIRE TO DO SO!

WAIT, LOIS!

BUT LOIS—!

YOU ASKED ME EARLIER IN THE EVENING WHY I AVOID YOU. I'LL TELL YOU WHY NOW! BECAUSE YOU'RE A SPINELESS, UNBEARABLE COWARD!

LET'S GET OUT OF HERE! I'LL SHOW THAT SKIRT SHE CAN'T MAKE A FOOL OUT OF BUTCH MATSON!

A FEW MINUTES LATER

A HIDDEN FIGURE OBSERVES BUTCH AND HIS FELLOW HOODLUMS LEAVE THE ROAD-HOUSE . . .

DUTCH FORCES LOIS'S TAXI INTO A DITCH!

PULL OVER THERE!

LET ME GO!

GET IN THAT CAR AND SHUT UP!

WHAT BURNS ME UP IS THAT I LET HER YELLOW BOY FRIEND OFF SO EASY!

WELL MAYBE YOU TWO MAY MEET AGAIN

THEN I HOPE IT'LL BE SOON!

HEY— WATCH OUT! OME ONE'S STANDING THE ROAD AHEAD OF US!

HA! HA! WATCH ME SCARE HIM OUT OF HIS WITS!

LOOK OUT! YOU'LL HIT HIM!

SUPERMAN HURDLES THE ONCOMING AUTO!

IT'S THE DEVIL HIMSELF!

BUTCH! STEP ON THE GAS! HE'S CHASING AFTER US !!!

BUTCH'S CAR LEAPS FORWARD LIKE A RELEASED ROCKET, BUT IS EASILY OVERTAKEN BY SUPERMAN

35

YE-EOW

THE OCCUPANTS OF THE CAR ARE SHAKEN OUT—

NEXT, SUPERMAN OVER TAKES BUTCH IN ONE SPRING..

—AND THE CAR, ITSELF, SMASHED TO BITS!

JUST A MINUTE, BUTCH!

DO YOU MIND?

THIS WILL TAKE BUT A FEW SECONDS

GET ME OFFA HERE!

OKAY! I'LL CUT YOU LOOSE!

DON'T!

YOU NEEDN'T BE AFRAID OF ME. I WON'T HARM YOU

BEARING LOIS IN HIS ARMS SUPERMAN HEADS TOWARD THE CITY — —

— — DEPOSITING HER UPON ITS OUTSKIRTS

I'D ADVISE YOU NOT TO PRINT THIS LITTLE EPISODE

NEXT MORNING

BUT I TELL YOU I SAW SUPERMAN LAST NIGHT!

ARE YOU SURE IT WASN'T PINK ELEPHANTS YOU SAW?

EDITOR

LOIS TREATS CLARK COLDER THAN EVER

I'M SORRY ABOUT LAST NIGHT— PLEASE DON'T BE ANGRY WITH ME

CLARK RECIEVES AN ASSIGNMENT

KENT, THE FRONT PAGE IS GETTING SO DULL I'VE EVEN GOT TO HEADLINE CARD-GAMES. —— THERE'S A WAR GOING ON IN A SMALL SOUTH AMERICAN RE-PUBLIC, SAN MONTE, AND TO STIR UP NEWS I'M SENDING YOU DOWN THERE AS CORRESPONDENT. TAKE ALONG A CAMERA AND TRY TO SEND BACK SOME GOOD SHOTS WITH YOUR ARTICLES

KENT TAKES A TRAIN, NOT TO-WARD SAN MONTE, BUT TO WASHINGTON D.C.

IN THE CAPITOL CITY, HE ATTENDS A SESSION OF CONGRESS, SITTING IN THE GALLERY

IS THAT SENATOR BARROWS SPEAKING?

YES.

UPON LEAVING THE SENATE CHAMBERS, CLARK SNAPS A PICTURE OF A FURTIVE MAN SPEAKING SWIFTLY TO SENATOR BARROWS

WHEN CAN I SEE YOU?

I TOLD YOU NEVER TO SPEAK TO ME IN PUBLIC!...UH.. MY HOME..TONIGHT AT 8:30

AT THE "MORGUE" OF A LOCAL NEWSPAPER....

WHO'S THE CHAP SPEAKING TO SENATOR BARROWS?

WHY, THAT'S ALEX GREER, THE SLICKEST LOBBYIST IN WASHINGTON. NO ONE KNOWS WHAT INTERESTS BACK HIM.

EIGHT-THIRTY P.M.! OUTSIDE SENATOR BARROWS' RESIDENCE... AN EAVESDROPPER LISTENS IN ON AN INTERESTING CONVERSATION!

I'VE TOLD YOU TO AVOID ME IN PUBLIC. WHAT WOULD PEOPLE THINK IF THEY KNEW I HAD ANYTHING TO DO WITH YOU?

QUIT SPUTTERING! I HAD TO SEE YOU. TELL ME: DO YOU THINK YOU'LL SUCCEED IN PUSHING THE BILL THRU?

THERE'S NO DOUBT ABOUT IT! THE BILL WILL BE PASSED BEFORE ITS FULL IMPLICATIONS ARE REALIZED. BEFORE ANY REMEDIAL STEPS CAN BE TAKEN, OUR COUNTRY WILL BE EMBROILED WITH EUROPE.

FINE! WE'LL TAKE CARE OF YOU FINAN- CIALLY FOR THIS!

I SUPPOSE YOU'RE GOING TO BE WELL TAKEN CARE OF YOURSELF?

YOU BET HE WILL!

--NOT UNLESS THEY TOUCH A TELEPHONE-POLE AND ARE GROUNDED!

92

OOPS! -- ALMOST TOUCHED THAT POLE!

YE-OW

93

LOOK! --THE CAPITOL! LET'S PAY IT A VISIT!

TAKE ME DOWN! TAKE ME DOWN!

94

WHAT A MAGNIFICENT VIEW!

HELP! HELP!

95

I WONDER IF WE COULD JUMP ALL THE WAY TO THAT BUILDING?

NO! DON'T!

96

DESPITE GREER'S FRENZIED PROTESTS, SUPERMAN LEAPS OUT INTO THE NIGHT!

MISSED -- DOGGONE IT!

97

TO BE CONTINUED

AND SO BEGINS THE STARTLING ADVENTURES OF THE MOST SENSATIONAL STRIP CHARACTER OF ALL TIME: SUPERMAN!

A PHYSICAL MARVEL, A MENTAL WONDER, SUPERMAN IS DESTINED TO RESHAPE THE DESTINY OF A WORLD!

Only in ACTION COMICS

CAN YOU THRILL AT THE DARING DEEDS OF THIS SUPERB CREATION!

DON'T MISS AN ISSUE!

98

SUPERMAN

by JEROME SIEGEL and JOE SHUSTER

As they topple like a plummet to the street below, eighty stories distant, Greer shrieks insanely the entire length of the building!

1.

As they strike the sidewalk, it bursts into fragments!

2.

SAY! WASN'T THAT FUN? -- LET'S DO IT AGAIN!

NO! I'LL TALK! - THE MAN BEHIND THE THREATENING WAR IS EMIL NORVELL, THE MUNITIONS MAGNATE. YOU'LL FIND HIM AT HIS LEXINGTON PARK ESTATE!

3.

Having secured the information he desires, SUPERMAN takes abrupt leave of Greer, springs to the top of the Washington Monument, gets his bearings then begins his dash toward Norvell's residence

4.

MEANWHILE --

I CAN'T EXPLAIN OVER THE PHONE, NORVELL, BUT YOU'RE ABOUT TO RECEIVE A VISIT FROM THE MOST DANGEROUS MAN ALIVE!

DON'T WORRY, GREER! -- I'LL TAKE CERTAIN PRECAUTIONS TO INSURE HE DOESN'T REMAIN ALIVE LONG!

6.

FIVE MINUTES ELAPSE -- THEN... ...SUPERMAN STEPS THRU THE WINDOW OF EMIL NORVELL'S STUDY AND CALMLY CONFRONTS HIM...

WHETHER YOU LIKE IT OR NOT, NORVELL, YOU'RE COMING WITH ME!

SORRY, BUT I HAVE OTHER PLANS!

AS HE SPEAKS, THE MUNITIONS MANUFACTURER SURREPTITIOUSLY REACHES BEHIND HIM TO PRESS A BUTTON ON HIS DESK.

WHAT ARE YOU HOLDING BEHIND YOU? -- GIVE IT TO ME!

ALL RIGHT BOYS! -- HE ASKED FOR IT! LET HIM HAVE IT!!

INSTANTLY SEVERAL PANELS ABOUT THE ROOM SLIDE ASIDE AND OUT STEP A NUMBER OF ARMED GUARDS! NEXT MOMENT SUPERMAN IS THE CENTER OF A DEAFENING MACHINE-GUN BARRAGE!

UNHARMED BY THE RAIN OF MACHINE-GUN BULLETS, SUPERMAN STREAKS TOWARD HIS WOULD-BE MURDERERS!

GOOD HEAVENS! HE WON'T DIE!

GLAD I CAN'T SAY THE SAME FOR YOU!

A MOMENT LATER A DOZEN BODIES FLY HEADLONG OUT THE WINDOW INTO THE NIGHT, THE MACHINE-GUNS WRAPPED FIRMLY ABOUT THEIR NECKS!

YOU SEE HOW EFFORTLESSLY I CRUSH THIS BAR OF IRON IN MY HAND? -- THAT BAR COULD JUST AS EASILY BE YOUR NECK!... NOW FOR THE LAST TIME! ARE YOU COMING WITH ME?

YES! YES! IMMEDIATELY!

SEVERAL MINUTES LATER...

YOU SEE THAT STEAMER? IT'S THE BARONTA. TOMORROW, IT LEAVES FOR SAN MONTE. UNLESS I FIND YOU ABOARD IT WHEN IT SAILS, I SWEAR I'LL FOLLOW YOU TO WHATEVER HOLE YOU HIDE IN, AND TEAR OUT YOUR CRUEL HEART WITH MY BARE HANDS!

I-I'LL BE ON IT!

NEXT DAY AN ODD VARIETY OF PASSENGERS BOARD THE SAN MONTE' BOUND STEAMER BARONTA... CLARK KENT AND LOIS LANE...

LOIS! WHY, WHAT ARE YOU DOING *HERE*?

OUR EDITOR DECIDED TO HAVE ME ACCOMPANY YOU TO THE WAR-ZONE AND SEND BACK DISPATCHES COLORED WITH MY DISTINCTIVE FEMININE TOUCH!

. . . A GROUP OF SULLEN-FACED TOUGHS WHO POSSIBLY INTEND TO ENLIST WITH ONE OF THE ARMIES AS PAID MERCENARIES . . .

LOLA CORTEZ, WOMAN OF MYSTERY, AN EXOTIC BEAUTY WHO FAIRLY RADIATES DANGER AND INTRIGUE . . . .

. . AND EMIL NORVELL, WHO HURRIES PASTY-FACED UP THE GANG-PLANK AND QUICKLY CONFINES HIMSELF TO HIS CABIN

HALF AN HOUR LATER THE *BARONTA* HOISTS ITS ANCHOR AND SLIPS OUT TO SEA, DESTINED FOR ONE OF THE STRANGEST VOYAGES THE WORLD HAS EVER KNOWN

IT IS THE FIRST NIGHT OUT . . . AS NORVELL NERVOUSLY PACES HIS CABIN, THERE COMES A KNOCK AT THE DOOR . . . HE ANSWERS IT . . . .

YOU!

YES -- I THOUGHT I'D DROP BY AND COMPLIMENT YOU ON HAVING HAD SENSE ENOUGH TO SHOW UP!

A MOMENT AFTER *SUPERMAN* DEPARTS . . . .

THAT'S HIM! REMEMBER! -- IF HE DIES, YOUR REWARD WILL BE FABULOUS!

HE'S AS GOOD AS DEAD RIGHT NOW!

AS SUPERMAN STANDS SILENTLY AT THE SHIP'S RAIL, ADMIRING THE MOONLIGHT, HE WHIRLS SUDDENLY AT THE SOUND OF FOOTSTEPS!

23

ALL TOGETHER, NOW! — GET HIM!

24

FOR AN INSTANT SUPERMAN BRACES HIMSELF AGAINST THE RAIL -- AND IN THAT SECOND IT GIVES WAY!

25

HE IS FLUNG, TWISTING AND TURNING INTO THE OCEAN!

26

THE THUGS REPORT BACK TO NORVELL

IT WAS SIMPLE! A LITTLE SHOVE AND HE TOPPLED OVERBOARD! -- NOW HOW ABOUT THAT DOUGH YOU PROMISED US!

YOU'LL GET NOTHING! GET OUT OF HERE, YOU TRUSTING FOOLS, AND BE GLAD I DON'T TURN YOU OVER TO THE POLICE!

27

MEANWHILE -- AT THAT VERY INSTANT SUPERMAN, SWIMMING VIGOROUSLY, HAS CAUGHT UP WITH THE STEAMER . .

28

. . BUT INSTEAD OF CLIMBING ABOARD, HE CONTINUES ONWARD UNTIL THE BARONTA IS OUT-DISTANCED FAR BEHIND!

SEE YOU LATER!

29

NEXT EVENING, A FEW MINUTES AFTER THE STEAMER LANDS NORVELL IS ATTACKED BY HIS DOUBLE CROSSED HENCHMEN

30

NORVELL IS SAVED BY THE TIMELY APPEARANCE OF *SUPERMAN*

HOLY CATS -- IT'S **HIM!**

RIGHT! -- AND HERE'S WHERE I EVEN A LITTLE SCORE!

SUPERMAN SUBJECTS THE TOUGHS TO THE SEVEREST THRASHING OF THEIR LIVES!

THE THUGS FLEE BEFORE HIS FURY!

YOU SAVED ME! -- BUT WHY?

BECAUSE THE FATE YOU ESCAPED IS PLEASANT INDEED COMPARED TO THE ONE I HAVE IN STORE FOR YOU!

W-WHAT ARE YOU GOING TO DO TO ME?

NOTHING -- IF YOU JOIN THE SAN MONTE ARMY!

LATER --- IN HIS HOTEL

IF I COULD ONLY DO SOMETHING! --- BUT IT'S SUICIDE TO RESIST THAT INHUMAN CREATURE!

I KNOW WHAT I'LL DO: I'LL ENLIST IN THE ARMY -- THEN ESCAPE AT THE FIRST OPPORTUNITY!

AFTER NORVELL ENLISTS --

YOU!

YES, I JOINED TOO -- I COULDN'T BEAR BEING PARTED FROM YOU!

45

ORDERS FROM HEADQUARTERS, SIR WE'RE TO MOVE TO THE FRONT.

39

THE NEW DETACHMENT MOVES IN TOWARD THE BATTLE-LINE

40

WHAT ARE YOU TRYING TO DO? — KILL US BOTH?

YOU'LL SEE!

41

WHAT I CAN'T UNDERSTAND IS WHY YOU MANUFACTURE MUNITIONS WHEN IT MEANS THAT THOUSANDS WILL DIE HORRIBLY

MEN ARE CHEAP -- MUNITIONS, EXPENSIVE!

42

AT THAT INSTANT — A SHELL WHINES OVERHEAD... THEN BURSTS!

43

THE COLUMN OF SOLDIERS DROPS FLAT, TO ESCAPE FLYING FRAGMENTS

44

THIS IS NO PLACE FOR A SANE MAN! I'LL DIE --!

45

I SEE! WHEN IT'S YOUR OWN LIFE THAT'S AT STAKE, YOUR VIEWPOINT CHANGES!

46

SHORTLY LATER, THE COMPANY PITCHES CAMP... RETIRES...

47

SENTRIES ARE PUZZLED BY A DARK SHADOW...

WHAT WAS THAT?

PROBABLY JUST A BIRD!

48

BUT IN REALITY IT IS SUPERMAN SPEEDING TO A STRANGE RENDEZVOUS

49

IN THE ENEMY CAMP...

BUT THE QUESTION, GENERAL, IS HOW STRONG ARE OUR LINES?

IMPENETRABLE!

50

AT THAT INSTANT A FIGURE BURSTS INTO THE TENT.

SMILE, PLEASE! —THANKS!

51

A FEW MOMENTS LATER --

GONE!— BUT HE WON'T ESCAPE!

GUARDS!

52

LATER THAT EVENING, CLARK KENT MAILS A PACKAGE...

WHERE TO?

THE EVENING NEWS... CLEVELAND, OHIO

53

THE EVENING-NEWS PRINTS A PICTURE-SCOOP...

EVENING NEWS

AMAZING WAR PICTURES!!

GENERALS CONFER

54

47

MEANWHILE, LOIS LANE AND LOLA CORTEZ HAVE REGISTERED AT THE SAME HOTEL

I'M A REPORTER DOWN HERE ON A NEWS ASSIGNMENT. AND YOU?

-- A WEALTHY TRAVELER.

55

AT THAT INSTANT, ARMY OFFICERS ENTERS THE HOTEL --

WHAT'S THE TROUBLE?

OFFICIAL BUSINESS.

56

SUDDENLY PANICKY, LOLA DARTS INTO AN ELEVATOR...

57

... AND HIDES A CERTAIN DOCUMENT IN LOIS' ROOM!

58

AN IMPORTANT DOCUMENT HAS BEEN STOLEN. MAY WE SEARCH THE GUESTS' ROOMS?

YOU HAVE MY PERMISSION

59

SORRY, MADAM!

I TOLD YOU THAT YOU WERE WASTING TIME SEARCHING MY ROOM!

60

THE PLANTED DOCUMENT IS DISCOVERED IN LOIS' ROOM!

SORRY, WE MUST PLACE YOU UNDER MILITARY ARREST!

BUT I KNOW NOTHING OF THIS!

61

SENTENCE IS PASSED --

BUT I'M INNOCENT!

IT IS THE JUDGEMENT OF THIS COURT THAT YOU SHALL BE EXECUTED AT DAWN FOR ESPONIAGE!

62

KENT, IN HIS DISGUISE AS A SOLDIER, OVERHEARS AN ASTOUNDING BIT OF INFORMATION

HAVE YOU HEARD? LOIS LANE, A SPY, IS TO BE EXECUTED THIS MORNING

YES! AND EXACTLY AT DAWN!

63

AT THAT VERY MOMENT LOIS IS BEING LED OUT TO HER DEATH . .

I TELL YOU! YOU'RE GOING TO KILL AN INNOCENT PERSON!

64

ALMOST FASTER THAN THE EYE CAN FOLLOW, A FANTASTIC FIGURE STREAKS PAST MILE AFTER MILE!

65

READY! AIM! FI —

DOWN — DOWN — INTO THE RANGE OF FIRE PLUMMETS SUPERMAN!

67

COVERING LOIS' BODY WITH HIS OWN, HE RECIEVES THE SHOTS MEANT FOR HER!

SHOOT AND BE HANGED!

68

YOU CAN'T DO THIS! — IT'S IMPOSSIBLE!

STOP!

THANKS FOR LETTING ME KNOW!

69

SUPERMAN!

RIGHT! AND STILL PLAYING THE ROLE OF GALLANT RESCUER! —

70

WHAT MANNER OF BEING ARE YOU?

SAVE THE QUESTIONS!

71

FINALLY SUPERMAN DROPS TOWARD THE GROUND INTO THE MIDST OF A TORTURER'S INQUISITION

YOU'LL TELL ME HOW MANY MEN THERE ARE IN YOUR DETACHMENT OR --!

LET ME GO! WHAT ARE YOU GOING TO DO?

GIVE YOU THE FATE YOU DESERVE YOU TORTURING DEVIL!

73

FOR AN INSTANT, SUPERMAN POISES THE TORTURER OVER HEAD...

74

...THEN TOSSES HIM AWAY AS THO HE WERE HURLING A JAVELIN!

75

THE TORTURER VANISHES FROM VIEW BEHIND A GROVE OF DISTANT TREES WITH A PITIFUL WAIL --

76

SUPERMAN UNTIES THE TORTURER'S CAPTIVES BONDS...

YOU'RE FREE TO FLEE! -- GOOD LUCK!

WE OWE OUR LIVES TO YOU!

77

LATER, AFTER DEPOSITING LOIS NEAR THE BARONTA, SUPERMAN ADVISES HER TO RETURN TO AMERICA.

BUT WHEN WILL I SEE YOU AGAIN!

WHO KNOWS? PERHAPS TOMORROW-- PERHAPS NEVER!

78

AND NOW TO ATTEND TO NORVELL!

79

BUT WHEN SUPERMAN RETURNS TO HIS DETACHMENT, HE FINDS ANTI-AIRCRAFT GUNS BOOMING

80

THE CAMP IS BEING MERCILESSLY RIDDLED BY A BLOOD-THIRSTY AVIATOR!

DIE! -- LIKE CRAWLING ANTS!

81

SUPERMAN LEAPS TO THE ATTACK! FOR THE FIRST TIME IN ALL HISTORY, A MAN BATTLES AN AIRPLANE SINGLE-HANDED!

82

THE PLANE ZOOMS TOWARD SUPERMAN'S FIGURE, GUNS BLAZING!

83

-- INTO A HEAD-ON CRASH!

84

ITS PROPELLER SHATTERED UPON SUPERMAN'S SKIN, THE AIRPLANE FALLS TO ITS DOOM!

85

NORVELL HAD WITNESSED THE CRASH

GOOD! -- THAT FINISHES MY NEMESIS!

86

51

BUT NEXT INSTANT --

HELLO! -- SURPRISED?

SUPERMAN! -- STILL ALIVE!!

87

O.K. -- BUT YOU'VE GOT TO QUIT MANUFACTURING MUNITIONS!

LET ME RETURN TO THE U.S. -- I'VE GROWN TO HATE WAR --

88

NORVELL HURRIES ABOARD THE BARONTA FOR THE RETURN TRIP...

FROM NOW ON, THE MOST DANGEROUS THING I'LL MANU-FACTURE WILL BE A FIRECRACKER!

NTA

89

THAT ABOUT CLEARS UP THINGS! NOW JUST ONE MORE MANEUVER AND MY MISSION HERE WILL BE FINISHED!

40

SHORTLY LATER, SUPERMAN EMERGES FROM A TENT WITH THE ARMY'S COMMANDER UNDER HIS ARM.

91

LATER, HE ALSO KIDNAPS THE HEAD OF THE OPPOSING ARMY

92

WHAT DO YOU WANT WITH US!

I'VE DECIDED TO END THIS WAR BY HAVING YOU TWO FIGHT IT OUT BETWEEN YOURSELVES

93

BUT WE--!

GO AHEAD! -- FIGHT! OR I'LL CLEAN UP ON BOTH OF YOU MYSELF!

94

BUT WHY SHOULD WE FIGHT?

WE'RE NOT ANGRY AT EACH OTHER!

95

THEN WHY ARE YOUR ARMIES BATTLING?

96

I DON'T KNOW! CAN YOU TELL ME?

NO, CAN YOU?

97

GENTLEMEN, IT'S OBVIOUS YOU'VE BEEN FIGHTING ONLY TO PROMOTE THE SALE OF MUNITIONS! — WHY NOT SHAKE HANDS AND MAKE UP?

98

AND SO, DUE TO THE CONCILIATORY EFFORTS OF SUPERMAN, THE WAR IS HALTED

99

WHEN KENT REPORTS BACK TO HIS EDITOR . . .

SINCE YOU'VE BEEN GONE, THERE'S BEEN NO SUPERMAN NEWS. MAYBE HE'S RETIRED FOR GOOD!

SOMEHOW, CHIEF, I'VE A HUNCH HE'LL MAKE HIS APPEARANCE AGAIN-- SOON!

THE END

100

SUPERMAN

by JERRY SIEGEL and JOE SHUSTER

Leaping over skyscrapers, running faster than an express-train, springing great distances and heights, lifting and smashing tremendous weights, possessing an impenetrable skin--these are the amazing attributes which *SUPERMAN*, savior of the helpless and oppressed, avails himself as he battles the forces of evil and injustice!

For the first time in its history, the city of Metropolis is ravaged by a terrible earthquake!

Editorial office of the DAILY PLANET..

I WANT FIRST-HAND EYE-WITNESS DETAILS OF THE QUAKE!

YOU'LL GET 'EM!

Unobserved, the meek reporter transforms himself into mighty *SUPERMAN*...!

AN EARTHQUAKE IN THIS LOCALITY--IT'S UNHEARD OF!

STORE ROOM

Shortly after--the man of TOMORROW'S figure streaks down toward the scene of terror!

 SPRINGING INTO ACTION, **SUPERMAN** SUPPORTS TOTTERING BUILDINGS WHILE TERRIFIED OCCUPANTS DASH TO SAFETY!

 HURRY! IT'LL GIVE WAY IN A FEW SECONDS!

 HIS AMAZING STRENGTH AND SPEED BRINGING HIM TO WHEREVER THERE IS NEED OF HIS ASSISTANCE!

MY BOY-- PINNED UNDER THAT WRECKAGE!

HE'LL BE FREE IN A MOMENT!

 WHEN THE EARTHQUAKE SUBSIDES, **SUPERMAN** LEAPS AWAY WITH THE GRATEFUL CHEER OF THOUSANDS RINGING IN HIS WAKE...!

⑧

 LATER NICE ARTICLE YOU HANDED IN-- PARTICULARILY THE **SUPERMAN** ANGLE!

I'VE LEARNED THAT THE DISTURBANCE WAS CAUSED BY A NEW WEAPON THE ARMY IS TESTING WHICH ARTIFICIALLY CAUSES EARTHQUAKES. THE MACHINE RAN WILD DURING THE TEST. - I'LL VISIT ITS INVENTOR FOR AN INTERVIEW.

⑨

 PROFESSOR MARTINSON? I'M CLARK KENT OF THE DAILY PLANET. HOW ABOUT A STORY CONCERNING YOUR NEW DISCOVERY!

I'D BE DELIGHTED!

⑩

 CLARK SEATS HIMSELF. WHILE HIS BACK IS TURNED--

MEDDLER!

⑪

 NOT A TICK! HE'S DONE FOR!

⑫ WHAT CLARK'S ASSAILANT DOES NOT REALIZE IS THAT KENT POSSESSES THE ABILITY TO TEMPORARILY HALT THE BEATING OF HIS HEART. CLARK IS PLAYING POSSUM TO LEARN WHAT THE SITUATION IS!

 OUT YOU GO--TO A MANGLED DEATH!

⑬

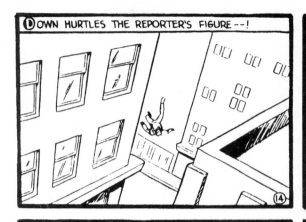

DOWN HURTLES THE REPORTER'S FIGURE --!

(14)

ABRUPTLY--OUT FLASHES ONE OF HIS HANDS, CLUTCHING THE SIDE OF THE SKYSCRAPER IN A STEELY GRIP, HALTING HIS PLUNGE!

TIME OUT!

(15)

IT TAKES BUT A FEW SECONDS TO REMOVE HIS OUTER GARMENTS .... THEN HE COMMENCES TO CLIMB SWIFTLY BACK TOWARD THE LABORATORY ---- AS *SUPERMAN!*

NOW IT'S *MY* TURN!

(16)

WITHIN THE LABORATORY ---

A SNOOPING REPORTER INTERFERED WHILE I WAS GOING THRU THE PROFESSOR'S DESK. BUT I DISPOSED OF HIM!

SPLENDID! BUT IT'S UNFORTUNATE YOU COULDN'T FIND THE PLANS WE SEEK!

(17)

AT A DISTANT SPOT...

("-*SUPERMAN* EAVESDROPPING! I'LL ATTEND TO HIM!-")

(18)

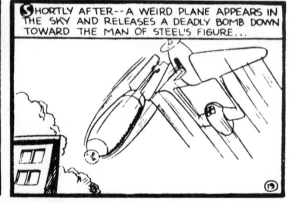

SHORTLY AFTER--A WEIRD PLANE APPEARS IN THE SKY AND RELEASES A DEADLY BOMB DOWN TOWARD THE MAN OF STEEL'S FIGURE...

(19)

THIS HAS GOT TO STOP BEFORE BOMBS FALL ON INNOCENT PEOPLE IN THE STREET!

(20)

A FLIP OF *SUPERMAN'S* WRIST, AND THE BOMB HURTLES BACK TO ITS SOURCE, DESTROYING THE PLANE!

(21)

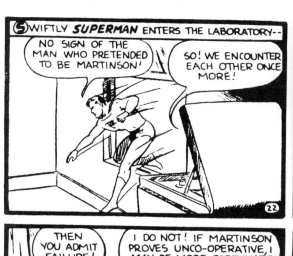

SUPERMAN TRAILS THE AUTOGYRO...

THE WORLD WILL NOT BE SAFE UNTIL LUTHOR NO LONGER EXISTS!

SUPERMAN-- PURSUING MY FUMBLING HIRELINGS!

SORRY TO DISAPPOINT THE MAN OF STEEL, BUT THAT PLANE WILL NEVER REACH HERE!

THE AUTOGYRO- DESTROYED BY A TERRIFIC EXPLOSION!

A CHALLENGE, SUPERMAN!

WHO SAID THAT?

!! ARE YOU WILLING TO DECLARE A TEMPORARY TRUCE?

THAT ALL DEPENDS--!

HERE IS MY PROPOSITION--AND CHALLENGE! IF YOUR MUSCLES CAN SURPASS MY SCIENTIFIC FEATS, I WILL ADMIT DEFEAT. BUT IF I CAN OUTDO YOU, THEN YOU ARE TO RETIRE AND LEAVE ME A CLEAR PATH!

DO YOU ACCEPT?

DEFINITELY!

SECONDS LATER...TWO WEIRD VESSELS SWOOP DOWN OUT OF THE SKY...

THAT'S WHAT I CALL PROMPT SERVICE!

ONCE AGAIN WE CONFRONT EACH OTHER!

CAN'T SAY THAT IT PARTICULARILY PLEASES ME!

QUIBBLING ASIDE--YOU AGREED TO MATCH ME AT ANY FEAT. WELL, IMPETUOUS ONE, ARE YOU PREPARED TO RACE MY SKY-VESSELS AROUND THE WORLD?

LET'S GO!

THEY'RE OFF--IN THE STRANGEST RACE THE WORLD HAS EVER SEEN--A *SUPERMAN* VERSUS SUPER-PLANES!

DEFYING TIME, THE WEIRD ADVERSARIES ANNI-HILATE ALL SPEED RECORDS IN A THRILLING RACE THAT SPANS CONTINENTS...

...AND OCEANS!

GET A HORSE!

FASTER! FASTER!--A HUMAN BEING OUTDISTANCE ONE OF MY SUPER-STRATO-LINERS? IMPOSSIBLE!

SORRY--I'M PRESSING THE MOTORS TO THE LIMIT!

LATER-WHEN THEY RETURN TO THE STARTING POINT...

IT APPEARS I AM THE VICTOR!

AND YOU DON'T LOOK THE LEAST BIT TIRED! - INCREDIBLE!

THE NEXT CONTEST?

ONE WHICH SHOULD CONFOUND YOU!--TO DETERMINE WHO CAN RISE THE HIGHEST ABOVE THE EARTH, AND STILL RETURN SAFELY!

46

AS ONE OF LUTHOR'S PLANES STREAKS UPWARD, *SUPERMAN* LEAPS IN ITS WAKE...

HERE WE GO!

47

UP ROCKET THE TWO--UP THRU FLEECY CLOUDS

GOOD THING I'M NOT SUBJECT TO VERTIGO!

48

--HIGHER AND HIGHER--INTO THE STRATOSPHERE--

49

--AND BEYOND!

WE'RE TOO HIGH! I'M LOSING CONTROL!

WE'RE BEYOND THE STRONG GRAVITATIONAL PULL!

50

HELPLESS, LUTHOR'S VESSEL DRIFTS TO CERTAIN DOOM IN THE CLAMMY CLUTCH OF OUTER-SPACE---!

51

KICKING FURIOUSLY, HIS FEET BLURRING LIKE PROPELLOR-BLADES, *SUPERMAN* BATTLES THE FORCES OF GRAVITATION...AND COMMENCES TO FALL TOWARD EARTH...!

52

CAN'T YOU THINK OF ANYTHING TOUGHER?

AGAIN YOU'VE TRIUMPHED!

53

INSTEAD OF FACING A SHRINKING VIOLET, THE WOLVES ARE FLUNG BACK...

DON'T CROWD ME!

I'D LIKE TO REMAIN AND TAME THESE WOLVES, BUT FIRST I'VE GOT TO TAKE CARE OF A HUMAN WOLF -- LUTHOR!

BUT AS *SUPERMAN* EMERGES FROM THE PIT, A POWERFUL NEW GAS IS RELEASED IN HIS FACE .... RENDERING HIM UNCONSCIOUS..

HE'S OUT!

LUTHOR WILL BE PLEASED!

LUTHOR'S HIRELINGS CARRY THE UNCONSCIOUS *SUPERMAN* TO A SPOT NEAR THEIR MASTER'S LABORATORY TOWER!

NOW TO PERMANENTLY REMOVE THIS FOE!

AS THE RAY STRIKES THE EARTH IT TREMBLES IN MIGHTY CONVULSIONS...CREVICES APPEAR IN THE GROUND...

SUPERMAN FALLS INTO ONE OF THEM!

NEXT INSTANT, THE CREVICE CLOSES, *BURYING SUPERMAN ALIVE!*

SUPERMAN

by JERRY SIEGEL and JOE SHUSTER

FOE OF ALL INTERESTS AND ACTIVITIES SUBVERSIVE TO THIS COUNTRY'S BEST INTERESTS, *SUPERMAN* LOSES NO TIME IN GOING INTO ACTION WHEN HE ENCOUNTERS A MENACE TO AMERICAN DEMOCRACY. SUPER-STRENGTH CLASHES WITH EVIL SUPER-CUNNING IN ANOTHER THRILLING, DRAMATIC ADVENTURE OF TODAY'S FOREMOST HERO, THE DARING DYNAMIC *MAN OF TOMORROW* --- SUPERMAN!!

EDITORIAL OFFICE OF THE *DAILY PLANET*...

WHAT'S ON THE FIRE FOR TODAY, CHIEF?

THE *DUKALIA-AMERICAN SPORTS FESTIVAL* IS BEING HELD TODAY AT THE *MUNICIPAL STADIUM*...I WANT BOTH YOU AND LOIS TO COVER IT...

THAT'S THE KIND OF ASSIGNMENT I LIKE. NOW IF YOU'D ONLY SEND US TO A BALL GAME TOMORROW.

BUT WHEN THE TWO REPORTERS REACH THE STADIUM, THEY DISCOVER TO THEIR DISCOMFITURE...

I DON'T LIKE THIS, CLARK! DUKALIA IS ON UNFRIENDLY TERMS WITH US -- AND THIS LOOKS MORE LIKE AN ANTI-AMERICAN DEMONSTRATION THAN ANYTHING ELSE!

SH-HH! NOT SO LOUD - OR WE MAY GET MORE THAN JUST DIRTY LOOKS!

SEE THAT MAN OVER THERE? IT'S EX-CAPTAIN LANG!

I REMEMBER -- HE WAS DISCHARGED FROM THE UNITED STATES NAVY FOR CONDUCT UNBECOMING AN OFFICER. -- LET'S GET OUT OF HERE, LOIS. I DON'T LIKE OUR COMPANY. WE'VE SEEN ENOUGH!

BUT SHORTLY AFTER...

WHAT'S THE MATTER NOW?

I MUST HAVE DROPPED MY FOUNTAIN PEN. WAIT HERE!

AS SOON AS HE IS OUT OF LOIS' SIGHT, CLARK WHIPS OFF HIS CIVILIAN GARMENTS STANDING REVEALED AS THE MIGHTY SUPERMAN...!

I'M CONVINCED THIS SPORTS FESTIVAL IS BUT THE FRONT FOR AN ORGANIZATION FOMENTING UNAMERICAN ACTIVITIES. THE DUKALIAN CONSUL IS ABOUT TO SPEAK—I'LL LEND AN EAR. AND IF I DON'T LIKE WHAT HE SAYS...

DUKALIAN CONSUL KARL WOLFF HOLDS HIS AUDIENCE SPELLBOUND

PRESENT HERE IS THE FLOWER OF DUKALIAN YOUTH! YOU HAVE SEEN THEM PERFORM PHYSICAL FEATS WHICH NO OTHER HUMAN BEINGS CAN. PROOF, I TELL YOU, THAT WE DUKALIANS ARE SUPERIOR TO ANY OTHER RACE OR NATION! PROOF THAT WE ARE ENTITLED TO BE THE MASTERS OF AMERICA!

STREAKING DOWN ONTO THE FIELD, INTERRUPTING THE CONSUL'S SPIEL—SUPERMAN!

LET'S SEE JUST HOW SUPERIOR YOU REALLY ARE!

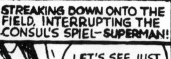

SO YOU'RE THE SHOT-PUTTER, EH? LET'S SEE IF WE CAN BREAK YOUR RECORD—OR YOUR NECK!

A HEAVE OF THE MAN OF STEEL'S MIGHTY ARM AND THE ATHLETE LANDS A DISTANCE AHEAD OF HIS SHOT-PUT....

NEXT, SUPERMAN SNATCHES THE POLE VAULT CHAMP....

SO THAT'S YOUR RECORD HEIGHT, EH?

NOW YOU CAN SAY YOU BEAT YOUR OWN RECORD-- WITHOUT THE AID OF THE POLE!

SEIZING ANOTHER ATHLETE BY THE NECK AND SEAT OF HIS PANTS, SUPERMAN PUSHES HIM BEFORE HIM IN THE FASTEST HUNDRED YARD DASH THAT HAS EVER BEEN RUN!

TWO SECONDS FLAT!

TAKING THE HURDLE CHAMPION UNDER HIS ARM, SUPERMAN CARRIES HIM OVER ALL THE HURDLES IN ONE GREAT LEAP....

HOW'S THAT?

LANG AT THAT UN-AMERICAN DEMONSTRA-TION! CLARK, I THINK HE DESERVES INVESTIG-ATION!

YOU'D JUST BE WASTING YOUR TIME, LOIS! ("-I MUST DIS-COURAGE HER. IF LANG IS IN-VOLVED IN SIN-ISTER ACTIV-ITIES, IT WOULD BE DANGEROUS FOR LOIS TO IN-TERFERE")

("-I MIGHT HAVE EXPECTED HIM TO DISCOURAGE ME. HE WANTS TO HOG THE STORY FOR HIMSELF.-") VERY WELL. IF YOU'RE NOT INTERESTED, GOODBYE!

SEE YOU LATER! ("-OF THAT, THERE CAN BE NO DOUBT!-")

LOIS MAKES A BEE-LINE FOR LIEUTENANT FERGUSON OF THE NAVAL INTELLIGENCE...

YOU KNOW YOU CAN TRUST ME. WHY WAS CAP-TAIN LANG DIS-CHARGED FROM THE NAVY?

HE SHOWED SUSPICIOUSLY UNDUE INTER-EST IN BATTLE-SHIP CON-STRUCTION PLANS.

I REMEMBER HAVING SEEN LANG IN THE LOBBY OF THE CART-WRIGHT HOTEL. THERE-FORE-- THAT'S MY NEXT STOP!

YOU'RE CERTAIN THAT LANG IS NOT IN?

I RANG HIS ROOM TWICE. THERE'S NO ANSWER FROM ROOM 221.

LATER-- LOIS RETURNS WITH A SUITCASE....

CAN I HAVE ROOM 219? I FOUND IT VERY QUIET ON MY LAST VISIT.

YOU'RE FORTUNATE. THE ROOM IS UNOC-CUPIED.

NO SOONER DOES LOIS ENTER ROOM 219 THAN SHE REMOVES A ROPE AND HOOK FROM THE SUITCASE AND SWINGS IT OUT SO THAT IT CATCHES ONTO A LEDGE OUTSIDE ROOM 221....

MADE IT THE FIRST TRY!

STEPPING THRU THE WINDOW, LOIS SWINGS OUT TOWARD HER DESTINATION.

I HOPE THAT HOOK HOLDS!

OOPS!-- ALMOST LOST MY GRIP THAT TIME!

WHAT--! SOMEONE INSERTING A KEY IN THE DOOR!

CAUTIOUSLY ENTERING THE DARKENED ROOM, THE MAN PLACES A PACKAGE IN THE TOP DRAWER OF THE DRESSER

("--IT'S ONE OF THE PRIZE-WINNING ATHLETES WHO ATTENDED THE SPORTS FESTIVAL!--")

AFTER THE ATHLETE DEPARTS, LOIS EMERGES FROM HER HIDING PLACE AND OPENS THE PACKAGE...

WHEW! BILLS OF HIGH DENOMINATION-- THEY MUST TOTAL AT LEAST FIFTY THOUSAND DOLLARS!

ABRUPTLY, STRONG FINGERS ENCIRCLE LOIS' NECK FROM BEHIND....

LOIS KICKS BACK SHARPLY, STRIKING HER ASSAILANT'S KNEE. AS THE GRIP ON HER THROAT QUICKLY RELAXES, SHE TEARS FREE AND DASHES TOWARD THE DOOR...

I'VE GOT TO GET OUT OF HERE!

BUT AS SHE OPENS THE DOOR--!

L-LANG!

WELL...I SEE I'VE COME NOT A MOMENT TOO EARLY!

REMEMBER--THE FIFTY THOUSAND DOLLARS WAS JUST FOR A DEMONSTRATION RIDE ON MY STARTLING INVENTION....

TRUE! AN ADDITIONAL TWO MILLION DOLLARS WILL BE PAID FOR THE INVENTION IF IT MEETS WITH MY COMPLETE SATISFACTION!

IF YOU HAVE MADE A GREAT MILITARY DISCOVERY, DON'T YOU THINK YOUR OWN COUNTRY IS ENTITLED TO IT?

I SWORE THIS COUNTRY WOULD PAY FOR DISMISSING ME FROM THE NAVY! I HAVE WOLFF'S ASSURANCE THAT WHEN DUKALIA CONQUERS AMERICA, I WILL RECEIVE AN IMPORTANT POST!

DUKALIA APPRECIATES GENIUS...AND LOYALTY!

WHEN LOIS HAD DEPARTED, CLARK REMOVED HIS OUTER GARMENTS AND TUCKED THEM BENEATH HIS **SUPERMAN** CLOAK.....

SO LOIS THINKS LANG COULD STAND INVESTIGATING! HM-MM! DOESN'T SOUND LIKE A BAD IDEA, AT THAT!

A GREAT LEAP LAUNCHES THE *MAN OF STEEL* TO A POSITION ATOP THE STADIUM...

LANG BELOW--WHISPERING TO SOMEONE IN THE CROWD.

WHAT **SUPERMAN'S** AMAZING SUPER-SENSITIVE HEARING ENABLES HIM TO OVERHEAR...

I ACCEPT YOUR TERMS!

SPLENDID!

AS EX-CAPTAIN LANG DRIVES OFF, SUPERMAN STREAKS DOWN AND SWINGS HIMSELF BENEATH THE CAR.....

GUESS I'LL BE A NON-PAYING PASSENGER!

AS LANG SWIFTLY ROUNDS A CURVE ON A MOUNTAIN ROAD, A HUGE TRUCK UNEXPECTEDLY LOOMS BEFORE HIM... THE DISCHARGED NAVAL OFFICER FRANTICALLY TWISTS THE WHEEL...

A SURE-CRASH!

A COLLISION IS NARROWLY AVOIDED! BUT--THE CAR'S WHEELS SLIP OFF THE ROAD!

THE AUTO COMMENCES TIPPING OVER, PREPARATORY TO BEGINNING THE TERRIBLE DOWNWARD PLUNGE!

BRACING HIS HAND AGAINST THE SIDE OF THE CLIFF, SUPERMAN SWERVES THE CAR BACK TO AN UPRIGHT POSITION ON THE ROAD. . . .

WHEW! I'VE NEVER COME CLOSER TO DEATH! I CAN THANK MY LUCKY STARS!

NO, LANG, YOU CAN THANK SUPERMAN!

LATER--PARKING NEAR THE WATERFRONT, LANG CAUTIOUSLY OPENS A HIGH GATE, THEN LOCKS IT AFTER HIMSELF. . . .

AN INSTANT LATER, THE *MAN OF STEEL* EASILY VAULTS OVER THE BARRIER . . . . .

THEY'LL HAVE TO BUILD THIS MUCH HIGHER IF THEY HOPE TO KEEP *ME* OUT!

TAKE IT OUT FOR A TRIAL SPIN!

AS YOU DIRECT, SIR!

SLOWLY, THE CRAFT MOVES SEAWARD, THEN COMMENCES TO SUBMERGE. . . .

PROVIDING YOU DELIVER THE MONEY AS PROMISED, I'M READY TO TAKE YOU ON A DEMONSTRATION VOYAGE AT ONCE!

NO NAME HAS BEEN MENTIONED BUT I COULD RECOGNIZE THAT VOICE ANYWHERE! LANG IS SPEAKING TO WOLFF!

AN INSTANT LATER, **SUPERMAN** IS AMAZED TO DISCOVER THAT THO HE MAKES USE OF HIS TELESCOPIC VISION. . . .

THAT STRANGE VESSEL--COMPLETELY DISAPPEARED--NO LONGER TO BE SEEN!

I CAN TAKE MY LEAVE, NOW! IF MY HUNCH IS TRUE, I'LL SOON HAVE COMPANY!

WH-WHAT HAS HAPPENED? WHERE IS THE INTRUDER?

WE WERE POWERLESS TO PREVENT HIS ESCAPE!

IT WAS THAT INCREDIBLY STRONG MAN WHO MADE FOOLS OF US AT THE STADIUM. HIS STRENGTH IS BEYOND ALL BELIEF!

JUST AS I HAD HOPED! WOLFF IS LOSING NO TIME MAKING A BEE-LINE FOR THAT WHARF!

AS WOLFF NOTES SUPERMAN'S SHADOW ON THE ROAD....

THAT HUGE SHADOW-- WHAT CAN CAUSE IT? --MUST BE A BIRD!

WOLFF JOINS LANG....

LOIS AMONG THEM--A CAPTIVE! I'VE GOT TO DO SOMETHING...!

SWIFTLY, SUPERMAN DONS HIS OUTER GARMENTS WHICH HE HAS CARRIED BENEATH HIS CLOAK....

ENTER CLARK KENT!

CLARK DELIBERATELY PERMITS HIMSELF TO BE CAPTURED...

GOT YOU!

UH-HHH!

CLARK! HOW-- HOW DID YOU GET HERE?

YOU'RE NOT THE ONLY ENTERPRISING REPORTER ON THE STAFF!

ANOTHER REPORTER, EH? I SUGGEST WE DISPOSE OF BOTH OF THEM IMMEDIATELY!

NO WE'LL TAKE THEM ALONG AS PRISONERS.-- PLENTY OF TIME TO ATTEND TO THEM LATER!

CAPTORS AND PRISONERS ENTER THE UNUSUAL VESSEL, AND AS THEY DO SO, THE HATCH CLOSES....

THE SIDES --MADE OF A TRANSPARENT PLASTIC! WE SEEM TO BE MOVING AT TERRIFIC SPEED!

YOU ARE VERY OBSERVANT... TOO MUCH SO FOR YOUR OWN GOOD!

YOU THINK THAT ASTONISHING? WATCH THIS!

AS LANG PULLS THE LEVER, THE VESSEL SLANTS SHARPLY UP INTO THE AIR!

THEN--AS IT DIVES BENEATH THE WATER'S SURFACE ONCE AGAIN

YOU SEE... MY SHIP CAN TRAVEL *ABOVE* WATER AS WELL AS *BENEATH* IT! -- QUITE AN IMPORTANT DISCOVERY FOR MODERN WARFARE, EH? AND ANYONE CAN OPERATE IT WITH THIS SIMPLE LEVER!

THAT'S ALL I WANT TO KNOW! HEAD FOR THE PANAMA CANAL-- AND FORGET ABOUT THE TWO MILLION... YOU'LL NEVER LIVE TO SEE IT!

YOU CAN PUT DOWN THAT GUN! THIS SIGNAL SUMMONS MY MEN!

AH--BUT I'VE ANTICIPATED YOU. HALL HAS ALREADY ATTENDED TO THEM... *SPY!* YOU CAN DROP THE POSE. I HAPPEN TO HAVE KNOWN ALL ALONG YOU STILL SERVE THE U.S. NAVY AND HAVE USED THIS NEW INVENTION TO SNARE FOREIGN SPYS!

YOU MUST BE COMPLETELY MAD! THIS CRAFT HASN'T THE SLIGHTEST CHANCE OF PENETRATING THE PANAMA CANAL DEFENSES!

YOU UNDERESTIMATE MY INGENUITY!

AS WOLFF HAD PREARRANGED, THE SKY-SUB IS MANEUVERED SO THAT IT IS ATTACHED TO A HOOK BENEATH A LARGE FREIGHTER...

WITH THE AID OF SPECIAL APPARATUS, TORPEDOES AND BOMBS ARE TRANSFERED FROM THE FREIGHTER TO THE SUB...

WHEN THE FREIGHTER APPROACHES THE PANAMA CANAL, IT WILL BE INSPECTED AND PASSED. NO ONE WILL KNOW THAT HIDDEN BENEATH IT IS A CRAFT THAT WILL BE RELEASED AT A VITAL SPOT TO BLOW UP THE CANAL!

YOU WON'T GET AWAY WITH IT!

BUT IT APPEARS HE IS!

77

AT THE CONSUL'S ORDERS, CLARK IS PLACED WITHIN AN EMPTY TORPEDO-TUBE....

PLEASE DON'T! THIS IS MURDER!

YOU'LL ONLY BE IN THE WAY NOW. YOU FIRST--THEN... THE OTHERS SHARE YOUR FATE!

YOU --YOU BUTCHER!

BUT DESPITE LOIS' PLEAS, THE TORPEDO BEARING CLARK IS SHOT INTO THE WATER...

THE SIDES OF THE TORPEDO SPLIT OPEN AS CLARK SMASHES HIS WAY OUT...

HERE'S WHERE' EXIT!

SWIFTLY CHANGING HIS GARMENTS, **SUPERMAN** HIDES HIS CIVILIAN GARMENTS BENEATH HIS CLOAK...

GOT TO GET BACK --BEFORE HE HARMS LOIS--!

SO HERE GOES!

SEIZING THE VESSEL, **SUPERMAN** FORCES IT UP TOWARD THE SURFACE...

GET MOVING!

LET THE GIRL AND LANG ALONE OPEN THE HATCH WHEN WE REACH THE SURFACE AND SEE WHAT THE TROUBLE IS!

WHAT CAN IT BE?

IT'S THAT INFERNALLY STRONG MEDDLER --GET HIM!

THIS BOMB OUGHT TO TAKE CARE OF HIM!

SORRY-- IT DIDN'T BOTHER ME A BIT!

TO THE FREIGHTER WITH YOU! JOIN YOUR PALS!

SWIFTLY, *SUPERMAN* DONS HIS CIVILIAN GARMENTS, AND HURRYING DOWN INTO THE SKY-SUB FREES LOIS AND LANE

CLARK! HOW DID YOU EVER ESCAPE?

SUPERMAN SAVED ME!

QUICK! FREE ME! WE'VE GOT TO SEE THAT THOSE CON-SPIRATORS DON'T ESCAPE!

UNDER LANG'S CONTROL, THE VESSEL ZOOMS UP INTO THE AIR...

LOOK--THE FREIGHTER'S CREW IS PULLING AWAY FROM THE SHIP IN LIFE-BOATS!

SMART LADS! THEY KNOW WHAT'S GOOD FOR THEM!

A CHARGE OF BOMBS DROPPED BY CLARK BLOWS THE FREIGHTER TO BITS...

THAT SHOULD RENDER THEM HARMLESS!

BUT THEY'LL ESCAPE!

NO THEY WON'T! I'LL BROAD-CAST A MESSAGE TO THE COAST GUARD!

SHORTLY AFTER...

I WANT TO THANK BOTH OF YOU-- FOR SAVING THE INVENTION, AIDING IN THE CAPTURE OF THOSE SPIES ... AND...

DON'T THANK US, THANK SUPERMAN!

LET'S PHONE IN THE STORY BEFORE SOME ONE BEATS US TO IT!

THE END

SUPERMAN

REG. U.S PAT OFF.

by JERRY SIEGEL and JOE SHUSTER

THE UNITY OF THE NATION IS THREATENED BY THE MACHINATIONS OF A CUNNING BEING KNOWN AS "THE LIGHT". **SUPERMAN,** *DEFENDER OF DEMOCRACY,* SWINGS INTO ACTION TO COMBAT A DARK MENACE THAT THREATENS TO ENGULF AND ENSLAVE A CONTINENT!

EDITORIAL OFFICE OF THE *DAILY PLANET....*

SENATOR BILLINGSLEY IS TO SPEAK AT *NATIONAL HALL.* I WANT BOTH OF YOU TO COVER THE EVENT.

A POLITICAL SPEECH!

WHY NOT ASSIGN US SOMETHING MORE INTERESTING?

I'VE BEEN INFORMED ON THE QUIET THAT SOMEONE NAMED "THE LIGHT" HAS ISSUED A WARNING THAT BILLINGSLEY WILL NEVER SPEAK AT THAT MEETING. ANYTHING MAY HAPPEN!

THAT'S *DIFFERENT!*

COME ON, CLARK!

LATER...

HE'S ALREADY LATE-- DO YOU THINK...?

I DON'T KNOW **WHAT** TO THINK! EXCUSE ME, LOIS. I'D LIKE TO MAKE A TELEPHONE CALL.

BUT INSTEAD OF APPROACHING THE TELEPHONE BOOTH, CLARK STEPS INTO AN EMPTY OFFICE AND REMOVES HIS OUTER GARMENTS...

"THE LIGHT" MAY NOT BE A CRANK AFTER ALL-- I'D BETTER LOOK INTO THIS-- AS **SUPERMAN...!**

MOMENTS LATER--THE COLOR- FUL COSTUMED FIGURE OF THE MIGHTY *MAN OF TOMORROW* STREAKS THRU THE FLEECY CLOUDS AT BREATH-TAKING SPEED....

THE SENATOR'S CAR SHOULD BE COMING ALONG THE *CARROLL HIGHWAY*. IT'S ENTIRELY POSSIBLE THAT I'M BEING UNDULY APPREHENSIVE, BUT...

THAT INSTANT--WITHIN SENATOR TOM BILLINGSLEY'S AUTO....

"THE LIGHT" MAY BE A JOKE TO YOU, SENATOR-- BUT WE'RE NOT TAKING ANY CHANCES!

NONSENSE! "THE LIGHT" IS A HARM- LESS POISON PEN WRITER.

TOWARD THE SENATOR'S CAR DRIVES A SEDAN.--UNUSUAL? DEFINITELY *NOT*! THAT IS, *UNTIL*...

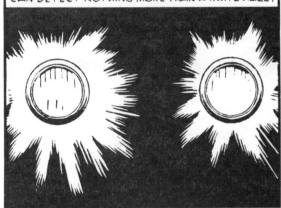

THE HEADLIGHTS OF THE NEARING CAR UN- EXPECTEDLY FLASH ON! FROM THEM EMERGES A BRILLIANCE OF SUCH STARK, BLINDING QUALITIES THAT THE HUMAN EYE INSTANTLY CAN DETECT NOTHING MORE THAN A WHITE HAZE!

THOSE HEAD- LIGHTS--! I--I CAN'T SEE!

WHAT --!!

NEITHER CAN I!

BLINDED, THE DRIVER OF THE SENATOR'S AUTO INSTINCTIVELY JAMS ON HIS BRAKES! THERE IS THE SOUND OF APPROACHING FOOTSTEPS--THEN SILENCE, EXCEPT FOR THE SHOUTS OF THE CONFUSED BODYGUARDS...

②

ABRUPTLY--THE GLARE IS GONE! IT TAKES SOME TIME FOR THEM TO ACCUSTOM THEIR EYES AGAIN TO NORMAL LIGHT, BUT WHEN THEY DO, THE GUARDS DISCOVER

HE'S GONE--! THE SENATOR IS **GONE**!

KID- NAPPED!

AT THAT MOMENT, THE *MAN OF STEEL* ALIGHTS BESIDE THE SENATOR'S CAR....

WHAT HAPPENED?

IT'S **SUPERMAN**!

HE MUST BE TO BLAME! GET HIM!

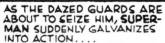
AS THE DAZED GUARDS ARE ABOUT TO SEIZE HIM, **SUPER-MAN** SUDDENLY GALVANIZES INTO ACTION....

WE'LL MAKE YOU TALK!

WHERE HAVE YOU TAKEN SENATOR BILLINGSLEY?

THE *MAN OF TOMORROW*, MOVING AT SUPER-SPEED, IS NO LONGER BEFORE THEM....

HUH? WHERE IS HE?

YOU MIGHT TURN AROUND, YOU KNOW!

I'VE NOTHING TO DO WITH THE SENATOR'S KIDNAPPING, I ASSURE YOU. --JUST WHAT DID HAPPEN?

YOU KNOW VERY WELL.--YOUR MEN TURNED ON THAT BLINDING LIGHT IN THEIR HEAD-LIGHTS--AND YOU SNATCHED THE SENATOR.

HE'S TRYING TO ESCAPE!

WHAT DO YOU MEAN "TRYING"? HE **IS** ESCAPING!

SAVE YOUR BULLETS, BOYS! THEY'RE AS HARM-LESS AS PEAS!

AN AUTO--ARMED WITH A BLINDING LIGHT THAT RENDERS THOSE WHO SIGHT IT HELPLESS! FANTASTIC! AND YET-- THERE'S NO DOUBT THAT THE SENATOR *HAS* DISAPPEARED!

A SPEED-ING AUTO BELOW-- MIGHT BE A JOY-RIDER --BUT I'LL GLANCE WITH-IN IT WITH MY X-RAY VISION.

WHAT **SUPERMAN**'S MARVELOUS SUPER-SIGHT REVEALS TO HIM!

THAT'S THE SENATOR... --NO DOUBT ABOUT IT! **HERE** I GO!!

DOWN IN THE VERY PATH OF THE ONRUSHING AUTO PLUMMETS **SUPERMAN**....!

WHOA, THERE!

THE CAR *INCREASES* SPEED! ON FLASH THE HEADLIGHTS, BOMBARDING THE *MAN OF STEEL* WITH BLINDING BEAMS...

WANT TO FIGHT, EH?

FULL INTO THE FIGURE OF **SUPERMAN** CRASHES THE MYSTERY-AUTO! UP INTO THE AIR HIS BODY IS WHIRLED...!

BUT--SOMERSAULTING--THE *MAN OF TOMORROW* ALIGHTS UPON THE AUTOMOBILE'S REAR BUMPER...!

CAN'T GET RID OF ME *THAT* EASILY!

ONE SWIFT MOVEMENT AND **SUPERMAN** RIPS OPEN THE BACK OF THE CAR....

I'VE BEEN MIGHTY PATIENT UP TO NOW, BUT DON'T GET ME *SORE*!

FRANTICALLY, THE SENATOR'S CAPTORS DISCHARGE BOLTS OF BLAZING BRILLIANCE TOWARD **SUPERMAN** FROM THEIR TINY RODS.... BUT TO NO AVAIL....

HERE'S SOME OF THE PUNISHMENT YOU'VE BEEN BEGGING FOR!

OUT OF CONTROL, THE AUTO PLUNGES TOWARD A RAVINE, BUT SEIZING THE LIMB OF A PROJECTING TREE, **SUPERMAN** HALTS THE MACHINE AT THE VERY EDGE OF THE SHARP INCLINE....

THAT'S FAR ENOUGH!

④

MOMENTS LATER--DOWN OUT OF THE SKY PLUMMETS THE AMAZING *MAN OF STEEL.* DEPOSITING THE CAR BEFORE THE ASTOUNDED GUARDS, HE SPRINGS OFF....

YOU'LL FIND THE SENATOR AND THE MEN WHO CAPTURED HIM IN THERE--CONFISCATE THEIR LIGHT-RODS!

FIRST YOU KIDNAP THE SENATOR, THEN RETURN HIM! I DON'T GET IT!

RETURNING TO *NATIONAL HALL,* **SUPERMAN** DONS HIS OUTER GARMENTS, ONCE AGAIN ASSUMING HIS IDENTITY OF THE MEEK *DAILY PLANET* REPORTER....

BETTER HURRY BACK TO LOIS BEFORE SHE BEGINS TO WONDER WHETHER I'M DICTATING A NOVEL OVER THE TELEPHONE!

IT CERTAINLY TOOK YOU LONG ENOUGH!

I MIGHT SAY THE SAME FOR THE SENATOR...

SHORTLY AFTER, SENATOR BILLINGSLEY ENTERS THE AUDITORIUM--HE LOSES NO TIME IN MAKING A SPECIAL ANNOUNCEMENT....

A FANATIC NAMED *"THE LIGHT"* PROPHECIED I WOULD NOT SPEAK TO YOU TODAY. HE TRIED TO MAKE THAT THREAT COME TRUE. -- FORTUNATELY, HE FAILED!

LATER--AS THE SENATOR MAKES THE ANNOUNCED ADDRESS, CLARK, KEEPING KEEN WATCH, OBSERVES A SUSPICIOUS INDIVIDUAL ENTER.

("--HE DELIBERATELY DROPPED A SMALL PILL BEHIND THAT VASE!--")

MOMENTS LATER--THERE IS A SUDDEN BLINDING FLASH--AN EYE-SCORCHING BLAZE OF LIGHT. THEN....

WHAT --!!

SHIELD YOUR EYES!

A MESSAGE IS TO BE SEEN ON THE WALL, WRITTEN IN LETTERS OF BLAZING *LIGHT!*

YOU MAY HAVE ESCAPED THIS TIME, SENATOR, BUT THERE WILL BE OTHER ATTEMPTS, AND THEY MAY NOT FAIL

--*"THE LIGHT"*

IN THE CONFUSION THAT FOLLOWS, CLARK ATTEMPTS TO FOLLOW THE SUSPICIOUS CHARACTER HE HAD OBSERVED, BUT LOIS BLOCKS HIS PATH....

LET GO, LOIS!

FORGET YOUR PANIC! GO TO THE PHONE AND CALL THE NEWSPAPER OFFICE!

THAT YOU, CLARK? GET BACK TO THE OFFICE AT ONCE! PROMINENT MEN ARE VANISHING BY THE DOZEN--KIDNAPPED BY *"THE LIGHT"*!

I'LL BE RIGHT THERE, WHITE!

AND TO THINK WE BELIEVED "THE LIGHT" MIGHT BE A HARMLESS CRANK!

THAT'S ALL CHANGED NOW! ("-I'D LIKE TO HAVE TRAILED THAT SUSPICIOUS CHAP, BUT THAT PLEASURE WILL HAVE TO BE INDEFINITELY POSTPONED.-")

UNKNOWN TO CLARK AND LOIS, THEY ARE PURSUED BY A SLEEK SEDAN....

WITHIN THE TRAILING CAR....

BUT WHY WASTE OUR TIME ON THESE TWO REPORTERS?

"THE LIGHT" CONSIDERS THEM DANGEROUS, AND THAT'S ENOUGH FOR ME.

DRAWING ABREAST OF THE REPORTERS' CAR, THE GOGGLED THUGS UNEXPECTEDLY FLASH THEIR ROD-WEAPONS AT CLARK....

("-I'LL PRETEND TO BE BLINDED.-")

I--I-- CAN'T SEE!

MY-- EYES--!

CLARK SLAMS ON THE BRAKES. HE AND LOIS, BOTH APPARENTLY DAZED, ARE DRAGGED INTO THE INTERIOR OF THE SEDAN....

WH-WHAT --??

NOT A PEEP OUTA EITHER OF YA-- GET IN THERE!

MINUTES LATER....

I SEE THE EFFECTS OF "THE LIGHT" HAVE WORN OFF!

I SEE, NOW! YOU'RE AGENTS OF "THE LIGHT"!

BRIGHT GIRL!

SHORTLY AFTER....THE TWO REPORTERS ARE FORCED INTO AN OUT-OF-THE-WAY BUILDING...

IN THERE!

WHAT-- WHAT ARE YOU GOING TO DO TO US?

THAT'S WHAT WE'D LIKE TO KNOW.

THE BOSS SAYS TO RUB 'EM OUT!

THERE'S YOUR ANSWER, LADY!

NO!

("-WHAT A PREDICAMENT!--I CAN'T PERMIT THESE THUGS TO GET AWAY WITH MURDER, YET--IF I ACT AS SUPERMAN I'LL BE FORCED TO REVEAL MY TRUE IDENTITY!-")

⑥

NOW?

SURE, WHY NOT?

LET'S GET IT OVER WITH!

THE THUGS WHIRL AT THE SOUND OF AN UNEXPECTED VOICE BEHIND THEM....

DROP THOSE GUNS!

WHA----!!

I DON'T SEE ANYONE!

BUT I HEARD A VOICE!

SO DID I!

ACTING AT TERRIFIC SPEED, SUPERMAN REMOVES HIS OUTER GARMENTS....

HOPE THIS LITTLE BIT OF VENTRILOQUISM DOES THE TRICK...!

OUT THRU THE DOOR HE SPEEDS FASTER THAN A GUST OF WIND...

...AROUND THE SIDE OF THE BUILDING....

THIS CALLS FOR SPEED...AND I MEAN SPEED PLUS!!

CRASHING IN THRU A WINDOW, SUPERMAN BANGS THE THUGS TOGETHER....

SURPRISE!

HEY! OUCH!

UH-HHH!

HUH!

...THEN, BACK AROUND THE HOUSE SPEEDS SUPERMAN RETRACING HIS STEPS....

ALL I HOPE IS THAT LOIS HASN'T YET HAD TIME TO GLANCE BACK TOWARD ME!

...SWIFTLY SUPERMAN DIVES INTO HIS OUTER GARMENTS AS LOIS COMMENCES TO TURN....

("-SECONDS... TO MAKE IT...!-")

CLARK-- DID YOU SEE THAT? SUPERMAN!

GOOD THING FOR US HE SHOWED UP!

("-AND A GOOD THING FOR ME LOIS DIDN'T TURN A SECOND SOONER!-")

CASEY? HURRY DOWN TO THE FOLLOWING ADDRESS--WE'VE GOT SOME OF *"THE LIGHT"*'S THUGS HERE--AND I'M NOT KIDDING!

WE'D BETTER GET THEM TIED BEFORE THEY REVIVE!

LATER....

SO YOU WEREN'T FOOLING, AFTER ALL! HOW DID YOU EVER CAPTURE ALL THOSE MEN SINGLE-HANDED, CLARK?

THE TRUTH IS THAT CLARK WAS STANDING BESIDE ME, WHILE *SUPERMAN* CLEANED UP THOSE CRIMINALS.

WHO IS *"THE LIGHT"*?

YOU'LL LEARN NOTHIN' FROM US, COPPER!

PERHAPS YOU'LL HAVE BETTER LUCK WITH THEM AT HEAD-QUARTERS, SERGEANT!

LATER--AT THE *DAILY PLANET*...

PROMINENT MEN THROUGHOUT THE COUNTRY ARE DISAPPEARING BY THE SCORE!

BUT WHAT CAN BE *"THE LIGHT"*'S MOTIVE--RANSOM?

I'M AFRAID IT MAY BE SOMETHING EVEN *MORE SINISTER*.

NEWS FLASH! GOVERNOR BENSON HAS JUST RECEIVED A THREAT FROM THE NOTORIOUS CRIMINAL KNOWN AS *"THE LIGHT"*!

COVER THAT STORY!

BUT AS LOIS AND CLARK EMERGE FROM THE *PLANET* BUILDING....

WHERE'S CLARK?--WELL, I CAN'T WASTE ANY TIME WAITING FOR THAT SLOW-POKE!

LOIS WOULD HAVE BEEN VERY SURPRISED TO KNOW THAT THE "SLOWPOKE" HAS NEARLY REACHED THE GOVERNOR'S RESIDENCE BY THIS TIME....

I'LL KEEP AN EYE ON THE GOVERNOR'S MANSION.

NO SOONER DOES THE MIGHTY *MAN OF STEEL* ALIGHT UPON A TREE LIMB HIGH ABOVE THE GOVERNOR'S ESTATE WHEN....

SO WE MEET AGAIN...

SUPERMAN'S TELESCOPIC VISION HAS REVEALED TO HIM THAT ONE OF THE GUARDS PATROLLING THE ESTATE IS THE SUSPICIOUS CHARACTER HE HAD SEEN AT *NATIONAL HALL*....

AS THE GUARD WALKS UNDER THE TREE, A HAND SUDDENLY JERKS HIM UP INTO THE FOLIAGE

ULP--!

THEN--TWO FIGURES HURTLE HIGH UP INTO THE SKY LIKE AN UNLEASHED BOLT....

LET GO! WHAT'S THE IDEA--?

DON'T PLAY INNOCENT! I KNOW YOU WERE PLANTED THERE BY *"THE LIGHT"*! WHAT ARE HIS PLANS?

PLANS? I DON'T KNOW WHAT YOU'RE TALKING ABOUT!

WOULDN'T IT BE A PITY IF I WERE TO LOSE MY GRIP?

A MOMENT LATER--AS THE *MAN OF STEEL* RELEASES HIS HOLD, DOWN PLUNGES THE SCREAMING GUARD....

YEEE-EEEE!

AS HE DROPS, A VOICE BOOMS OUT OF THE CLOUDS NEAR HIM...

WHERE ARE YOU?

HERE I AM! CATCH ME! CATCH ME!

STRANGE--BUT UNLESS YOU'RE WILLING TO TALK, I'M AFRAID I WON'T BE *ABLE* TO FIND YOU!

I'LL TALK! I'LL TALK!

THAT'S BETTER!

I'LL TELL YOU ANYTHING YOU WANT TO KNOW-- ANYTHING!

⑨

GRADUALLY, THE BEAM CHANGES COLORS. — BLUE, RED, ORANGE, GREEN, YELLOW, PURPLE — *"THE LIGHT"* WHISPERS HYPNOTICALLY TO HIS CAPTIVE....

THOSE LIGHTS — BEATING INTO YOUR BRAIN — ROBBING YOU OF ALL INITIATIVE.

THE LIGHTS — THE PRETTY COLORED LIGHTS...

NOW — FREE HIM!

MOMENTS LATER, THE CAPTIVE RISES AT *"THE LIGHT"*'S COMMAND.

NOW WILL YOU OBEY ME?

YOU ARE MY MASTER, I SHALL DO AS YOU DIRECT...

YOU SEE HOW HE IS NOW AN INSTRUMENT OF MY WILL? SO SHALL IT BE WITH ALL OF YOU! YOU ARE ALL PROMINENT MEN IN YOUR LINES — WITH YOUR HELP, VICTORY IS ASSURED!

SOMEONE IS COMING!

SUPERMAN! I MIGHT HAVE EXPECTED HIS APPEARANCE — AND SO I AM PREPARED!

PLUNGING STRAIGHT AT *BARROWS' RIDGE*, SUPERMAN CLEARS A WAY FOR HIMSELF THRU THE SOLID ROCK....

HERE'S WHERE I PUT OUT *"THE LIGHT"*!

INTO THE VILLAINOUS SCIENTIST'S LABORATORY CRASHES THE *MAN OF TOMORROW*....

WE MEET AT LAST!

A MOMENT I HAVE LONG AWAITED!

THE MECHANISM BLASTING FORTH VARI-COLORED BEAMS OF LIGHT STRIKES AT THE *MAN OF STEEL*...

CAN'T MOVE!

HE'S HELP-LESS! AND NOW — I HAVE PLANS FOR SUPERMAN!

MY INSTRUCTIONS ARE AS FOLLOWS — COMPLETELY DESTROY ANY MILITARY MATERIALS THAT MAY BE USED AGAINST ME! GO!

I — OBEY!

SHORTLY AFTER...THE *MAN OF STEEL* PLUNGES DOWN OUT OF THE SKY BEFORE A GOVERNMENT ARMORY....

CRUSH-- DESTROY --!!

DRIVING BY, LOIS HALTS HER AUTO AS SHE SIGHTS THE *MAN OF TOMORROW*....

IT'S-- SUPERMAN!

WHAT'S HAPPENED TO YOU-- YOUR EYES...

"THE LIGHT" HAS COMMANDED ME TO CAUSE WHOLE-SALE DESTRUCT-ION--AND I MUST OBEY!

BUT YOU MUSTN'T-- YOU CAN'T-- YOU'VE ALWAYS FOUGHT EVIL... NEVER CHAMPIONED IT!

FOUGHT EVIL... FOUGHT IT...!

AIDED BY LOIS' APPEAL, **SUPERMAN**'S MIND CLEARS OF *"THE LIGHT"*'S INFLUENCE....

I--I'M ALL RIGHT NOW. YOU'LL NEVER KNOW HOW CLOSE I CAME TO...

I KNOW. BUT HADN'T YOU BETTER HURRY AND STOP *"THE LIGHT"* BEFORE IT'S TOO LATE?

MEANWHILE...

NOW TO MAKE ALL OF YOU MY SLAVES!

ABRUPTLY--IN THRU THE WALL CRASHES...

SUPERMAN! BUT I THOUGHT--

THAT I'D BE BUSY SPREADING DESTRUCTION? GUESS AGAIN!

AND AS FOR YOUR HYP-NOTIZING THESE MEN TO DO YOUR WILL... THAT'S *OUT*!

YOU'VE DESTROYED THE CONTROL-BOARD... BUT I'VE AN ACE UP MY SLEEVE!

12

SUPERMAN

by JERRY SIEGEL and JOE SHUSTER

SUPERMAN MEETS A STRANGE FOE IN THE MYSTERIOUS BEING KNOWN ONLY AS *"THE ARCHER"*. VICTIMS ARE GIVEN THE CHOICE OF PAYING A HEAVY FEE OR PERISHING BEFORE THE UNIQUE CRIMINAL'S DEADLY ACCURACY WITH THE BOW AND ARROW!

LIMOUSINE AFTER LIMOUSINE PULLS UP BEFORE THE *GAYFORD MANSION*....

THE REASON: WEALTHY THOMAS GAYFORD IS HOLDING ONE OF HIS INTERNATIONALLY FAMOUS PARTIES....

HAVE FUN, FOLKS! I'M FOOTING THE BILLS!

LATER--AS THE GUESTS LINE UP AROUND A BANQUET TABLE....

YOU'LL NEVER KNOW JUST HOW GLAD I AM TO HAVE ALL OF YOU HERE. YOU SEE, I HAVE HERE AN ANONYMOUS NOTE, SIGNED *"THE ARCHER"*. IT IT PROPHESIES THAT SINCE I HAVE FAILED TO PAY A DEMANDED RANSOM, I SHALL DIE TONIGHT.

WHAT?

SURELY YOU'RE JOKING!

NOT AT ALL. BUT THE JOKE'S ON *"THE ARCHER"*! I'VE POSTED GUARDS ABOUT THE PLACE. IT WILL BE IMPOSSIBLE FOR HIM TO ENTER!

BUT UNKNOWN TO GAYFORD --AT THAT VERY MOMENT ONE OF THE GUARDS LIES STILL IN DEATH...!

①

A GREEN-CLAD FIGURE LAUNCHES ITSELF FROM THE LIMB OF A HIGH TREE TO A BALCONY ON THE SIDE OF THE MANSION....

A TOAST, FRIENDS-- TO 'THE ARCHER'-- WHO MISSED HIS MARK!

LOOK!

UP THERE!

AAAGH HHH!!

GET "THE ARCHER"!

HE'S GONE!

CALL THE POLICE!!

EDITORIAL OFFICE OF THE DAILY PLANET....

WHERE IN BLAZES ARE LOIS LANE AND CLARK KENT?

THEY'RE NOT TO BE FOUND ANYWHERE, MR WHITE!

FINE THING! JUST WHEN THE BIGGEST NEWS STORY OF THE YEAR IS BREAKING, THEY HAVE TO PLAY HIDE-AND-SEEK!

ER-- MR. WH-WHITE...

YES?

I'LL BE GLAD TO COVER THE STORY FOR YOU!

YOU'LL COVER IT?

I--I'D LIKE TO BECOME A REAL REPORTER-- LIKE CLARK KENT, AND IF YOU'D ONLY GIVE ME A CHANCE...

HMM...YOU'D PROBABLY DO A BETTER JOB THAN CLARK, AT THAT. TELL YOU WHAT I'LL DO, KID. COME BACK AGAIN IN FIVE OR TEN YEARS.....AND I MAY GIVE YOU A BREAK....

T-TEN YEARS? --THAT'S A LONG TIME!

CLARK AND LOIS RETURN TO THE NEWSPAPER OFFICE.....

SO HERE YOU ARE! WHERE HAVE YOU TWO BEEN?

OUT LOOKING FOR MATERIAL --BUT NOT A THING IS STIRRING!

NOTHING, EH? GET DOWN TO THE GAYFORD MANSION! -- THOMAS GAYFORD HAS BEEN SLAIN BY A MYSTERIOUS PERSON NAMED "THE ARCHER". HE REFUSED TO PAY THE AMOUNT DEMANDED!

WHAT --?!

"THE ARCHER"! SOUNDS MELO- DRAMATIC!

--AND EXCITING

YOU, EH? IT DOESN'T TAKE YOU LONG TO SHOW UP WHEREVER NEWS IS BEING MADE!

THAT'S OUR BUSINESS!

HAVE YOU ANY IDEA WHO THIS "ARCHER" MAY BE, CASEY?

NONE AT ALL--YET, BUT WE HAVE SOME INTERESTING CLUES.

WHY DON'T YOU COOK UP A NEW COME-BACK?

THAT ONE'S A LITTLE SHOP- WORN!

QUIET, YOU TWO--OR I'LL HAVE YOU RUN OFF THE PLACE!

③

AT THAT MOMENT----

A NOTE-- PINNED TO THE WALL BY THE ARROW!

WHAT DOES IT SAY?

KEEP BACK. THIS IS CONFIDENTIAL POLICE BUSINESS!

WELL --??

NO HARM IN LETTING YOU KNOW. "THE ARCHER" SAYS HE KILLED GAYFORD TO SHOW THAT HE MEANS BUSINESS WHEN HE MAKES HIS DEMANDS!

QUICK, A TELEPHONE!

AS THEY DRIVE OFF, CLARK'S QUICK EYES NOTE....

("-AN ARROW-- STREAKING DOWN TOWARD US!-")

SWIFTLY, CLARK RAISES HIS HAND SO THAT THE ARROW BOUNCES OFF BEFORE IT REACHES LOIS....

WHAT WAS THAT NOISE?

I DIDN'T HEAR ANYTHING!

BUT THEN-- AS THEY SPEED DOWN AN INCLINE... CLARK MAKES ANOTHER STARTLING DISCOVERY....

("-THE BRAKES --THEY DON'T WORK--!-")

CLARK'S X-RAY VISION REVEALS TO HIM THAT THE BRAKES OF HIS CAR HAVE BEEN TAMPERED WITH....

("-COMING AROUND THAT CURVE AHEAD-- A TRUCK! THERE'S SURE TO BE A COLLISION--UNLESS...!-")

CAREFUL, CLARK!

SWIFTLY CLARK FOCUSES HIS EYES HYPNOTICALLY UPON LOIS LANE SO THAT SHE IS SWIFTLY AND PAINLESSLY RENDERED UNCONSCIOUS....

SHE'S OUT!

NO TIME TO CHANGE TO MY SUPERMAN COSTUME!

AS THE TRUCK HURTLES TOWARD HIM, KENT HEAVES HIS ROADSTER UP...!

HOPE THE TRUCK DRIVER DOESN'T GET A GOOD LOOK AT ME!

...AND VAULTS OVER THE ONCOMING TRUCK, ROADSTER AND ALL...!

THAT DOES IT!

THERE! THE BRAKE'S ARE OKAY AGAIN! BUT NOW TO START DRIVING AGAIN!

I--I MUST HAVE FALLEN ASLEEP!

YOU CERTAINLY DON'T FIND MY COMPANY VERY INTERESTING!

⑤

GOODNIGHT, LOIS,-- PLEASANT DREAMS!

I DOUBT IF I'LL SLEEP A WINK--NOT WITH "THE ARCHER" LOOSE...!

ONE THING I KNOW DEFINITELY--"THE ARCHER" DISLIKES INQUISITIVE REPORTERS!

WHEN CLARK REACHES HIS APARTMENT....

THIS DEMANDS FURTHER INVESTIGATION--FROM SUPERMAN!

SHORTLY AFTER, THE COLORFUL *MAN OF TOMORROW* HURTLES THRU THE DARK SKY...

TRACKING DOWN SOMEONE AS COLD AND CRUEL AS *"THE ARCHER"* WILL BE NO CINCH!

AND LATER--HE ALIGHTS ATOP THE BALCONY OUTSIDE THE *GAYFORD MANSION*....

ONE CLUE HE'S *SURE* TO HAVE LEFT BEHIND!

HIS FOOTPRINTS! MY MICROSCOPIC VISION MAKE THEM APPEAR AS CLEAR AS SIGN POSTS!

SUPERMAN LEAPS DOWN TO THE ROAD BELOW AND FAILS TO SIGHT SHADOWS CREEPING TOWARD HIM...

AND HERE'S WHERE HE STOOD WHEN HE TAMPERED WITH MY CAR'S BRAKES!

SUDDENLY, SEVERAL POLICEMEN SPRING AT THE *MAN OF STEEL*..

IT'S SUPERMAN!

GRAB HIM!

A MOMENT BEFORE THE POLICE REACH HIM, SUPERMAN DIVES AT THE GROUND AND BURROWS OUT OF VIEW...!

I'D BETTER EXIT!

STOP HIM!

AN INSTANT LATER HE POPS OUT OF THE GROUND BEHIND THE OFFICERS...

WERE YOU GENTLEMEN PAGING ME?

THERE HE IS!

DON'T LET HIM GET AWAY!

BUT OFF RACES SUPERMAN SO SWIFTLY THAT HE IS OUT OF VIEW IN MOMENTS...!

IT WOULD BE USELESS TO ATTEMPT TO REASON WITH THEM!

6

NEXT MORNING....

WHERE'S LOIS?

AT THE CARNAHAN RESIDENCE-- "THE ARCHER" HAS STRUCK AGAIN!

WAIT, MR. KENT! CAN I GO WITH YOU?

NOT NOW, JIMMY, SOME OTHER TIME, PERHAPS.

LATER...

HAS "THE ARCHER" REALLY DABBLED IN MURDER AGAIN?

YES, BUT IF YOU'RE LOOKING FOR NEWS, YOU'RE A LITTLE LATE. I'VE ALREADY TELEPHONED IN THE STORY.

AND HE LEFT ANOTHER NOTE. SAYS MANY MORE MEN WILL DIE--UNLESS THEY LEARN TO PAY PROMPTLY....

--IN THE DOORWAY!

IT'S--

"THE ARCHER"!

STAND BACK, OR...

SIMULTANEOUSLY, CLARK AND THE SERGEANT LEAP FOR THE MENACING FIGURE, BRINGING IT DOWN....

GOT HIM!

GET THE BOW OUT OF HIS HAND!

CLARK--YOU SURPRISE ME!

I GUESS IT WAS REFLEX ACTION!

AND NOW, MR. ARCHER, TO SEE WHO YOU ARE!

HUH? I'VE NEVER SEEN YOU BEFORE!

WHO ARE YOU?

ROBIN HOOD!

THIS-- "THE ARCHER"? --I WONDER...

I HEARD A RADIO NEWS FLASH AND HURRIED OVER TO DEMONSTRATE MY SKILL WITH THE BOW AND ARROW!

LATER--AT HEADQUARTERS....

REMEMBER TO MENTION IN THE PAPER THAT IT WAS ME WHO CAPTURED THIS DANGEROUS CRIMINAL.

IF YOU ASK ME, I THINK THIS FELLOW IS A HARMLESS NUT WHO IMAGINES HIMSELF TO BE THE REAL "ARCHER"!

AMOS KENDRICK, THE JEWELER, CALLED. --HE CLAIMS TO HAVE RECEIVED A THREAT FROM "THE ARCHER"!

PAY NO ATTENTION TO HIM. HE'S GOT NOTHING TO WORRY ABOUT NOW THAT "THE ARCHER" IS BEHIND BARS.

("--ID BETTER EXIT!--")

FAR FROM THE POSSIBILITY OF SCRUTINY, CLARK REMOVES HIS OUTER GARMENTS....

IT'S MY PERSONAL OPINION THAT KENDRICK MAY BE VERY MUCH IN DANGER!

SHORTLY AFTER...THE MAN OF TOMORROW ALIGHTS ATOP THE ROOF OF KENDRICK'S RESIDENCE...

NOW TO MAKE USE OF MY X-RAY VISION!

WHAT THE MAN OF STEEL SIGHTS...

WHY DON'T THE POLICE ARRIVE? THIS SUSPENSE IS DRIVING ME MAD!

SUDDENLY-- IN THRU THE WINDOW SPEEDS A DEADLY SHAFT...!

IN A TWINKLING, SUPERMAM RIPS AN OPENING IN THE ROOF....

NO TIME TO SEARCH FOR ANOTHER ENTRANCE!

8

DOWN PLUMMETS THE *MAN OF TOMORROW* AS THE ARROW NEARS ITS GOAL....

A RACE, EH?

...KNOCKING IT ASIDE IN THE NICK OF TIME...

--AND CLOSE, TOO!

WHAT --??

YOU WON'T GET ME! KEEP BACK!

PUT DOWN THAT GUN! WANT TO HURT YOURSELF?

BUT KENDRICKS FIRES IN UNREASONING TERROR...!

THE BULLETS-- THEY GLANCED OFF YOU LIKE PEAS...!

YOU'D BE BETTER OFF WITH A PEA-SHOOTER, AT THAT!

THIS DELAY HAS GIVEN *"THE ARCHER"* AMPLE TIME TO SLIP AWAY!

THEN-- YOU AREN'T HE!

NO SIGN OF HIM! *"THE ARCHER"* MADE GOOD HIS ESCAPE!

SOMETIME LATER....

I MESSED UP A BEAUTIFUL OPPORTUNITY TO SNARE "THE ARCHER". MIGHT AS WELL CHANGE NOW.

THIS NOTE CAME FOR MR. KENT. THE MESSENGER SAID IT WAS ABOUT "THE ARCHER".

THANKS, I'LL TAKE IT, JIMMY.

HM-MM! IT SAYS FOR CLARK TO COME TO BINSTON AND ANNEX AVENUES IF HE WANTS TO KNOW WHO "THE ARCHER" IS! WHAT A BREAK FOR ME!

CLARK ENTERS THE DAILY PLANET EDITORIAL OFFICE TWO MINUTES LATER....

CONGRATULATIONS, CLARK! THIS IS YOUR LUCKY DAY!

YES?

A TIP HAS COME IN THAT THERE'S A BIG STORY BREWING AT 1411 WINGATE ROAD! I'D COVER IT MYSELF, ONLY IT'S TOO SENSATIONAL.

THANKS, LOIS. I CERTAINLY APPRECIATE YOUR GENEROSITY.

BUT AS CLARK CHANGES TO HIS IDENTITY AS SUPERMAN...

THIS UNSELFISHNESS ON LOIS' PART IS ALMOST TOO MUCH FOR ME. IT'S RATHER UNUSUAL FOR A REPORTER TO PASS UP A GOOD STORY!

WAIT TILL CLARK FINDS OUT WHAT I'VE UNCOVERED WHILE HE'S ON A WILD-GOOSE CHASE!

UNKNOWN TO LOIS, JIMMY THE OFFICE BOY, CONCEALS HIMSELF IN THE TRUNK AT THE REAR OF HER CAR....

IF I WAITED FOR A CHANCE TO BE HANDED TO ME, IT MAY NEVER COME! I'VE GOT TO BE LIKE LOIS-- MAKE MY OPPORTUNITIES!

MEANWHILE....
THIS IS 1411 WINGATE ROAD, ALL RIGHT. -- BUT THERE'S NOTHING HERE EXCEPT AN EMPTY LOT! IF THIS IS LOIS' IDEA OF A JOKE...!

SUPERMAN RETURNS TO THE *DAILY PLANET* IN HIS IDENTITY AS CLARK KENT....
THIS NOTE ON LOIS' DESK EXPLAINS EVERYTHING! SHE SENT ME OUT TO NO-MAN'S-LAND SO SHE'D HAVE AN OPPORTUNITY TO INVESTIGATE THAT TIP ABOUT *"THE ARCHER"* WITHOUT INTERFERENCE FROM ME!

ONCE AGAIN AS *SUPERMAN*, CLARK SPEEDS TOWARD BINSTON AND ANNEX AVENUES....
FOOLISH GIRL! SHE MAY BE GETTING INTO TERRIBLE DANGER!

HE ALMOST GOT ME --AGAIN!

BENEATH THAT LEDGE -- A PERFECT HIDING PLACE!

LOIS AND JIMMY HUDDLE IN SILENT TERROR BENEATH THE LEDGE, UNAWARE THAT *THE ARCHER"* APPEARS ATOP THE LEDGE BEHIND THEM AND TAKES CAREFUL AIM,....

DOWN FLASHES AN ARROW TOWARD LOIS' UNPROTECTED BACK...!

BUT FROM A GREAT HEIGHT, *SUPERMAN* SIGHTS LOIS' DANGER
GOT TO OVERTAKE THAT ARROW!

NECK AND NECK!

THE *MAN OF TOMORROW* SWOOPS DOWN BEHIND LOIS, RECEIVING THE ARROW UPON HIS OWN SUPER-TOUGH SKIN....

SUPER-MAN!

WHAT A GENIUS YOU ARE, LOIS-- FOR GETTING INTO TROUBLE!

OFF RACES *"THE ARCHER"* IN FRANTIC FLIGHT....

IF I CAN ONLY REACH MY CAR...!

UP WITH YOU!

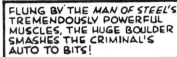

FLUNG BY THE *MAN OF STEEL'S* TREMENDOUSLY POWERFUL MUSCLES, THE HUGE BOULDER SMASHES THE CRIMINAL'S AUTO TO BITS!

LET GO!

THAT MASK IS COMING OFF!

IT'S QUIGLEY --THE FAMOUS BIG-GAME HUNTER!

I--I THOUGHT HUNTING HUMAN BEINGS WOULD PROVE MORE PROFITABLE!

ANY KID COULD TELL YOU THAT CRIME DOESN'T PAY, MR. QUIGLEY.

I'LL BIND HIM FOR YOU-- THEN SEE TO IT THAT POLICE GET HERE PROMPTLY!

LATER--AT THE *DAILY PLANET...*

TELL ME, JIMMY-- HOW DOES IT FEEL TO GET YOUR FIRST BY-LINE?

SWELL. AND I OWE IT TO BOTH OF YOU!

LET SOME OF THE CREDIT GO TO SUPERMAN, JIMMY.

⑬

THE END

SUPERBOY

The ADVENTURES of SUPERMAN WHEN HE WAS A BOY!

TAKE A GOOD LOOK AT THE YOUNG GIRL SHAKING HANDS WITH YOUNG CLARK KENT! RECOGNIZE HER? IT'S **LOIS LANE!** THE SAME LOIS WHO KEEPS **SUPERMAN** BUSY RESCUING HER! BUT THIS IS LOIS AS A YOUNG GIRL... AND YOUNG CLARK HAS TO GO THROUGH A ROUTINE HE WILL REPEAT AS A MAN! HERE, AT LAST, IS THE STORY OF HOW THE CLARK KENT–LOIS LANE–**SUPERMAN** TRIANGLE BEGAN. READ ALL ABOUT IT IN –

"How Clark Kent Met Lois Lane!"

1

NOW, KIDS, HOW ABOUT A LITTLE COMPETITION? THE ONE WHO BRINGS IN THE BEST STORY OF THE DAY GETS IT ON THE FRONT PAGE...WITH A BYLINE!

GEE!

I'LL WIN...NATURALLY! ANY GIRL IS SUPERIOR TO A BOY... THAT IS, ANY BOY BUT SUPERBOY... AND YOU'RE NO SUPERBOY!

IF YOU ONLY KNEW.'

HOW ABOUT A LITTLE PRIVATE BET? THE LOSER TREATS THE WINNER TO AN ICE CREAM SUNDAE?

I NEVER BET... BUT I'LL MAKE AN EXCEPTION IN YOUR CASE.'

LATER ... AS THE TWO WALK THE BUSY STREETS, A STREET-WATERING TRUCK RUMBLES NEAR...

SUDDENLY... THE NOZZLES SPRAY ...NOT WATER... BUT SLEEPING GAS!

GAS!

OHHH!

UHHH!

AS THE GAS DOES ITS WORK, BANDITS EMERGE FROM THE TRUCK AND SWIFTLY ENTER A FASHIONABLE JEWELLERS SHOP...

OKAY, BOYS! ANY COP THAT ISN'T SLEEPING BY NOW IS TOO BUSY OUTSIDE!

③

WHILE **SUPERBOY** RESTORES THE BILLBOARD, THE BANDITS MAKE THEIR GETAWAY!

FOAMY SOAP

OH-OH! LOIS IS RETURN-ING! GOT TO SWITCH BACK FAST!

BUT LOIS HAS ALREADY REACHED THE ALLEY, AND...

SO YOU'RE AWAKE NOW? BUT WHY IS YOUR JACKET OFF?

I...I...

I.. I'M USING IT AS A FAN TO BLOW THE GAS AWAY FROM YOU!

HMMPH! THANKS... BUT **SUPERBOY** BEAT YOU TO IT... AND YOU SHOULD'VE SEEN THE FAN **HE** USED!

I WAS CONSCIOUS ALL THE TIME AND HAVE I GOT A **SCOOP!** TOO BAD **YOU** WERE SLEEPING AND DIDN'T SEE IT!

BACK AT THE *DAILY PLANET*...

IT LOOKS LIKE LOIS IS GOING TO GET THAT ICE CREAM, CLARK! SHE CERTAINLY SCOOPED YOU!

AW...THE DAY ISN'T OVER YET!

SILLY! DO YOU THINK YOU CAN GET A MORE EXCITING STORY THAN ONE ABOUT **SUPERBOY**?

FINE THING! LOIS GETS A SCOOP AND I DON'T... AND ALL BECAUSE I CAN'T REVEAL MY **SUPER-** IDENTITY! HOW LONG CAN I KEEP THIS UP?

FOR A LONG, LONG TIME, CLARK! AFTER ALL, YOU'RE ONLY A **BOY** NOW! IT WILL GET WORSE WHEN YOU'RE A **MAN!**

⑤

LATER... LOIS GOES ON AN INSPECTION TOUR OF THE NEWSPAPER OFFICES...

YEP... THIS IS THE NEWSPAPER "MORGUE"! HERE'S WHERE WE FILE OLD STORIES ABOUT PEOPLE AND THINGS! TAKE A LOOK...

BY SHEER CHANCE, LOIS READS THIS WEEK-OLD CLIPPING!

ROAD BUILDER DIES

TITUS KORY DIED TODAY, DISINHERITING HIS NEPHEW AND LEAVING HIS MILLIONS TO CHARITY. HIS WILL STATED, "TO MY NEPHEW, PAUL, I LEAVE 3 PIECES OF ENGINEERING EQUIPMENT, WITH THE HOPE THAT HE REFORMS AND USES THEM TO START AN ENGINEERING CAREER." PAUL KORY WAS RECENTLY RELEASED FROM PRISON AFTER SERVING A TERM FOR BURGLARY.

HMM-MM! I'VE GOT A HUNCH...

LATER... AT THE TITUS KORY LOT ON THE OUTSKIRTS OF TOWN...

PAUL KORY WAS A BURGLAR ... MAYBE HE'S STILL AT IT! THERE'S THE WATER TRUCK ... AND IT'S LIKE THE ONE USED IN THE GAS ROBBERY! I'LL LISTEN AT THE DOOR OF THAT SHED!

PAUL, IT AIN'T EXACTLY WHAT YOUR UNCLE WANTED... BUT YOU'RE A SUCCESSFUL ENGINEER! HAW!

YES, INDEED! MY UNCLE'S EQUIPMENT IS PERFECT—FOR ENGINEERING CRIME!

AHHH! I THOUGHT I HEARD SOMEONE SNEAK ACROSS THE GROUNDS TO OUR DOOR!

WITH HIS BARE HANDS, **SUPERBOY** TWISTS THE CRANE'S STEEL GIRDERS... FORMING A MAKESHIFT JAIL-CELL!

THERE, KORY... LET'S SEE YOU ENGINEER AN ESCAPE!

SUPERBOY! WAIT FOR ME!

SHE'S AFTER ME AGAIN! I WISH SHE WAS AS EAGER FOR CLARK KENT!

LATER... LOIS DELIVERS HER STORY...

WHAT A SCOOP! CLARK, WHY CAN'T **YOU** GET STORIES LIKE THIS?

SO... CLARK PAYS OFF HIS DEBT!

HOW MANY SCOOPS?

TWO!

SCOOPED AGAIN!

A WEEK PASSES QUICKLY...AND SUDDENLY IT'S TIME FOR PARTING...

'BYE! GIVE MY REGARDS TO **SUPERBOY** WHEN YOU SEE HIM!

SHE'S GOING! I WONDER IF I'LL EVER SEE HER AGAIN? I WONDER IF WE'LL MEET SOME DAY... WHEN I'M **SUPERMAN**?!?

The END

10

SORRY I CAN'T DRIVE YOU HOME AS USUAL TODAY, LOIS—BUT I'M TAKING THE TIRE-RATIONING CRISIS SERIOUSLY.

EVERY-ONE SHOULD—IT'S THE PATRIOTIC THING TO DO!

BUT AS CLARK STRUGGLES TOWARD THE TRAIN WITH LOIS, HIS X-RAY VISION BRINGS TO HIM A STARTLING SCENE...

HURRY, CLARK—BEFORE THE DOOR CLOSES!

(PUFF!) RIGHT WITH YOU!

("—WHAT'S THAT?—")

WHAT CLARK'S AMAZING VISION REVEALS TO HIM... A SECTION OF THE SUBWAY TRACK—MISSING...!

AS LOIS IS CROWDED INTO THE PACKED CAR, THE DOOR SLIDES SHUT AND SHE DISCOVERS...

CLARK DIDN'T MAKE IT! HE'S STILL ON THE PLATFORM!

BUT AT THAT MOMENT THE DAILY PLANET REPORTER IS STREAKING THRU THE MOB ON THE SUBWAY PLATFORM AT SO GREAT A SPEED THAT NO ONE CAN OBSERVE HIM—AND AS HE RACES, HE SWITCHES TO HIS WORLD-FAMOUS ACTION-COSTUME...

IMPOLITE OF ME TO DASH AWAY FROM LOIS LIKE THIS—BUT SUPERMAN HAS WORK TO DO!

DOWN ONTO THE TRACKS LEAPS THE MAN OF TOMORROW, AND AS THE SUBWAY TRAIN BEGINS TO MOVE HE FLASHES AHEAD OF IT AT FULL SPEED...

ALMOST AT THE SPOT WHERE THE RAIL IS MISSING—NO ROOM HERE FOR HALF-MEASURES!

BAYS

WHIRLING, SUPERMAN PITS HIS STRENGTH AGAINST THE SPEEDING SUBWAY TRAIN...

NOT ANOTHER INCH DO I BUDGE!!

2

THE COLORFULLY-CLAD FIGURE SUCCEEDS IN HALTING THE TRAIN'S FORWARD PLUNGE BARELY IN TIME...

ANOTHER FOOT OR SO-- AND THERE'D HAVE BEEN... DISASTER!

WHAT HAPPENED?

I HEARD SOMEONE SAY SUPERMAN STOPPED THE TRAIN!

SUPERMAN! HERE!!

HERE IT IS-- THE PART OF THE RAIL THAT'S MISSING!

SO POWERFUL IS SUPERMAN'S STRENGTH THAT HE MOLDS THE RAIL SECTION BACK INTO PLACE AS THO THE STEEL WERE PUTTY...

THERE! AN EMERGENCY JOB-- BUT IT SHOULD BE SATISFACTORY!

SECONDS LATER, THE MAN OF TOMORROW VAULTS ONTO THE PLATFORM OF THE NEXT STATION AND WHIPS BACK INTO HIS CIVILIAN GARMENTS...

NOW TO PHONE IN THE STORY TO WHITE.

THAT'S RIGHT. SUPERMAN AVERTED A SUBWAY TRAIN WRECK!

BUT AS CLARK LEAVES THE PHONE BOOTH....

ULP!

CLARK! HOW DID YOU GET HERE? I LEFT YOU BACK ON THE PLATFORM AT THAT OTHER STATION!

("--IT'S GOING TO TAKE SOME **FAST THINKING** TO **GET OUT** OF **THIS** SPOT! LOIS KNOWS I WAS LEFT BEHIND ON THAT OTHER SUBWAY PLATFORM. WHAT SORT OF FAIRLY LOGICAL EXPLANATION CAN I OFFER HER WITHOUT REVEALING MY **SUPERMAN** IDENTITY?--")

WELL--YOU SEE--I--I--ER...I TOOK AN EXPRESS TRAIN AND GOT HERE FIRST! YES, THAT'S IT!

YOU DID, EH? WELL, LET ME AT THAT TELEPHONE! I'VE A GREAT YARN TO TELEPHONE IN. **SUPERMAN** JUST HALTED A SUBWAY WRECK!

BUT, LOIS...

QUIET! CAN'T YOU SEE I'M TRYING TO TALK INTO THE TELEPHONE!

WHAT'S THAT? YOU SAY--CLARK **ALREADY** REPORTED THE STORY??!

HOW DID YOU MANAGE TO TELEPHONE THAT STORY IN FIRST? **HOW** DID YOU EVER KNOW MY TRAIN WAS INVOLVED IN AN ENCOUNTER WITH **SUPERMAN!**

I--I--ER...

("--NOW I'M IN AN EVEN **WORSE** SPOT!--")

UH--UH--...NEWS LIKE THAT TRAVELS FAST. IF I WERE TO LET YOU IN ON ALL MY METHODS, YOU'D FOREVER BE SCOOPING ME. HEH! HEH! ("--I'M AFRAID THAT FELL KINDA FLAT.--")

THERE'S SOMETHING SUSPICIOUS HERE.

LATER...OUTSIDE LOIS' APARTMENT...

COME TO THINK OF IT, **SUPERMAN** HIMSELF COULDN'T HAVE ACTED ANY **FASTER!**

YOU'RE JUST MAKING IT APPEAR MORE MYSTERIOUS THAN IT REALLY WAS.

WHEW! THAT WAS THE CLOSEST I'VE EVER COME TO HAVING MY IDENTITY DISCOVERED. THANK GOODNESS LOIS WILL FORGET THE INCIDENT!

BUT **WILL** LOIS FORGET?

119

"--BUT **SUPERMAN'S** OPERATIONS WERE OFTEN INTERNATIONAL IN SCOPE! I REMEMBER THE TIME HE HALTED A WAR SINGLE-HANDED!--"

"--STILL, HE IS ALWAYS ALERT TO AID THE LITTLE FELLOW, THE COMMON MAN SUFFERING FROM INJUSTICE. THE TIME HE AIDED EUSTACE WATSON WAS A CLASSIC!--"

"--HE ENCOUNTERED AND BESTED SOME OF THE WORST SCOUNDRELS THE WORLD HAS EVER SEEN. THERE WAS **ULTRA**, WHO TRIED HIS BEST TO ERASE THE **MAN OF TOMORROW**, BUT HIS BEST WASN'T GOOD ENOUGH!--"

"--AND, OF COURSE, I'M NOT FORGETTING **LUTHOR** WHO SIMPLY REFUSES TO RECOGNIZE THAT **SUPERMAN** IS THE BETTER MAN!--"

"--HE IS ALWAYS QUICK TO AID ANY GOOD CAUSE: *KIDTOWN*, SLUM ELIMINATION, CHARITY DRIVES, ETC.--"

"--**SUPERMAN** WAS THE DOWNFALL OF MANY A POLITICAL GRAFTER!--"

HOW COULD I HAVE IMAGINED THAT MEEK, SHRINKING CLARK KENT COULD BE DYNAMIC **SUPERMAN**? A SILLY THOUGHT, AND THE SOONER I FORGET IT, THE BETTER!

AFTER LOIS RETIRES THAT EVENING, CLARK FINDS THAT A PERSISTENT THOUGHT PREVENTS SLEEP. HE CHANGES TO **SUPERMAN.**

THAT SUBWAY RAIL WASN'T MISPLACED BY ACCIDENT! THERE'S SOMETHING WRONG GOING ON IN THE LABYRINTHS OF THE SUBWAY SYSTEM AND I'M GOING TO TRACK IT DOWN!

SHORTLY AFTERWARD, AS THE **MAN OF TOMORROW** RACES ALONG A SUBWAY TUNNEL, HIS SUPER-SENSITIVE HEARING DETECTS...

MASSIVE DYNAMOS—!

AVAILING HIMSELF OF HIS X-RAY VISION AND SUPER-HEARING, HE DETECTS A STARTLING SIGHT IN A NEARBY BUILDING....

THE WIRES HAVE BEEN CONNECTED TO THE SUBWAY TRACKS... AFTER I FLING THIS SWITCH, THE TREMENDOUS ELECTRICITY GENERATED BY THESE DYNAMOS WILL SURGE INTO THE TRACKS...THE PASSENGERS ABOARD TRAINS PASSING THIS SECTION, WILL BE **ELECTROCUTED**...!

WE KNOW ALL THAT! THROW THE SWITCH!

THE TALON DOESN'T LIKE DELAYS!

THRU THE EARTH BURROWS THE **MAN OF TOMORROW** AT DESPERATE SPEED...!

GOT TO PREVENT A MASS EXECUTION!

SUPERMAN!

AND NOT TOO LATE, I HOPE!

THROW THE SWITCH!

8

OUT OF MY WAY!

YOU'RE TOO LATE!!

THE SUBWAY TRACKS CRACKLE WITH ELECTRICAL ENERGY--AND A SHORT DISTANCE OFF A TRAIN HURTLES TOWARD THE WAITING DOOM,....!!

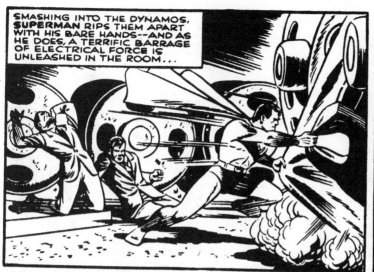

SMASHING INTO THE DYNAMOS, **SUPERMAN** RIPS THEM APART WITH HIS BARE HANDS--AND AS HE DOES, A TERRIFIC BARRAGE OF ELECTRICAL FORCE IS UNLEASHED IN THE ROOM...

THE THREAT'S BANISHED--BUT THE TALON'S HIRELINGS WERE SLAIN BY THEIR OWN ELECTRICAL APPARATUS! ONLY MY SUPER-PHYSIQUE SAVED ME!

EARLY MORNING--LOIS IS ROUSED BY THE SHOUTING OF NEWSBOYS...

WHA--?

EXTRA! DAILY PLANET EXTRA! SUPERMAN SMASHES SABOTEURS!!

DRESSING HASTILY, LOIS PURCHASES A COPY...

ANOTHER SCOOP BY CLARK KENT! THAT SETTLES IT! I'M GOING TO FIND OUT ONCE AND FOR ALL IF CLARK IS **SUPERMAN** OR NOT!

LATER...

THIS ARTICLE OF MINE STATES THAT I KNOW ALL ABOUT **THE TALON** AND HIS WORKING METHODS. IF ANYTHING WILL MAKE **THE TALON** BETRAY HIS HAND, THIS OUGHT TO!

BUT IT'S A DANGEROUS TRICK, LOIS!

DON'T LET HER DO IT!

BUT CLARK'S PROTESTS ARE OF NO AVAIL... WHIRLING PRESSES PRINT LOIS' ARTICLE IN GREAT QUANTITIES--THE NEWSPAPER'S LATEST EDITION IS DISTRIBUTED THROUGHOUT THE CITY....

AND IN THE TALON'S HIDEAWAY...

GET-- THAT-- GIRL!!

WHILE LOIS TURNS TOWARD THE STAKE, **SUPERMAN** WHIPS PAST HER AT SUPER-SPEED...

("-GOT TO MAKE IT BEFORE SHE COMPLETELY TURNS!-")

SWISH!

EMPTYING THE RAGS, HE DONS HIS OUTER GARMENTS AND ADJUSTS THE ROPES IN PLACE...

("-SHE'S ALMOST GOT HER EYES ON ME!-")

COME TO, CLARK! **SUPERMAN** SAVED US! WE'VE GOT TO GET TO THE SUBWAY SYSTEM HEADQUARTERS AND WARN THEM OF **THE TALON'S** THREAT!

I--I WANT TO KEEP AS FAR AWAY FROM **THE TALON** AS I CAN!

LATER... IN THE PRIVATE OFFICE OF ALBERT CALDWELL, PRESIDENT OF **METROPOLIS SUBWAY, INC....**

BUT I INSIST IT'S TRUE! THE TALON IS GOING TO DESTROY YOUR SUBWAY!

MELO-DRAMATIC NONSENSE!

("-MY X-RAY EYESIGHT... I SEE SOMETHING INTERESTING!-") NO SENSE WASTING TIME HERE, LOIS. I'M GOING BACK TO THE *PLANET* TO TURN IN WHAT WE'VE LEARNED!

BUT ONCE HE IS OUTSIDE THE OFFICE, CLARK CHANGES TO **SUPERMAN** AND RACES BACK IN....

SUPERMAN! STRANGE HOW YOU SHOWED UP SO SOON AFTER CLARK'S DEPARTURE!

WHAT DOES THIS INTERRUPTION MEAN?

I WAS WONDERING, CALDWELL, IF YOU DABBLE IN AMATEUR THEATRICALS?

OF COURSE NOT!

THEN THERE'S ONLY ONE OTHER EXPLANATION FOR THE TRACES OF YELLOW PIGMENT AND GREASE PAINT I CAN STILL DETECT ON YOUR SKIN, TALON!

MR. CALDWELL-- THE TALON!

HE'S MAD!

I'M BETTING HE'S THE BIRD WE'RE AFTER!

OBOY! IT'S OFF FOR THE *DAILY PLANET* FOR ME!

IF I'M FAST ENOUGH I MAY BE ABLE TO SCOOP CLARK!

SUPERMAN STUNTS DIZZILY, BUT WITH NO APPARENT RESULT...

READY TO TELL ME WHERE THE FORCES OF DESTRUCTION ARE TO BE UNLEASHED?

I KNOW NOTHING, I TELL YOU-- NOTHING!

DID I GET YOU HERE FAST ENOUGH, LADY?

FAST ENOUGH TO EARN ME A FRONT PAGE BY-LINE... I HOPE!

RUNNING INTO THE SUBWAY TUNNEL, SUPERMAN RACES BACK AND FORTH THRU THE ENTIRE SUBWAY SYSTEM AT SUPER-SPEED, DODGING IN AND OUT, ABOVE AND BELOW THE TRAINS.

AT THE SPEED I'M GOING WE'RE SURE TO BE ON THE SCENE OF THE DISASTER WHEREVER IT HAPPENS! WILL YOU TALK?

YES-- IN THE TUBE BENEATH THE CHANNEL RIVER! A TIME BOMB!

SPEEDING TO THE SCENE OF THE IMPENDING DISASTER, SUPERMAN HURTLES TOWARD THE BOMB--AND AS HE DOES... IT EXPLODES....

YOU'RE UNHARMED! AND SO IS THE TUNNEL!

YES. MY BODY ABSORBED MOST OF THE EXPLOSION'S FORCE. YOU'RE HEADED FOR A CELL!

LATER--AT THE POLICE STATION....

BUT WHY DID CALDWELL DISGUISE HIMSELF AS THE TALON AND TRY TO DESTROY THE SUBWAY SYSTEM?

HE IS A FASCIST SYMPATHIZER, A FIFTH COLUMNIST, AND TRIED TO SABOTAGE THE CITY'S TRANSPORTATION SYSTEM, SO THAT THE CONQUEST OF OUR NATION BY THE AXIS WOULD BE THAT MUCH SIMPLER.

SEVERAL MOMENTS LATER....

KENT AROUND? NO. I HAVEN'T SEEN HIM. WHY DO YOU ASK?

SWELL! THIS ONE TIME I SCOOPED HIM!

DID SOMEONE MENTION MY NAME?

YOU HERE? ER--I--I GUESS I WAS MISTAKEN.

HERE'S A FULL EXPOSE OF THE TALON, WHITE.

THE END

BUT ARE LOIS' SUSPICIONS OF CLARK'S TRUE IDENTITY COMPLETELY ALLAYED? ONLY FUTURE RELEASES OF YOUR FAVORITE STRIP WILL TELL! DON'T MISS A SINGLE ADVENTURE OF-- SUPERMAN!

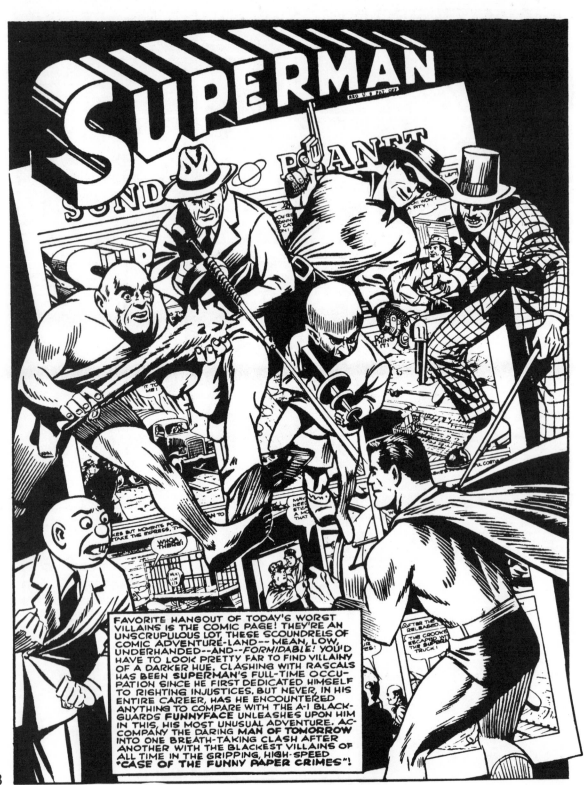

FAVORITE HANGOUT OF TODAY'S WORST VILLAINS IS THE COMIC PAGE! THEY'RE AN UNSCRUPULOUS LOT, THESE SCOUNDRELS OF COMIC ADVENTURE-LAND--MEAN, LOW, UNDERHANDED--AND--FORMIDABLE! YOU'D HAVE TO LOOK PRETTY FAR TO FIND VILLAINY OF A DARKER HUE. CLASHING WITH RASCALS HAS BEEN SUPERMAN'S FULL-TIME OCCUPATION SINCE HE FIRST DEDICATED HIMSELF TO RIGHTING INJUSTICES. BUT NEVER, IN HIS ENTIRE CAREER, HAS HE ENCOUNTERED ANYTHING TO COMPARE WITH THE A-1 BLACK-GUARDS FUNNYFACE UNLEASHES UPON HIM IN THIS, HIS MOST UNUSUAL ADVENTURE. ACCOMPANY THE DARING MAN OF TOMORROW INTO ONE BREATH-TAKING CLASH AFTER ANOTHER WITH THE BLACKEST VILLAINS OF ALL TIME IN THE GRIPPING, HIGH-SPEED "CASE OF THE FUNNY PAPER CRIMES"!

ATOP A FREIGHT CAR PRECARIOUSLY RUMBLING ACROSS A HIGH TRESTLE, TWO FIGHTING FIGURES DESPERATELY WAGE A GRIM BATTLE, WITH DEATH THE LOSER'S PENALTY...

YOU'VE TRAILED ME ACROSS A CONTINENT, DETECTIVE CRAIG! BUT NOW THAT YOU'VE FOUND ME, YOU DIE!

IT'S TOO EARLY TO FORECAST THIS STRUGGLE'S OUTCOME, MACHINE-GUN MIKE!

IN STORIES, THE DETECTIVE ALWAYS WINS OUT OVER THE CROOK! BUT THIS IS REAL LIFE!

DOWN OFF THE HIGH TRESTLE PLUMMETS A SHRIEKING BODY--DOWN TOWARD THE TURBULENT RIVER FAR BELOW! SOMEONE IS GOING TO DIE--BUT WHO--DETECTIVE CRAIG, OR MACHINE-GUN MIKE?!

YA-AA-A!

TO BE CONTINUED!

I DIDN'T REALIZE YOU WERE A COMIC STRIP FAN!

AVID IS THE WORD FOR IT! GOSH, TAKE THIS DETECTIVE CRAIG STRIP, FOR EXAMPLE. I WON'T BE ABLE TO SLEEP TONIGHT, WORRYING WHETHER OR NOT CRAIG OR MACHINE-GUN MIKE IS THE ONE WHO WILL DIE.

The DAILY PLAN

MIND IF I LOOK AT THE COMIC PAGE? I WANT TO SEE HOW PRINCE PERIL IS DOING!

SO YOU LIKE THE FUNNIES TOO, EH? WELL, WHEN YOU COME DOWN TO IT, WHO DOESN'T?

ODD HOW THOSE IMPOSSIBLE CHARACTERS GET A GRIP ON YOU. TAKE TORGO, FOR INSTANCE-- THE MENACING GIANT IN *PRINCE PERIL*. YOU KNOW AND I KNOW THAT IT'S IMPOSSIBLE FOR SUCH CREATURES TO EXIST-- YET WE ENJOY READING ABOUT THEM.

AND EVEN AS CLARK SPEAKS...

LOOK!

UP THERE!

IT'S FRIGHTFUL!

A COLOSSAL GIANT TOWERS OVER THE *NATIONAL BANK* IN *METROPOLIS'* FINANCIAL SECTION...

WHAT IS IT?

MY GOSH! IT'S--

TORGO-- THE MONSTER-GIANT IN THE *PRINCE PERIL* COMIC STRIP!

GALVANIZING INTO ACTION, THE HORRENDOUS TITAN RIPS THE ROOF OFF THE BANK BUILDING-- SCOOPS UP HANDFULS OF LOOT...

SWISH-H-H

.. THEN RACES OFF, LOADED WITH BOOTY!

GET DOWN TO THE *NATIONAL BANK*-- A REPORT HAS JUST COME IN THAT A MONSTER-GIANT HAS ROBBED IT!

HURRY, CLARK!

YOU CAN GO ALONE. IT SOUNDS LIKE A HOAX TO ME!

IN AN EMPTY HALLWAY, CLARK KENT SWITCHES TO THE WORLD'S MOST FAMOUS ACTION COSTUME.

HOAX OR NO HOAX, IT'S UP TO *SUPERMAN* TO LOOK INTO THE SITUATION!

UP-- UP-- AND AWA-AAY!!!

IN BARE INSTANTS, THE MAN OF TOMORROW ARRIVES AT HIS DESTINATION...

NO DOUBT ABOUT IT-- SOMEONE WENT ON A RAMPAGE!

WHO WAS RESPONSIBLE, CASEY?

THEY TELL ME THE CULPRIT WAS TORGO, THE GIANT IN THE PRINCE PERIL COMIC.

TORGO? ALIVE? !-- I'LL KNOW SOON ENOUGH WHETHER THAT'S A JOKE OR REALITY!

IT IS REALITY!

I STILL CAN'T BELIEVE IT! BUT IF THAT VISION IS JUST A WALKING NIGHTMARE, IT'S GOING TO FEEL THE IMPACT OF REAL FISTS PRETTY SOON!

UNEXPECTEDLY, A PREHISTORIC MONSTER MATERIALIZES OUT OF THE EMPTY AIR...

WHOA! WHAT NOW?!

TWO AGAINST ONE!

HERE'S WHERE I PROVE THE MATHEMATICIANS ARE WRONG, AND THAT ONE IS GREATER THAN TWO--ESPECIALLY WHEN THE ONE HAPPENS TO BE ME!

BUT TO SUPERMAN'S AMAZEMENT...

WHIZZED RIGHT THRU!

BUT NEXT TIME...!

THEY'RE-- GONE...!

YES, YOU POOR, HELPLESS AND BEWILDERED EX-SUPERMAN ...GONE!

AND WHO IN BLAZES ARE YOU?

NOW WOULDN'T YOU LIKE TO KNOW!

TELL ME...OR I'LL SOCK THAT SILLY GRIN CLEAR DOWN TO YOUR TOES!

YOU MAY CALL ME FUNNY- FACE!

BUT BEFORE HE CAN REACH THE APPARITION-- IT VANISHES...

FIRST A GIANT OUT OF A COMIC STRIP... NEXT A PREHISTORIC MONSTER... THEN A SILLY-FACED GALOOT NAMED FUNNYFACE... AND THEY ALL VANISHED!

I'M NOT KIDDING, CHIEF! THAT BANK ROBBERY WAS PULLED BY NONE OTHER THAN TORGO, THE FUNNY PAPER MENACE IN PRINCE PERIL!

IMPOSSIBLE-- ABSURD! I SUPPOSE NEXT YOU'LL BE TELLING ME THAT DETECTIVE CRAIG'S FOE, MACHINE-GUN MIKE IS RUNNING WILD.

CALLING ALL CARS! MACHINE-GUN MIKE ROBBING MINTON MUSEUM!

HUH?!

ONLY ONE EXPLAN- ATION, BOSS! YOU'RE PSYCHIC!

THE WORLD HAS GONE MADHOUSE! GET DOWN TO THE *MINTON MUSEUM* BUT THIS TIME TURN IN A YARN THAT MAKES *SENSE!*

I'LL TRY!

INSIDE THE MUSEUM...

HURRY!

WOTSA RUSH? WE GOT ALL TH' TIME IN TH' WORLD...

AS LONG AS GOOD OLD *MACHINE-GUN MIKE* IS OUT THERE COVERIN' THE PLACE!

A GIANT SIZED **MACHINE-GUN MIKE** KEEPS THE POLICE AT BAY AS HIS MEN FLEE THE MUSEUM WITH THE COSTLY PAINTINGS...

OKAY, BOSS! WE GOT A FORTUNE IN VALUABLE PAINTINGS!

GET INTO THE CAR AND SCRAM!

HEY! WHAT GOES ON--?!

WHERE ARE TH' PICTURES ???

BACK WHERE YOU BELONG!

NO WONDER THINGS GOT TANGLED--LOOK WHO JUST RAN OUTA TH' MUSEUM!

SUPERMAN!

STEP ON IT!!

SLOW DOWN!!

WAIT FOR ME!

QUICK! LET'S BEAT IT WHILE WE CAN!

TRYING TO RUN OUT, EH?

I PROMISED YOU'D GO TO A CELL-- AND I KEEP MY PROMISES!

GOOD WORK, SUPERMAN! IF YOU ONLY COULD HAVE CAPTURED MACHINE-GUN MIKE, TOO...!

YOU CAN'T HAVE EVERYTHING, SERGEANT CASEY!

IN A NEARBY ALLEY, SUPERMAN CHANGES TO CLARK KENT...

IT MIGHT BE A GOOD IDEA IF I WERE SEEN HEREABOUTS IN MY IDENTITY AS CLARK KENT... SO THE QUESTION WON'T ARISE AS TO HOW I GOT MY FACTS...

CLARK! SO HERE YOU ARE!

BEEN LOOKING FOR ME, LOIS?

I'LL SAY I HAVE! WHAT'S THE IDEA OF RUNNING OFF AND COVERING THIS STORY YOURSELF?

SORRY, LOIS-- BUT THIS CASE FASCINATED ME SO... VILLAINS OUT OF THE COMICS... IT'S ALMOST AS THO SOMEONE WERE USING THE COMIC PAGE AS A CHART FOR CRIME...

CHART FOR CRIME...! HM-MM. MAYBE YOU'VE GOT SOMETHING THERE, CLARK. IF THAT WERE TRUE, THE NEXT VILLAIN TO POP UP WOULD BE THE BLACK RAIDER FROM THE SOLITARY RIDER COMIC.

IF IT WERE TRUE! BUT UNDOUBTEDLY IT ISN'T. FORGET THE IDEA, LOIS. IT'S SILLY.

("-SILLY, EH? I WONDER? HM-MM. THE MOST LOGICAL PLACE FOR THE BLACK RAIDER TO STRIKE IN METROPOLIS WOULD BE THE STOCKYARDS. THEREFORE, THAT'S MY NEXT STOP!-")

SHORTLY AFTER--WHEN LOIS REACHES THE ADMINISTRATIVE BUILDING OF METROPOLIS' HUGE STOCKYARDS....

BUT I'M ALMOST POSITIVE OF IT!

WHAT UTTER NONSENSE! THE BLACK RAIDER ROB US? PREPOSTEROUS!

UP WITH YOUR HANDS -- THIS IS A HOLDUP!

WHO IS RESPONSIBLE FOR THIS OUTRAGE?

LOOK OUT THE WINDOW-- AND YOU'LL SEE!

THE BLACK RAIDER!

I TOLD YOU SO!

STOP THAT GIRL! SHE DUCKED INTO THE NEXT ROOM!

I'LL WARN-- BLACK RAIDER!

SLAM!

CLARK--I'M CALLING FROM THE STOCKYARDS! THE BLACK RAIDER HAS--EEE-EEEEE!!

LOIS-- LOIS... WHAT IS IT??! --THE LINE WENT DEAD!

LET'S GO, MEN!

LET ME GO-- YOU BIG STIFF!

CHANGING TO HIS SUPERMAN COSTUME, THE MAN OF TOMORROW STREAKS TO THE STOCK-YARD TO SIGHT AN AMAZING SCENE...

A CARAVAN OF CATTLE-LOADED TRUCKS!

OCKYARDS

HIT THE ROAD! I'M TAKING OVER THOSE TRUCKS!

AT THE TERRIFIC SPEED OF WHICH ONLY HE IS CAPABLE, *SUPERMAN* SPEEDS BACK AND FORTH, RETURNING THE TRUCKS TO THE STOCKYARD WITH THEIR STOLEN CARGO...

HERE YOU ARE! THE LAST OF THEM!

STOP BLACK RAIDER! HE'S SPED OFF WITH A GIRL REPORTER!

GIRL REPORTER! ...THAT SOUNDED LIKE A DESCRIPTION OF LOIS, AND SURE ENOUGH-- IT IS. I'LL SOON FREE HER!

I BEG TO DIFFER!

HEY! STOP IT!!

HO! HO! CAN'T TAKE IT, EH?

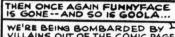

THEN...

GONE-- FUNNYFACE --BLACK RAIDER-- LOIS...BUT WAIT... WHAT'S THAT UP IN THE SKY?

HOVERING OVER A TRAIN LOADING A GOLD CARGO, A SPACE-VESSEL LOWERS A ROD THAT SUCKS THE GOLD INTO THE VESSEL'S INTERIOR...

IT'S--GOOLA-- THE MARTIAN VILLAIN IN *STREAK DUGAN!*

BUT AS HE SEEKS TO ENGAGE HIS FOE IN COMBAT--AGAIN... FUNNYFACE!

WHAT IS THIS--A BALLOON BARRAGE?

THEN ONCE AGAIN FUNNYFACE IS GONE--AND SO IS GOOLA...

WE'RE BEING BOMBARDED BY VILLAINS OUT OF THE COMIC PAGE! THAT LEAVES ONLY VIPER, THE VILLAIN OF THE *HAPPY DAZE* STRIP. I RECALL THAT IN THE COMIC VIPER IS ATTEMPTING TO ROB THE OLD FOLKS HOME OF ITS CAMPAIGN FUND.

LATER...

PERHAPS MY FEAR IS BASELESS, BUT I THOUGHT I OUGHT TO WARN YOU AGAINST THE CHARACTER NAMED VIPER.

YOUR WARNING WAS UNNECESSARY.

BECAUSE I AM VIPER!

AND SO YOU ARE!

OLD FOLKS HOME

141

143

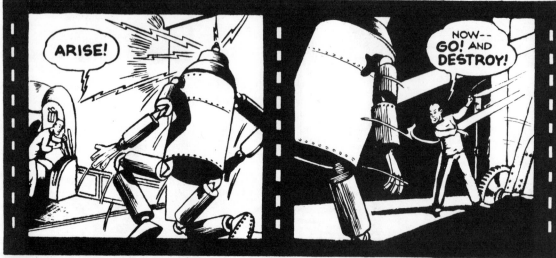

144

145

146

147

148

149

151

152

CAMP TOWNE, TRAINING BASE FOR THE FINEST FIGHTING MEN ON EARTH, IS AGOG WITH EXCITEMENT TODAY!

JUST THINK-- SUPERMAN IS COMING HERE IN PERSON!

I CAN HARDLY WAIT TO SEE HIM IN ACTION!

THE MEN ARE CERTAINLY KEYED UP OVER THE SUPERMAN PROGRAM THE U.S.O. HAS ARRANGED, COLONEL!

CONFIDENTIALLY, CAPTAIN-- SO AM I!

AT THE MAIN GATE...

HALT! WHO GOES THERE?

LOIS LANE AND CLARK KENT OF THE DAILY PLANET! WE'RE GOING TO WRITE UP SUPERMAN'S VISIT!

HERE'S OUR PASS...

LUCKY YOU! I'M DYING TO SEE SUPERMAN -- BUT I'VE GOT TO STAY AT MY POST!

THAT'S TOO BAD!... COME ON, CLARK!

UH--I DON'T FEEL SO WELL! ("GOT TO FIND AN EXCUSE TO SLIP AWAY, OR THERE WON'T BE ANY SHOW!-")

BUT LOIS HAS NO INTENTION OF LETTING HER FELLOW-REPORTER OUT OF HER SIGHT...

NONE OF YOUR THREAD-BARE EXCUSES! THIS IS ONE TIME YOU'RE NOT GOING TO DISAPPEAR IN THE MIDDLE OF AN ASSIGNMENT AND LEAVE ME TO DO ALL THE WORK!

("-I'M AFRAID SHE'S GOING TO BE DIFFICULT, AND I CAN'T RISK DOING ANYTHING THAT WOULD REVEAL THAT I REALLY AM SUPERMAN!-")

THOUSANDS OF MEN LINED UP ON THE PARADE GROUND TO RECEIVE SUPERMAN WITH SUPER-MILITARY HONORS!

AND HE SHOULD BE THERE NOW! I--I THINK I'LL GET A DRINK OF WATER!

THAT WON'T WORK, EITHER! THERE'S A DRINKING FOUNTAIN-- AND THERE'S COLONEL MCNAB WAITING FOR US!

IT SEEMS YOU'RE RIGHT ON ALL THREE COUNTS!

SLOW MINUTES DRAG BY WHILE EAGER SOLDIERS WAIT IMPATIENTLY FOR THEIR FIRST GLIMPSE OF THE MAN OF TOMORROW...

HE'S LATE...IT WOULD BE A TERRIBLE LET-DOWN FOR THE MEN IF SUPERMAN DIDN'T SHOW UP AT ALL!

HE'LL BE HERE, COLONEL, IF HE HAS TO MOVE MOUNTAINS TO MAKE IT! HE'D NEVER DISAPPOINT OUR FIGHTERS!

("-MOVING MOUNTAINS WOULD BE COMPARATIVELY EASY!-")

155

159

9

161

THE MIGHTIEST BATTLER OF THEM ALL WATCHES THE DRAMA FROM A NEUTRAL POINT...

I WOULDN'T HAVE MISSED THIS FOR THE WORLD!

AREN'T OUR BOYS MAGNIFICENT?

THE BLUES' OWN GUNS ARE TURNED AGAINST THEM...

THIS SAVES US THE TROUBLE OF BRINGING UP OUR OWN HEAVY EQUIPMENT!

AND THE END COMES SOON!

DON'T FORGET OUR BET, SAM! MY SIDE WON-- SO YOU OWE ME TWO DOLLARS!

I DON'T MIND! IT'S WORTH IT--FINDING OUT THAT'S THE KIND OF BUDDIES I'M GOING TO HAVE WITH ME WHEN WE HIT THE REAL THING!

CONGRATULATIONS, GENERAL! THE BEST MAN WON, EVEN THOUGH WE HAD **SUPERMAN** ON OUR SIDE!

NONSENSE, GENERAL! YOU'RE STILL THE BEST MAN!

GENTLEMEN, STOP FLATTERING EACH OTHER! NEITHER OF YOU WON! THE VICTORY BELONGS TO THE MEN IN THE RANKS!

I'VE BEEN WITH YOU IN A HUNDRED ADVENTURES, SUPER-MAN--BUT I'VE NEVER BEEN AS THRILLED AS TODAY!

BACK IN CAMP TOWNE, **SUPERMAN** MAKES HIS SCHEDULED APPEAR-ANCE, AFTER ALL!

PIPE DOWN, FELLOWS! IT'S THE WINNER WHO RATES THE CHEERS-- AND I WAS ON THE LOSING SIDE TODAY!

HOORAY FOR SUPERMAN!

NOR I!

⑪

165

A BUSY TRAFFIC INTERSECTION IN CROWDED **METROPOLIS** IS DISTURBED BY AN OFFICER'S FRANTIC WHISTLE BLAST..

STOP

TWEET TWEET

THAT POOR LITTLE FELLOW-- HE'LL BE KILLED!

HEAVEN HELP ME! I CAN'T STOP IN TIME!

I COULDN'T HELP IT, I TELL YOU! HE WALKED RIGHT IN FRONT OF ME!

IF YOU'D BEEN DRIVING AT A REASONABLE SPEED, THIS TRAGEDY WOULDN'T HAVE HAPPENED. CARELESS DRIVERS LIKE YOU SHOULD GET THE ELECTRIC CHAIR!

THIS MAN IS DEAD!

LET'S GET HIM INTO THE AMBULANCE!

P-POOR LITTLE GUY!

WHAT'S DELAYING YOU?

WE CAN'T BUDGE HIM!

HE-- HE SEEMS TO WEIGH A TON!

169

170

171

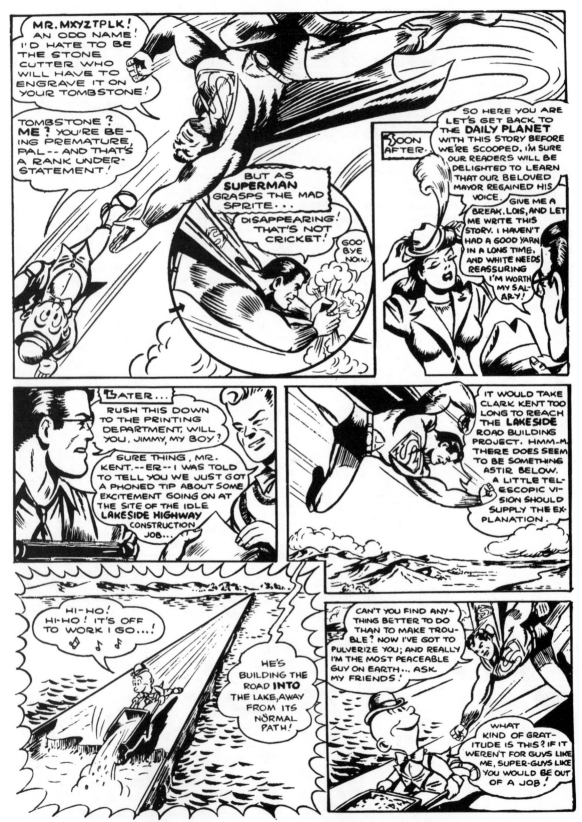

173

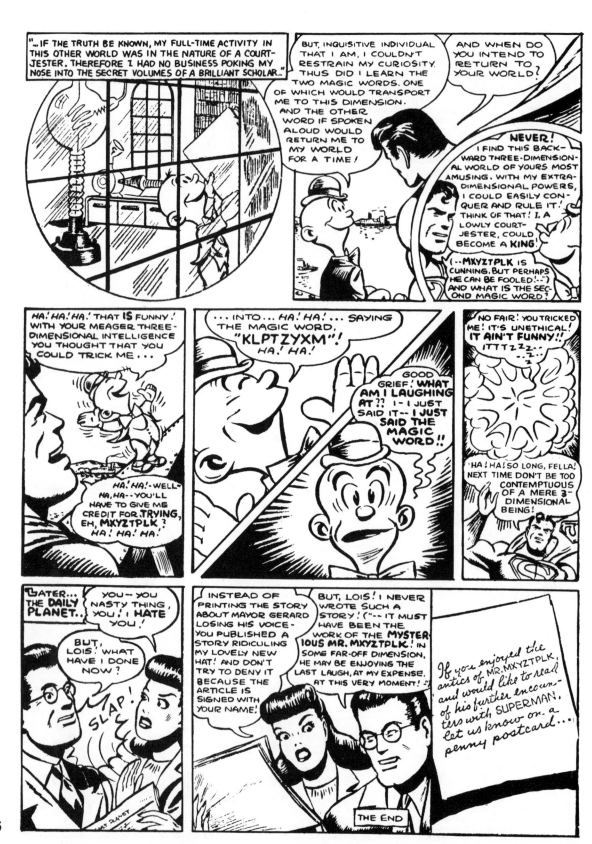

176

AT THE DAILY PLANET OFFICE— LOOK AT THAT FRONT PAGE! MURDER! ROBBERY! ARE WE RUNNING A YELLOW JOURNAL? CAN'T WE EVER HAVE A NICE HUMAN INTEREST STORY? AFTER ALL, LIFE HAS ITS TENDER MAGIC, TOO!

SPEAKING OF MAGIC, HOW ABOUT A STORY ON THOSE TWO MAGICIANS WHO RECENTLY PERFORMED SUCH UNUSUAL FEATS?

YOU MEAN HOCUS AND POKUS? WHY, THEY'RE JUST A COUPLE OF PEDDLERS!

HOCUS AND POCUS AREN'T MAGICIANS! SUPERMAN REALLY DID THEIR "MAGIC"!

MAGICIANS... GOOD! LOIS—I THINK YOU'VE GOT A STORY!

BUT CHIEF—WE'RE REPORTERS! NOT PRESS AGENTS FOR MAGIC PEDDLERS!

I WANT THAT STORY! GO GET IT!!

LATER... WHY, THE LETTERING ON THAT OFFICE DOOR ALONE IS A STORY!

I'LL HAVE TO KILL THIS MAGIC ANGLE, OR I'LL BE UP TO MY NECK IN IT!

HOCUS & POCUS
MAGICAL ENGINEERS

ALL MAGIC GUARANTEED OR MONEY REFUNDED

COME IN

②

WE GOT NO NEWS FOR YOUSE! OUR BUSINESS IS ON THE SKIDS 'CAUSE DOC'S MAGIC IS ON THE BLINK!

SEE! I YELL ABRACADABRA TILL I'M BLUE IN THE FACE, AND NOTHING OCCURS!

179

182

AFTER LOIS FINISHES HER STORY...

ER-UH — VERY INTERESTING STORY, LOIS! A WAVE OF A MAGIC WAND AND YOU'RE JUST LIKE **SUPERMAN!** ER-EXCUSE ME A MINUTE...

THEN, LOIS FINDS SHE DOESN'T KNOW HER OWN STRENGTH!

JUST A SECOND, CHIEF! I'M NOT CRAZY— I CAN PROVE IT. LOOK! I CAN LIFT YOU!

HEY! LET ME DOWN!

ER-UH-C-CALL UP NEW ROSES HOSPITAL! T-TELL THEM I WANT THEIR BEST PADDED CELL!

RELAX, CHIEF, WHILE I ANSWER THIS!

WHAT? YOU'RE **SURE?** ALL THREE OF THEM? WHERE? YES—YES! FINE! THANKS!

HUH? WHAT IS IT?

SOME WAITRESS SAYS SHE OVERHEARD THE **BBB** GANG PLANNING A HOLD-UP! I'LL PROVE I'M **REALLY** AS GOOD AS **SUPERMAN** BY BRINGING IN THAT TRIO SINGLE-HANDED!

NOW — MEET THE **BBB** GANG, WHOSE VICIOUS CRIMES BLOT THE POLICE LEDGERS OF 16 STATES! COLD, VIOLENT, INHUMAN, **THESE** ARE THE BRUTES LOIS SINGLE-HANDEDLY CHALLENGES!

WANTED

REWARD

BRUTE

BUZZARD

BEAR

⑦

AND NOW — TO RESUME OUR STORY...

WHERE'S LOIS? STOP HER!

TOO LATE, CHIEF! SHE — SHE JUST JUMPED OUT THE WINDOW!

HERE SHE GOES AGAIN! WHAT A MESS! WHEN'LL I EVER GET TIME TO DO ANYTHING BUT RESCUE HER?

WAIT'LL CLARK HEARS OF MY CAPTURING THE BBB GANG SINGLE-HANDED!

MEANWHILE, NEAR A HIGHWAY OUTSIDE THE CITY, THE BBB GANG WAITS...

HERE COMES THE ARMORED TRUCK! GET SET.

LET'S GO!

WAIT'LL CLARK HEARS HOW I DID THIS WITHOUT THE AID OF SUPERMAN!

WELL, IN A WAY SHE'S RIGHT! OFFICIALLY, I'M NOT HERE.

IT MUSTA HIT A ROCK AND SWERVED!

A DAME! WHERE'D SHE COME FROM?

DROP THOSE GUNS! YOU'RE UNDER ARREST!

8

185

188

THANKS FOR EVERYTHING, **SUPERMAN**! BUT AREN'T YOU GOING TO TURN THOSE HOODLUMS OVER TO THE POLICE?

NOW THAT YOU'RE OUT OF HARM'S WAY, MISS LANE, I'LL GIVE THAT LITTLE MATTER MORE SERIOUS THOUGHT!

BUT AS THE WORLD'S MOST FAMOUS CHAMPION OF JUSTICE RESUMES THE GUISE OF A MILD-MANNERED REPORTER...

THOSE SMALL-TIME CROOKS ARE FOLLOWERS, NOT LEADERS! INSTEAD OF TAKING THEM IN FOR MOLESTING LOIS, I'LL COME BACK AND FIND OUT WHO THEIR BOSS IS AND WHAT HE'S UP TO!

PRESENTLY...

NOTHING OUT OF THE ORDINARY OVER MY WAY, LOIS... DID YOU FIND ANYTHING?

ENOUGH TO MAKE THE FRONT PAGE OF THE *PLANET* SIZZLE! LET'S GO!

MEANWHILE, IN A SECRET UNDERGROUND WORKSHOP, AN OLD ENEMY OF **SUPERMAN** CHUCKLES TO HIMSELF...

SUCCESS AT LAST! THE MOST POTENT WEAPON EVER INVENTED IS MINE—PROVED AND PERFECTED—READY TO BRING ME WHATEVER I DESIRE!

LUTHOR, WHOSE VAST SCIENTIFIC KNOWLEDGE IS EQUALED ONLY BY HIS CRIMINAL AMBITIONS, PLANS ANOTHER FANTASTIC BID FOR RICHES AND POWER!

HO, HO, HO! THE WORLD AT MY FEET! WEALTH BEYOND THE WILDEST IMAGININGS OF ORDINARY STUPID MEN!... AND SUDDEN DEATH FOR **SUPERMAN** IF HE SHOULD DARE TO INTERFERE WITH THIS FINAL FLOWERING OF MY GENIUS.

BUT THE NEXT MINUTE....

WHAT'S THIS?.... HAVE YOU FOOLS BEEN FIGHTING AMONG YOURSELVES?

NAW, BOSS! WE MADE DA MISTAKE OF TRYIN' TA GRAB LOIS LANE, NOT KNOWIN' **SUPERMAN** WAS KEEPIN' AN EYE ON HER!

YOU UNSPEAKABLE IDIOTS-- DO YOU MEAN TO TELL ME YOU LET HER ESCAPE AFTER SHE HAD SEEN THE WORK OF MY MOLECULAR IMPULSION BEAM ON STEEL, ROCKS AND TREES?

TAKE IT EASY, CHIEF! SHE AIN'T WISE TO DA REAL LOWDOWN-- AN' SUPERMAN AIN'T NEITHER!

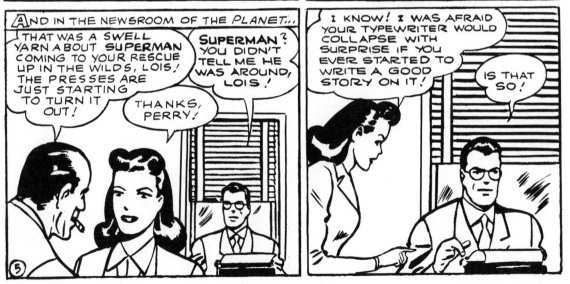

194

WITH BARE HANDS, THE **MAN OF STEEL** STRAIGHTENS HEAVY ROLLERS!

WHY NEW PRESSES? NOTHING'S THE MATTER WITH THESE, EXCEPT THE SHAPE THEY'RE IN!

DOGGONED IF I DON'T BELIEVE YOU'RE RIGHT!

THE PAPERS MIGHT HIT THE STREETS A FEW MINUTES LATE!

FOR A WHILE, IT LOOKED AS IF THEY'D NEVER GET OUT!

LET 'EM ROLL! I'VE GOT PRESSING BUSINESS ELSEWHERE!

THEY'RE ROLLING — SMOOTHER THAN EVER!

OUTSIDE, BELLS AND SIRENS SHRIEK!

WHAT'S ALL THE EXCITEMENT?

SUPERMAN! SOMETHING'S GONE WRONG IN THE FINANCIAL DISTRICT!

WHEEERRR...

DING! DONG.

SOMETHING HAS GONE WRONG, INDEED, WHEN CONCRETE PAVEMENTS BECOME A STICKY BOG THAT TRAPS POWERFUL VEHICLES!

EVERYTHING'S STOPPED! NOT A WHEEL TURNING IN THE WHOLE AREA!

YOU CAN'T WALK, EITHER.

I'LL BE BACK!

AND HERE IS THE SOURCE OF THE TROUBLE!

WITH THE PLANET OUT OF BUSINESS, I CAN CONCENTRATE ON NUMBER ONE TARGET! NOW THAT THE PAVEMENT IS SOFTENED, I'LL SET THE FREQUENCY FOR THE SPECIAL STEEL OF THE TRUSLOW TRUST COMPANY VAULT!

⑧

HE'S SPOTTED *ME!* NO DOUBT HE THINKS HIMSELF SAFE BECAUSE HIS ATOMIC STRUCTURE IS DIFFERENT FROM THAT OF ORDINARY PEOPLE, AND MY MOLECULAR PROPULSION BEAM DID NOT HARM THEM!

BUT HE IS A FOOL! I'LL TURN ON THE POWER FULL FORCE AND BLAST HIM INTO ETERNITY— AND BE RID OF HIM FOR GOOD! *HO, HO, HO!*

LIKE A CRIMSON-AND-BLUE BULLET, THE **MAN OF TOMORROW** STREAKS TOWARD THE SHIP, WHICH PLUNGES OMIN-OUSLY TO MEET HIM, HURLING FORTH A BEAM OF INCREDIBLE POWER!

HE MUST BE PRETTY SURE OF HIMSELF, COMING TO MEET ME!

THIS IS THE SUPREME MOMENT OF MY LIFE!

A CRACKLING ROAR ECHOES ACROSS THE SKY!

WHAT---? AAA-AAA-A-A-A...

BOOM

AND **SUPERMAN** — NO LONGER EARTH'S MIGHTIEST WARRIOR— DROPS LIKE A STONE!

I'VE DONE IT! THE WORLD IS MINE FOR THE TAKING! WHAT IF THE RECOIL DID SMASH MY RAY PROJECTORS? I CAN BUILD NEW ONES— A THOUSAND OF THEM, IF NECESSARY!

HE'S FALLING TOWARD THE CONDENSER AT THE POWER PLANT!

HE'LL BE CRUSHED FLAT AND BURNED TO A CINDER!

⑩

ON AN ANCIENT ROOFTOP, STEEL RINGS AGAINST STEEL AS TWO SWORDSMEN FIGHT A DUEL TO THE DEATH...

SUDDENLY, A FATAL THRUST, AND ONE OF THE COMBATANTS PLUNGES FROM THE PARAPET...

AND AS THE DEFEATED SWORDSMAN LIES IMMOBILE ON THE GROUND, ABRUPTLY A VOICE SHOUTS THE COMMAND—"CUT!"

CUT!!

YES, "CUT!" FOR THIS IS A MOVIE SET IN THE HEART OF THE ALPS, THE LAST SCENE OF THE HISTORICAL PICTURE, "BLACK MAGIC", STARRING ORSON WELLES AS THE SINISTER MAGICIAN, CAGLIOSTRO, HAS JUST BEEN PUT ON FILM.

AND DON'T FORGET THE FANCY DRESS BALL TONIGHT. AS YOU KNOW, ALL OF YOU ARE GOING IN YOUR "BLACK MAGIC" COSTUMES!

LATER, AS WELLES, AND ACTRESS NANCY GUILD DRIVE UP A STEEP MOUNTAIN ROAD, HEADED FOR THE TOWN WHERE THE COSTUME BALL IS TO BE HELD...

I'LL BE QUITE SORRY TO TAKE OFF THIS COSTUME—I ENJOYED PLAYING THE VILLAINOUS CAGLIOSTRO!

AND I ENJOYED PLAYING MARIE ANTOINETTE!

SUDDENLY...

LOOK! WHAT'S THAT?

IT LOOKS LIKE A ROCKET SHIP! LET'S STOP—I WANT TO GET UP CLOSE TO IT!

ORSON WELLES IS RIGHT, THOUGH HE DOESN'T KNOW IT YET. FOR ON THE OTHER SIDE OF THE HILL IS GATHERED A VAST CONCOURSE OF PEOPLE BREATHLESSLY AWAITING THE LAUNCHING OF THE FIRST ROCKET SHIP TO MARS!

...AND THIS SPACE SHIP, THE RESULT OF COOPERATION AMONG ROCKET SOCIETIES OF THE WORLD, MARKS A MILESTONE IN SCIENCE...

THIS BABY LOOKS POWERFUL ENOUGH TO REACH ANOTHER PLANET!

MEANWHILE, CURIOUS ABOUT THE STRANGE PROJECTILE ORSON WELLES ENTERS ITS INTERIOR THROUGH AN OPEN PORTHOLE..

NO DOUBT THE PAPERS HAVE CARRIED THE NEWS OF THE SHIP, BUT I'VE BEEN CUT OFF FROM CIVILIZATION SINCE WORKING ON THE PICTURE!

AS ORSON EXAMINES THE SHIP'S CONTROLS, THROUGH AN OPEN PORTHOLE FLOAT THE WORDS OF THE DIRECTOR OF THE INTERNATIONAL ROCKET SOCIETY..

I AM PRESSING THE BUTTON. IN TEN SECONDS, THE PORTHOLES WILL CLOSE AND THE FIRST PILOTLESS ROCKET WILL TAKE OFF FOR MARS!

"PILOTLESS ROCKET... TEN SECONDS...CLOSED PORTHOLES"— I'VE GOT TO GET OUT OF HERE!!

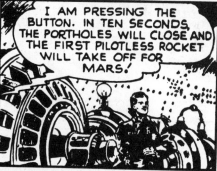

THE PORTHOLES WILL NOT OPEN AGAIN UNTIL THE SPACE-SHIP REACHES MARS, WHEN THE ROBOT INSTRUMENTS WILL BROADCAST BACK, BY RADAR, INFORMATION ABOUT THE PLANET...

211

FRANTIC, ORSON DASHES TO THE PORTHOLE, BUT THE THICK GLASS CLOSES IN HIS FACE!

I'M TRAPPED-- IN A MARTIAN ROCKET SHIP!

VOLCANO-LIKE BLASTS ERUPT FROM THE JETS OF THE ROCKET SHIP, PROPELLING IT AWAY FROM EARTH AT INCREDIBLE VELOCITY...

AND, AS THE ROCKET SHIP PLUNGES INTO THE BLACK ABYSS OF OUTER SPACE, ORSON WELLES TAKES A LAST LOOK AT HIS OWN PLANET!

WHEN I FOOLED THE WORLD WITH MY MARTIAN INVASION BROADCAST-- I NEVER DREAMED I WOULD INVADE MARS MYSELF!

INSIDE THE ROCKET SHIP'S CABIN, ORSON WELLES FLOATS LIKE A FEATHER, FOR THERE IS NO GRAVITY TO HOLD HIM TO THE FLOOR!

I'VE READ AND WRITTEN ABOUT THIS IN SCIENCE FICTION STORIES, BUT I NEVER THOUGHT IT WOULD ACTUALLY HAPPEN TO ME!

TWO HOURS LATER, THE SPACE SHIP ARRIVES WITHIN THE GRAVITATIONAL PULL OF MARS. REVERSING ITSELF, IT FALLS BASE DOWNWARDS WITH THE ROCKET'S BLAST NOW ACTING AS A BRAKE. THE STRANGE RED PLANET APPROACHES FAST.

SOON, THE ROCKET SHIP LANDS. THE PORTHOLES OPEN AUTOMATICALLY. AND ORSON STEPS OUT...ONTO THE SOIL OF ANOTHER WORLD!

SECONDS LATER, WELLES MEETS *MARTIANS!*

HAIL, WELLES! WE HAVE COME TO TAKE YOU BEFORE OUR MASTER, THE GREAT MARTLER!

THEY LOOK LIKE NAZIS—AND "MARTLER"... SOUNDS LIKE HITLER!

YOU SPEAK ENGLISH!!

FOR MANY YEARS, WE HAVE STUDIED YOU EARTHLINGS BY MEANS OF A DEVICE SIMILAR TO YOUR TELEVISION. WE HAVE LEARNED YOUR LANGUAGE AND MUCH ABOUT YOU!

INSIDE THE PALACE OF MARTLER, RULER OF MARS...

...I ADMIRED YOUR HITLER AND HIS NAZIS. I AM MARTLER, AND WITH MY SOLAZIS I WILL BLITZKRIEG THE SOLAR SYSTEM! I WILL START MY CONQUEST WITH EARTH, FOR YOU HAVE URANIUM WHICH WE LACK. MY FLEET OF SPACE SHIPS IS ABOUT TO LEAVE TO INVADE YOUR WORLD! TO YOU, WELLES, I OFFER THE POST OF PROPAGANDA MINISTER ON EARTH!

IF ONLY I COULD WARN EARTH.

VENUS

SATU

EARTH

MERCURY

YOU'RE NOTHING BUT AN OLD-FASHIONED DICTATOR! GET BACK OR I'LL RUN YOU THROUGH!

AT SWORD'S POINT, ORSON WELLES ENTERS THE NEARBY MARTIAN BROADCASTING STUDIO...

SHOW ME HOW TO BROADCAST TO EARTH— OR I'LL KILL YOU!

I'LL... I'LL SHOW YOU...

ATTENTION, **SUPERMAN!** THIS IS ORSON WELLES, BROADCASTING FROM MARS. I HAVE NO TIME TO TELL YOU HOW I COME TO BE HERE. I HAVE TIME ONLY TO WARN YOU THAT THE MARTIANS ARE COMING WITH A FLEET OF ROCKET SHIPS TO INVADE EARTH AND THAT THEY WILL BE THERE WITHIN HOURS!

BUT THE EARTH LAUGHS AT THE WARNING, FOR THIS IS THE SECOND TIME THAT ORSON WELLES HAS CRIED "WOLF"! AND IN THE OFFICE OF THE *DAILY PLANET*...

...YOU MUST BELIEVE ME... THE MARTIANS REALLY *ARE* COMING! AT THIS VERY MOMENT, THEY ARE THREATENING ME WITH RAY GUNS... *HELP, SUPERMAN!*

IT'S ANOTHER HOAX!

WHOM DOES ORSON THINK HE'S KID-DING?

MY TELESCOPIC VISION WILL SOON TELL ME WHETHER THIS IS A JOB FOR SUPERMAN!

5

SECONDS LATER, IT'S "UP, UP, AND AWAY!" AS **SUPERMAN** BRIDGES THE ASTRONOMICAL DISTANCE BETWEEN EARTH AND MARS, AT COMET SPEED!

THAT HOAX OF ORSON'S, YEARS AGO, ABOUT A MARTIAN INVASION, SURE BACKFIRED! NOW, EVEN THOUGH HE'S TELLING THE TRUTH, NO ONE WILL BELIEVE HIM!

MEANWHILE, THE WORLD REGARDS ORSON'S FRANTIC WARNINGS AS THE BEST JOKE OF THE YEAR!!

THEY'RE CLOSING IN ON ME.!... I CAN'T HOLD THEM OFF ANY LONGER...THEY'RE GOING TO BLAST ME WITH THEIR RAY GUNS...PREPARE FOR THE MARTIAN ROCKET SHIPS.!!

THIS IS THE FUNNIEST THING I'VE HEARD IN AGES!

BETTER THAN BOB HOPE!

IN THE MARTIAN RADIO STUDIO, WELLES FIGHTS DESPERATELY WITH AN ANCIENT SWORD AGAINST THE RAY GUNS OF THE SOLAZIS!

... THIS IS THE END! BEWARE, EARTH... PREPARE! THE MARTIANS ARE COMING!

AS THE RAY GUN TRIGGER TIGHTENS, AND THE DEADLY BEAM STABS OUT... ENTER SUPERMAN!

THEN, ON THE INTER-COMMUNICATION TELEVISION SCREEN APPEARS THE IMAGE OF THE MARTIAN DICTATOR...

THE **MAN OF STEEL** TAKES ON HIS OWN INDESTRUCTIBLE CHEST THE MAN-DESTROYING BEAM WHICH WOULD HAVE SHRIVELED ORSON WELLES TO ASHES!

IT TICKLES!

STOP THIS NONSENSE, ALL OF YOU! I WISH TO SEE **SUPERMAN** AND TALK WITH HIM!

216

217

THE FIRST PART OF THE **SUPERMAN**-ORSON WELLES PLAN WORKS AS THE MOON REACHES THE ROCKET SHIP FLEET AND PULLS THE SPACE SHIPS WITHIN ITS ORBIT. THE ROCKET SHIPS ARE POWERLESS TO CONTINUE AND ARE NOW MERE SATELLITES OF THE MOON!

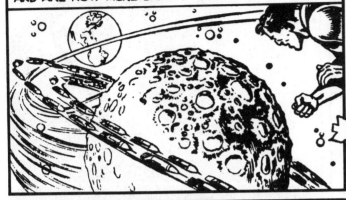

IT WORKED — AND JUST IN TIME! ANOTHER FEW MINUTES AND THE MARTIAN ROCKET SHIPS WOULD HAVE REACHED EARTH! NOW TO WORK OUT A PLAN WITH ORSON TO MAKE SURE THAT MARS NEVER AGAIN TRIES TO INVADE THE EARTH!

SWIFTLY, ORSON WELLES AND **SUPERMAN** PUT THEIR SECOND PLAN INTO OPERATION...

I'VE LEARNED ENOUGH OF THE MARTIAN LANGUAGE TO MAKE MR. MARTLER SAY A FEW WORDS TO HIS MARTIAN SUBJECTS!

AND WITH MY X-RAY VISION, I'VE LEARNED ENOUGH ABOUT THIS MACHINERY TO MAKE THE TELECAST! LET'S GO!

SCAN MARS

FELLOW MARTIANS, THERE MUST BE NO MORE WAR. WE WILL STAY ON OUR OWN PLANET!

YOU WILL RULE YOURSELVES — AND I SHALL RETIRE —

GREAT NEWS! NOW WE CAN GO HOME TO OUR FAMILIES! I NEVER DID WANT TO FIGHT ANYWAY!

⑪

...BUT...I DON'T WANT TO RETIRE..I *LIKE* BEING DICTATOR OF MARS!

THAT'S JUST WHY YOU'RE *GOING* TO RETIRE!

TO AN ASTEROID WHERE YOU CAN'T HURT ANYONE EXCEPT YOURSELF!

WITH *SUPERMAN* FOR AN ENGINE, THE ROCKET SHIP TAKES OFF FOR THE RETURN TRIP TO EARTH...

LET'S HOPE MARS WILL BE MORE PEACEFUL WITHOUT MARTLER!

BUT YOU CAN'T LEAVE ME HERE BY MYSELF... WITH NO ONE TO BOSS!

THERE IS ENOUGH FOOD TO SUPPORT YOU FOR THE REST OF YOUR LIFE!

YOU'RE LUCKY NOT TO BE HANGED LIKE THE NAZI LEADERS YOU ADMIRED AND IMITATED!

BACK ON EARTH, AT THE HEADQUARTERS OF THE INTERNATIONAL ROCKET SOCIETY...

OUR SPACESHIP BACK—WITH ALL THE MARTIAN DATA RECORDED ON THE INSTRUMENTS! THANK YOU, SUPERMAN!

GLAD TO HELP BRING SPACE TRAVEL CLOSER.

HE MIGHT NOT BELIEVE THE WHOLE STORY, SO I'D BETTER KEEP QUIET!

ENROUTE, THE MAN OF STEEL LANDS THE SPACESHIP ON AN ASTEROID WHIRLING BY ITSELF THROUGH THE LONELY REACHES OF INTERSTELLAR SPACE!

WITH TRANSPORTATION PROVIDED BY SUPERMAN, ORSON IS IN TIME FOR THE COSTUME BALL THAT EVENING. THE ENTIRE ADVENTURE HAS TAKEN LESS THAN EIGHT HOURS SINCE THE COMPLETION AT NOON OF THE FILMING OF "BLACK MAGIC"!

TELL ME, ORSON, WAS YOUR BROADCAST THIS TIME ANOTHER HOAX... A PUBLICITY STUNT... OR THE TRUTH?

ASK SUPERMAN!

LATER, AT THE DAILY PLANET EDITOR PERRY WHITE THROWS A SHEET OF PAPER INTO HIS WASTEPAPER BASKET...

CLARK—THIS IS A NEWSPAPER—NOT A SCIENCE-FICTION MAGAZINE! GET DOWN TO 10TH AND WESTERN AND COVER THAT FIRE—IF YOU WANT TO KEEP WORKING HERE!

ORSON WELLES REALLY ON MARS! Martian Menace Genuine By Clark Kent In an exclusive interview with Superman your Planet reporter...

THE END

IN SMALLVILLE, ONCE THE HOME-TOWN OF *SUPERBOY*, AN OLD NEIGHBOR OF CLARK KENT'S TAKES A MOMENTOUS STEP!

GOOD LUCK, LANA! I KNOW HOW MUCH YOU WANT A NEWSPAPER CAREER... PERHAPS YOU CAN FIND IT IN METROPOLIS!

OH, I KNOW I CAN. CLARK KENT IS A REPORTER FOR THE *DAILY PLANET* NOW... HE'LL HELP ME!

MEANWHILE, IN METROPOLIS, MIGHTY *SUPERMAN*, WHO, IN HIS OTHER IDENTITY OF "TIMID" CLARK KENT, ONCE LIVED NEXT DOOR TO LANA, COMPLETES A ROUTINE MISSION...

NEXT STOP FOR THESE BANDITS IS THE POLICE STATION! BUT WHAT'S THE MATTER WITH ME? I'VE HAD COLD CHILLS DOWN MY BACK ALL DAY, AS THOUGH TROUBLE WAS COMING!

AND IT ARRIVES, NEXT MORNING, AT THE PLANET OFFICE!

HELLO, CLARK... REMEMBER ME? I'M LANA LANG!

WHY... ER... LANA! YOU'VE GROWN UP! WHAT ARE YOU DOING IN METROPOLIS?

I WANT A JOB AS A REPORTER... AND I WAS SURE YOU'D HELP ME, CLARK, FOR OLD TIME'S SAKE!

ER...WELL, SURE, LANA, I'LL DO WHAT I CAN! WE'LL ASK PERRY WHITE!

NOW I KNOW WHY I HAD THAT FEELING YESTERDAY... LANA ALWAYS SPELLED TROUBLE FOR ME BACK IN SMALLVILLE!

PERRY WHITE EDITOR

NO, I'M SORRY, MISS LANG! I CAN'T USE AN INEXPERIENCED SMALL-TOWN GIRL REPORTER!

THANK GOODNESS! I DON'T THINK I COULD STAND *BOTH* LOIS AND LANA IN MY HAIR!

BUT LANA NEVER DID GIVE UP EASILY!

BUT IF YOU GIVE ME, A SMALL-TOWN GIRL, A CHANCE ON YOUR PAPER, THINK HOW IT WILL HELP YOU GET CIRCULATION IN SMALL TOWNS ALL OVER THE COUNTRY!

MISS LANG, THAT'S A CLEVER IDEA, AND SHOWS YOU HAVE THE MAKINGS OF A REPORTER! I'LL GIVE YOU A CHANCE! CLARK, WILL YOU ASK LOIS LANE TO COME HERE?

2

223

LOOK, LANA... IT *IS SUPERMAN* COMING!

BY INHALING MY BREATH, I'LL DRAW DOWN THAT *BALLOON-DUMMY* OF *SUPERMAN* I FIXED UP OUTSIDE... AND MY SUPER-VENTRILOQUISM WILL COMPLETE THE ILLUSION!

HELLO, GIRLS!

SORRY I CAN'T STAY FOR DINNER... I PROMISED TO HELP THE PHONE COMPANY WITH ITS HARBOR CABLE REPAIRS!

A PUFF OF SUPER-BREATH WILL SEND THE DUMMY ON ITS WAY... AND I'D BETTER GO, TOO, BECAUSE I *DID* PROMISE TO HELP!

WHAT A PITY! BUT THAT'S *SUPERMAN*... ALWAYS BREAKING DATES TO DO SOME BIG FEAT!

SAY, I'M GOING TO COVER *THAT* STUNT... I'LL SEE YOU LATER, TOO!

HM, ALL THIS IS FAMILIAR! IT WAS THE SAME WAY WITH SUPER-*BOY* AND CLARK, TOO!

MINUTES LATER, AT THE HARBOR, IT'S A WORRIED SUPERMAN WHO KEEPS TRAFFIC MOVING WHILE A CABLE IS REPAIRED...

WE'LL REPAIR THE CABLE, *SUPERMAN,* IF YOU CAN KEEP THE SHIP TRAFFIC FLOWING!

SURE, I'LL GIVE ALL SHIPS A LIFT!

LANA SEEMS AS SUSPICIOUS AS EVER! I WONDER WHAT SHE AND LOIS ARE TALKING ABOUT?

TROUBLE, SUPERMAN... THAT'S WHAT THEY'RE TALKING ABOUT! FOR LANA...

I'M CONVINCED BY THAT TRICK AND I NEVER WAS CONVINCED! AND I'M DETERMINED TO FIND OUT ONCE AND FOR ALL IF CLARK KENT IS REALLY *SUPERMAN!*

I'D LIKE TO KNOW THE ANSWER MYSELF... BUT I'D KEEP IT SECRET! LANA WOULD BROADCAST IT, AND RUIN *SUPERMAN'S* CAREER!

NEXT MORNING, IN PERRY WHITE'S OFFICE...

MR. WHITE, STORIES ABOUT *SUPERMAN* ALWAYS INTEREST OUR READERS! HOW ABOUT ME DOING A SERIES OF ARTICLES CALLED "I REMEMBER SUPERBOY"? I KNEW HIM SO WELL!

THAT'S A TERRIFIC IDEA, LANA! GO AHEAD ON IT!

4

SO LANA BEGINS A DRAMATIC SERIES THAT CAN HAVE MOMENTOUS CONSEQUENCES!

"...I REMEMBER HOW *SUPERBOY* ONCE ENCOUNTERED AN ESCAPING BANDIT GANG IN SMALLVILLE..."

"HE STOPPED THEM BY SWIFTLY SHAPING A ROCK INTO A GREAT PRISM THAT DAZZLED THEM WITH MAN-MADE RAINBOWS!"

"I ALSO REMEMBER THE TIME AN AVALANCHE BROUGHT A GREAT ROCK-FALL TO THREATEN SMALLVILLE..."

THESE HOME-RUNS WILL *SAVE* HOMES! AND THEY'LL FALL IN THAT UNINHABITED SWAMP!

"I ALSO REMEMBER HOW, WHEN CRIMINALS USING STOLEN ARMY TANKS THREATENED SMALLVILLE, *SUPERBOY* CONVERTED A LOCOMOTIVE INTO A HUGE MAGNET TO SAVE THE DAY!"

LOOK, SUPERBOY HAS GRABBED UP THOSE TANK-MOBSTERS!

5

MEANWHILE, AS FATE WOULD HAVE IT, "LENS" LEWIS, THE CAMERAMAN CROOK, *IS* ABOUT TO BE RELEASED FROM THE *METROPOLIS PRISON,* WHERE HE HAS JUST FINISHED *SERVING THE SENTENCE* FOR HIS CRIME...

WHY, LANA'S TALKING TO THAT CRIMINAL WHO WAS JUST RELEASED! NOW WHAT ON EARTH...

SURE, THERE WAS FILM IN THAT CAMERA! I FIGURED I COULD USE A FILM OF THE ROBBERY TO FORCE THE BOYS INTO GIVING ME A BIGGER CUT!

IF IT'S STILL WHERE YOU HID IT, WILL YOU SELL IT TO ME? I WANT A SOUVENIR OF THAT CASE!

SURE, WHY NOT? I HID IT SO IT COULDN'T BE USED AS EVIDENCE AGAINST ME, TOO... BUT I'VE SERVED MY TIME AND THE FILM CAN'T HURT ME NOW!

I THINK I CAN GUESS WHAT'S ON THAT FILM... AND I'VE GOT TO MAKE SURE LANA DOESN'T USE IT!

SOON, IN A SECLUDED SPOT OUTSIDE SMALLVILLE...

I DUCKED IT HERE WHEN I WAS TRYING TO GET AWAY FROM *SUPERBOY*... AND IT'S STILL SAFE!

WONDERFUL! I HAVE YOUR MONEY, MR. LEWIS!

BUT AS "LENS" LEWIS WALKS AWAY...

BY WRAPPING THIS LEAD FOIL I BROUGHT ALONG AROUND THE FILM, IT WILL PREVENT *SUPERMAN* FROM FOGGING IT WITH X-RAY VISION AND... WHY, LOIS! YOU FOLLOWED ME

LANA, IF THAT FILM CONTAINS THE SECRET OF *SUPERBOY'S* IDENTITY, YOU MUSTN'T USE IT! IT WOULD WRECK *SUPERMAN'S* CAREER!

OF COURSE, IF *SUPERMAN* WERE *MY* BOY FRIEND, I MIGHT FEEL ABOUT IT AS YOU DO!

ALL RIGHT... *SIGH!*...I'LL GIVE HIM UP TO YOU IF YOU'LL DESTROY THAT FILM!

OH, NO, YOU DON'T! I CAN USE THE FILM NOW...TO LEARN *SUPERMAN'S* IDENTITY! DON'T TRY ANYTHING...THIS GUN I HID WITH THE CAMERA STILL WORKS!

7

227

SOON, HEADING BACK TOWARD METROPOLIS IN LANA'S CAR...

THE SECRET OF *SUPERMAN'S* IDENTITY! WHY, I CAN MAKE A FORTUNE SHOWING THIS, AND CHARGING EVERY CROOK IN METROPOLIS A GRAND TO SEE IT!

I HOPE YOU'RE SATISFIED WITH WHAT YOU'VE DONE, LANA!

MEANWHILE, BACK AT THE *PLANET* OFFICE, PERRY WHITE HAS A PROBLEM...

LANA LANG WENT OFF TO TALK TO SOME CROOK GETTING OUT OF PRISON, AND HASN'T COME BACK! HER *"I REMEMBER SUPERBOY!"* ARTICLE FOR TODAY ISN'T FINISHED!

WHY DON'T YOU GET LOIS TO DO IT?

SHE'S DISAPPEARED, TOO! *YOU'LL* HAVE TO FINISH THE ARTICLE, CLARK!

WELL...ER...ALL RIGHT, BUT MY TYPEWRITER'S NOT WORKING WELL! I'LL HAVE TO USE THE ONE IN THE NIGHT EDITOR'S OFFICE!

IN THE PRIVACY OF THE SMALL OFFICE, CLARK KENT BECOMES *SUPERMAN* FOR AN URGENT REASON!

THAT UNFINISHED ARTICLE OF LANA TELLS ME WHAT SCHEME SHE HAD IN MIND... AND IT MIGHT WORK! I CAN GUESS WHERE SHE AND THAT CROOK WOULD GO, AND I'D BETTER GET THERE FAST!

BUT, ZIPPING AT SUPER-SPEED OVER THE COUNTRY-SIDE TOWARD SMALLVILLE...

IT WAS NEAR HERE I CAUGHT LENS AFTER THE HOLD-UP, SO HE MUST HAVE HIDDEN HIS CAMERA SOME-WHERE NEAR... OH, OH! THAT CAR... MY TELESCOPIC VISION TELLS ME THAT LANA AND LOIS ARE *BOTH* IN IT, AND IN TROUBLE!

SO THERE *WAS* FILM IN THAT CAMERA... I DIDN'T DREAM THERE COULD BE, SINCE IT WAS A FAKE "MOVIE"! NOW I'VE GOT TO GET HOLD OF IT SOMEWAY, BUT I CAN'T ENDANGER THE GIRLS!

UNWILLING TO RISK HARM TO LANA OR LOIS, THE MAN OF STEEL FOLLOWS UNSEEN TO THE OUT-SKIRTS OF METROPOLIS!

I REMEMBER LEWIS HAD A HOUSE AND PHOTOGRAPHIC STUDIO... AND THAT WOULD BE IT! BUT WHAT'S HIS PLAN? IF I CAN EAVESDROP WITH SUPER-HEARING!...

I'LL DEVELOP THIS FILM QUICK AND THEN I'M GIVING A MOVIE... AT A THOUSAND DOLLARS A SEAT!

OH, WHAT A TERRIBLE MISTAKE I MADE!

I CAN'T JUST GRAB LOIS AND LANA...THEY MIGHT GET SHOT! AND IF I JUST GRAB THE FILM, THE GIRLS WOULD STILL BE SURE THAT CLARK KENT WAS SUPERBOY... ER, I MEAN, IS SUPERMAN... ER, ANYWAY, I HAVE AN IDEA!

SOON, IN A DESERTED TRACT OF LAND SOME DISTANCE FROM METROPOLIS, AN ASTOUNDING ACTIVITY BEGINS!

THAT PATCH OF FOREST HAD TO BE CLEARED ANYWAY FOR A NEW ROAD... AND THIS TIMBER AND THE STONE I QUARRIED WILL PROVIDE ALL THE MATERIALS I NEED!

FASTER THAN AN ARMY OF CONSTRUCTION MEN COULD WORK, THE MAN OF STEEL STARTS HIS TASK...AND ON THE PLAIN THERE RISES A STREET OF GIANT SIZE!

THANKS TO MY PHOTOGRAPHIC MEMORY, EVERY DETAIL WILL BE PERFECT... AND IN EXACT SCALE!

SMALLVILLE BANK

BANK

9

THESE ADULT-SIZED TEEN-AGED CLOTHES AND THE OVERSIZED SCHOOL BOOKS OUGHT TO DO THE TRICK! THEN TO SET UP THAT AUTOMATIC MOVIE CAMERA I BORROWED...

NOW FOR SOME ACTING! BUT THIS MAKES ME FEEL STRANGE... AS THOUGH I REALLY WAS A BOY AGAIN, WALKING HOME FROM SCHOOL!

THEN, QUICKLY SETTING UP ANOTHER SCENE...

I'LL NEED THIS SCENE FOR A CONVINCING DOUBLE-EXPOSURE... AND THOSE OVERSIZED MECHANICAL DUMMIES I MADE WILL DO VERY WELL FOR BANDITS!

AGAIN DONNING THE SUPERMAN COSTUME, THE MAN OF STEEL APPEARS AS THE BOY OF STEEL AGAINST THE BACKGROUND OF GIANT BUILDINGS!

WHEN I COMBINE THIS PICTURE WITH THE ONE I JUST TOOK, IT SHOULD CONVINCE EVEN LANA THAT SHE'S WRONG!

MOMENTS LATER AFTER DISMANTLING HIS GIANT SET...

NOW TO RETURN THIS CAMERA AND DO SOME SUPER-FAST DEVELOPING ON THIS FILM!

MEANWHILE, THE JUBILANT "LENS" LEWIS GETS ON WITH HIS PLAN TO MAKE A FORTUNE...

YEAH, I'M RUNNING THE FILM TONIGHT... AND IT'LL COST A THOUSAND CASH DOLLARS TO SEE IT!

A THOUSAND BUCKS IS CHEAP TO SEE THAT FILM, IF IT REALLY GIVES AWAY SUPERMAN'S IDENTITY!

10

"LENS" KEEPS THE PHONE WIRES HOT...AND PRESENTLY HIS AUDIENCE BEGINS TO ARRIVE...

HERE'S MY GRAND, LENS!

THANKS! I'LL SHOW THE FILM IN A FEW MINUTES!

WHAT ARE WE GOING TO DO, LANA?

BUT "LENS" ALSO HAS A VISITOR HE DOESN'T KNOW ABOUT!

GOT TO MOVE CAREFULLY NOW... MY X-RAY VISION TELLS ME NO ONE'S WATCHING THE TABLE WITH HIS FILM ON IT!

NOW TO SWITCH THE FILMS SO SWIFTLY NO ONE CAN SEE IT! THERE, IT'S DONE!

A MOMENT LATER, THE UNSUSPECTING "LENS" THREADS THE SUBSTITUTE FILM INTO THE PROJECTOR, AND THE FABULOUS MOVIE BEGINS...

MY PRYING CAUSED THIS, ALL THIS... SUPERMAN'S SECRET WILL BE OUT NOW, AND IT'S ALL MY FAULT! I'VE GOT TO STOP IT...SMASH THE PROJECTOR...

SMALLVILLE BANK

LOOK, THERE'S YOUNG CLARK WALKING PAST THE BANK!

LANA'S A GOOD SCOUT AFTER ALL... SHE RISKED ANYTHING TO STOP THE SHOW!

HEY, YOU, WHAT KIND OF A SWINDLE IS THIS?

YOU SAID THE FILM WOULD SHOW SUPERBOY'S IDENTITY, BUT IT ONLY SHOWS HIM CATCHING THE BANDITS!

BUT... BUT...

WHY, THERE'S CLARK AND SUPERBOY!

SMALLVILLE BANK

ONE DAY, AT AN AMUSEMENT PARK IN THE OUTSKIRTS OF METROPOLIS, WE SEE AN OLD AND FAMIL... WELL, NOT *QUITE* SO FAMILIAR A FIGURE...

HA,-HA,-HA! THIS CRAZY MIRROR MAKES ME LOOK ALL OUT OF SHAPE!

YES, IT IS *SUPERMAN'S* OLD ENEMY--THE PRANKSTER.

AND ELSEWHERE IN THE SAME AMUSEMENT PARK...

THIS GIANT DUCK IS LIKE ONE OF MY TOYS--THAT I USED IN CRIME! SIGHH! THOSE WERE THE GOOD OLD DAYS, BEFORE *SUPERMAN* DROVE ME OUT OF BUSINESS!

YOU GUESSED IT, DEAR READER, THIS PLUMP FELLOW IS NONE OTHER THAN THE TOYMAN!

BY A STRANGE COINCIDENCE, A THIRD WELL-KNOWN GENIUS IS ALSO PRESENT...

BAH! IF I WANTED TO DEVOTE MY GENIUS TO SUCH INVENTIONS, WHAT A SENSATION I COULD CREATE!

THIS THIRD CHARACTER IS LUTHOR, RENEGADE MASTER-MIND OF SCIENCE AND ARCH-FOE OF *THE MAN OF STEEL!*

SHORTLY AFTERWARDS, A WHIM OF FATE BRINGS THE 3 MASTERS OF MENACE TOGETHER IN A SURPRISING FASHION!

WHY DON'T YOU WATCH WHERE-- SAY, YOU'RE THE TOYMAN!

AND YOU'RE THE PRANKSTER!

LOOK OUT!

LUTHOR!

OUCH! WHY BLESS ME, THAT'S WHO HE IS.

MOMENTS AFTER THEIR EXPLOSIVE MEETING...

THIS CHANCE MEETING MAY BE THE LUCKIEST THING THAT EVER HAPPENED! WHAT HAVE YOU FELLOWS BEEN DOING LATELY?

IT'S *SUPERMAN,* YOU KNOW. HE'S ALWAYS INTER-FERING!

NOT MUCH!

WHY DON'T THE THREE OF US COMBINE OUR TALENTS AND FIGHT *SUPERMAN*? HE'S HAD TROUBLE ENOUGH BEATING ANY ONE OF US! HOW COULD HE DEFEAT ALL THREE?

SOUNDS LIKE A GREAT IDEA, LUTHOR!

LATER..

WE'VE AGREED TO BECOME PARTNERS! NOW WE'LL DRAW LOTS TO DECIDE WHICH ONE OF US PLANS THE FIRST CRIME!

I WIN! I DREW THE SLIP WITH THE X MARKED ON IT!

I'VE GOT JUST THE PRANK FIGURED OUT FOR THIS JOB, TOO. I ALWAYS WANTED TO TRY IT BUT I DIDN'T HAVE THE NERVE! THIS OUGHT TO BE FUN!

AND THE NEXT DAY, AS A CROWD GATHERS TO VIEW A DAZZLING JEWELRY STORE EXHIBIT...

GOLLY! LOOK AT THAT MODEL OF METROPOLIS BRIDGE--ALL MADE OF PRECIOUS STONES! IT'S WORTH A FORTUNE!

HMM! WHAT'S THIS?

DON'T TRY TO PICK IT UP, MISTER! SEE THAT STRING ATTACHED? THE KIDS WILL YANK IT OUT OF SIGHT BEFORE YOU TOUCH IT!

SAY, YOU'RE RIGHT! THAT'S AN OLD CHILDREN'S PRANK!

THE KIDS IN THIS NEIGHBORHOOD ARE FULL OF MISCHIEF! SEE WHAT'S HAPPENING TO THAT GENTLEMAN!

GREAT SCOTT! IT'S *LUTHOR*, THE CRIMINAL SCIENTIST!

HEY!

SUDDENLY, FROM THE STRANGE HAT ON THE PAVEMENT, THERE POURS CHOKING CLOUDS OF SUFFOCATING GAS!

GAS? I--I CAN'T BREATHE!

BUT EVEN AS THE FUMES FELL THE OTHERS, REPORTER CLARK KENT CHANGES COSTUMES TO BECOME SUPERMAN!

THE GAS IS HARMLESS--SO I CAN CONCENTRATE ON CATCHING LUTHOR! QUEER--THIS DOESN'T SEEM TO BE THE SORT OF CRIME LUTHOR WOULD HAVE PLANNED!

BUT I GUESS EVEN AN OLD DOG CAN LEARN NEW TRICKS!

SUPERMAN!

AS SUPERMAN'S STEELY FINGERS CLOSE ON HIS QUARRY, THE PRANKSTER PULLS THE REST OF HIS PLAN INTO ACTION!

I KNEW NOBODY WOULD TOUCH THIS WALLET -- THINKING IT TO BE A CHILDISH PRANK! HA-HA! ACTUALLY, THAT STRING IS ATTACHED TO A DETONATOR THAT SETS OFF DYNAMITE PLANTED BY THAT BUILDING WALL!

BOOM!

SO THAT'S IT! DURING THE CONFUSION, YOUR HENCHMEN ARE BLASTING THEIR WAY INTO THE JEWELRY BUILDING! WELL, I'LL JUST PUT YOU HERE FOR SAFEKEEPING!

AND THEN I'LL TAKE CARE OF... GOOD GLORY! THE PRANKSTER AND THE TOYMAN!

ULP!

4

PUFFS OF SUPER-BREATH WRENCH THE JEWELED BRIDGE MODEL FROM THE PRANKSTER'S GRASP AND SEND HIM HURTLING BACK...

UGHHH! QUICK, TOYMAN! *DO* SOMETHING!

I ALWAYS HAVE SPECIAL TOYS PREPARED FOR EMERGENCIES!

AND THERE'S NO DENYING *THIS* IS AN EMERGENCY!

WHA-? TINY, FLYING PUPPETS OF ME!

THAT ISN'T ALL, *SUPERMAN!* EACH PUPPET IS A TINY HAND GRENADE -- THAT EXPLODES ON CONTACT WITH ANYTHING IT TOUCHES!

ANOTHER OF YOUR DEADLY TOYS, EH? I'VE GOT TO STOP THEM!

CAN'T RISK THE EXPLOSION DESTROYING THIS MODEL BRIDGE! SO I'LL SET OFF THE GRENADES-- WITH MY TEETH!

AT DAZZLING SPEED, *SUPERMAN* INTERCEPTS THE EXPLOSIVE PUPPETS BEFORE THEY TOUCH ANYTHING! ALL EXCEPT ONE...

I CAN'T EXPLODE THAT GRENADE -- WITHOUT DANGER OF FLYING PARTICLES HURTING THAT WOMAN! ONLY ONE THING TO DO!

OPENING HIS MOUTH WIDE, THE *MAN OF STEEL* SWALLOWS THE DEADLY GRENADE!

HMM! THIS FLAVOR IS DELICIOUS!

5

BUT WHILE SUPERMAN IS VERY BUSY, THE THREE OUT-LAWS MAKE GOOD THEIR ESCAPE IN ONE OF LUTHOR'S INVENTIONS.

FORTUNATELY, I HAD MY JET-MOBILE READY! WE'LL BE MILES AWAY BEFORE SUPERMAN STARTS TO LOOK FOR US!

DON'T FORGET! IT WAS MY TOYS THAT KEPT SUPERMAN BUSY AND GAVE US THE CHANCE TO ESCAPE!

WE CARRIED OUT OUR PART OF THE JOB PERFECTLY, TOYMAN! IT WAS THE PRANKSTER'S FAULT THAT WE FAILED!

THE NEXT JOB IS MINE, THOUGH! AND I'VE ALREADY FIGURED OUT WHAT IT WILL BE! THERE WILL BE NO MISTAKES THIS TIME!

SEVERAL DAYS LATER, IN THE DAILY PLANET OFFICE WHERE REPORTERS CLARK KENT AND LOIS LANE ARE EMPLOYED...

I GUESS LUTHOR, THE PRANKSTER AND THIS TOYMAN HAVE GIVEN UP TRYING TO DEFEAT SUPERMAN AFTER THEIR FIRST ATTEMPT FAILED!

MORE LIKELY, THEY'RE WAITING FOR THE RIGHT OPPORTUNITY TO STRIKE AGAIN!

HMM! AND THIS FRONT PAGE STORY COULD BE IT!

LATER, WHEN CLARK KENT IS ALONE...

THAT STORY MENTIONED THE "JACK IN THE BOX" CONTEST! IT TOLD ABOUT A CONTEST IN WHICH $1,000,000 IN PRIZE MONEY IS TO BE GIVEN AWAY TO SOME LUCKY WINNER!

THAT'S JUST THE SET-UP THAT WOULD INTEREST THE TOYMAN! EVEN THE NAME OF THE CONTEST IS THAT OF A TOY!

AT THIS MOMENT, OUTSIDE THE BUILDING WHERE THE CONTEST IS BEING HELD...

CAREFUL WITH THOSE CRATES! THEY'RE MARKED "HANDLE WITH CARE"!

THEY SURE ARE HEAVY! I WONDER WHAT'S IN 'EM--AND WHY WE GOT ORDERS TO LEAVE THEM RIGHT HERE ON THE SIDEWALK?

JACK IN THE BOX CONTEST HEADQUARTERS

THIS SIDE UP

HANDLE WITH CARE

THIS SIDE UP

HANDLE WITH CARE

AS YOU'VE GUESSED, READER, THESE ARE NO ORDINARY CRATES! IN FACT, THEY CONCEAL...

6

...THE TOYMAN'S NEWEST TRICK!

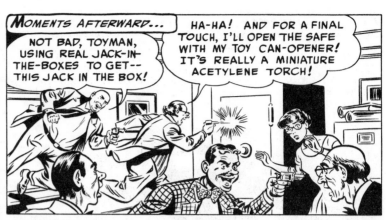

MOMENTS AFTERWARD...

NOT BAD, TOYMAN, USING REAL JACK-IN-THE-BOXES TO GET-- THIS JACK IN THE BOX!

HA-HA! AND FOR A FINAL TOUCH, I'LL OPEN THE SAFE WITH MY TOY CAN-OPENER! IT'S REALLY A MINIATURE ACETYLENE TORCH!

BUT SUDDENLY... SUPERMAN AGAIN!

OH, NO! NOBODY'S LUCK CAN BE THIS BAD!

SWIFTLY, THE TERRIBLE TRIO TAKES TO FLIGHT...

TO THE ROOF! IT'S OUR ONLY CHANCE!

OUT OF MY WAY!

THE SAFE-- IT'S FALLING! THE TOYMAN'S TINY TORCH CUT THROUGH THE FLOOR SUPPORT!

THAT HEAVY SAFE WILL PLUNGE THROUGH TO THE LOWER FLOORS OF THE BUILDING! IT'S BOUND TO HURT SOMEBODY!

SORRY TO BOTHER YOU, MISS!

EEEK! YOU SAVED MY LIFE, SUPERMAN!

239

BUT WHEN THE MAN OF TOMORROW WINGS HIS WAY TO THE ROOF...

THEY MANAGED TO ESCAPE WHILE I WAS BUSY CATCHING THAT SAFE! BUT *HOW?* WHERE COULD THEY HAVE GONE?

FIFTY THOUSAND FEET STRAIGHT UP...

GULP! I--I THINK I LEFT MY STOMACH A COUPLE OF MILES BACK DOWN THERE!

STOP COMPLAINING, TOYMAN! IF IT WASN'T FOR MY STRATOSPHERE ROCKET, WE'D BE PRISONERS OF *SUPERMAN* RIGHT NOW! LUCKILY, I KEPT IT IN READINESS ON THE ROOF!

FRANKLY, I'M DISAPPOINTED IN YOUR CRIME SCHEMES! YOU BOTH HAVE INFLATED REPUTATIONS! BUT NOW YOU WILL HAVE A CHANCE TO SEE A REAL GENIUS AT WORK--*ME!* AND I WILL *DEFEAT SUPERMAN!*

LATER, WITH SUPREME INSOLENCE, LUTHOR BROADCASTS A CHALLENGE TO *SUPERMAN!*

PREPARE FOR THE WORST, *SUPERMAN!* I, LUTHOR, HAVE UNLEASHED MY MOST TERRIFIC MENACE! *THE FLOATING LAND MINES!* UNLESS EVERY COUNTRY PAYS A BILLION DOLLARS BLACKMAIL, THESE MINES WILL DESTROY THEIR CAPITAL CITIES!

LUTHOR IS AS GOOD AS HIS WORD! AT ALMOST THE MOMENT OF HIS BROADCAST, MONSTROUS MINES OF MENACE APPEAR OVER THE VARIOUS CAPITALS OF THE WORLD!

SACRE BLEU! WE ARE LOST!

LUTHOR CAN SEND THE MINES DOWN BY THE PUSH OF A BUTTON--AND BLOW US ALL UP!

BUT THEN, A FAMILIAR BLUE-CLAD FIGURE HURTLES INTO SPECTACULAR ACTION...

A NEW PRODUCT, IF I SAY SO MYSELF! AND THE MINE CAN'T HURT ANYONE WHEN IT EXPLODES THIS HIGH IN THE AIR!

BLAMMM!

8

241

SECONDS LATER, THE BLACK VACUUM OF SPACE IS SHATTERED BY A BLINDING EXPLOSION!

IT WORKED! THE BLAST I SET OFF CAN'T HURT ME -- AND IT'S SCATTERED THE KRYPTONITE PARTICLES TOO FAR TO AFFECT ME ANY LONGER!

BAROOOM

MEANWHILE, AT LUTHOR'S HEADQUARTERS...

NOW, WILL YOU TWO IMITATION MASTERMINDS ADMIT THAT I, LUTHOR, AM THE ONLY REAL GENIUS? MY SUCCESS IN DEFEATING SUPERMAN PROVES THAT I'M THE GREATEST...

WAS I DEFEATED?

TELL ME MORE, LUTHOR -- BUT WHILE I LISTEN, I'LL JUST TIE YOU UP WITH THIS ROPE I'M MAKING OUT OF THE DRAPERIES!

I--I DON'T UNDERSTAND! MY PLAN WAS FOOLPROOF! W-WHAT COULD HAVE GONE WRONG?

10

SECONDS LATER, ON THE WAY TO PRISON...

HA, HA, HA! YOU THOUGHT YOU WERE A GENIUS!

LUTHOR GOT US ALL CAPTURED BY SUPERMAN! HA, HA, HA!

THE PRANKSTER AND THE TOYMAN ARE SO HAPPY LUTHOR CAN'T GLOAT OVER THEM--THAT THEY DON'T EVEN MIND GOING TO PRISON! WHAT A PRIZE PACKAGE OF CONCEITED HAMS THESE THREE ARE!

THE END

COMING...SUPER-ATTRACTIONS!

JULY SUPERBOY COMICS NOW ON SALE

Featuring "The BOY with ULTRA-POWERS!"

INTO SMALLVILLE ONE DAY COMES A MYSTERIOUS YOUTH WHO HAS POWERS EVEN MORE FANTASTIC THAN SUPERBOY'S! UNDERNEATH HIS ORDINARY OUTER GARMENTS IS THE COLORFUL ACTION COSTUME OF... ULTRA-BOY; HIS MISSION--TO EXPOSE THE BOY OF STEEL'S SECRET IDENTITY!

Why is he doing this? WE CHALLENGE YOU TO GUESS!

JULY Jimmy Olsen COMICS NOW ON SALE

ELASTIC LAD is BACK!

SEE WHAT HAPPENS WHEN JIMMY S-T-R-E-T-C-H-E-S HIMSELF SO HIGH AND SO THIN THAT HE IS ABLE TO ENTER A NARROW HOLE IN THE PHANTOM ZONE!

Extra! JIMMY OLSEN VISITS THE PAST AND BECOMES GOLIATH'S Best PAL!

JULY ACTION COMICS NOW ON SALE

By Popular Demand! ANOTHER ALL "RED KRYPTONITE" ISSUE!

SEE HOW RED K. CHANGES THE MAN OF STEEL INTO... "HALF A SUPERMAN!"

SEE HOW RED K. GIVES SUPERGIRL A SHOCKING NEW POWER!

242

243

"INSTANTLY, I FOCUSED THE HEAT OF MY X-RAY VISION ON THE WHEELS' RUBBER TIRES..."

NOW THE TIRES WILL MELT -- AND THE STICKY RUBBER WILL SLOW UP THE CHAIR LONG ENOUGH FOR ME TO RUN TO IT AT NORMAL SPEED!

"THE SUDDEN STOPPING OF THE CHAIR THREW THE GIRL OFF--AND INTO MY ARMS!"

"A LOVELY FACE LOOKED UP AT ME GRATEFULLY, AND I STARED INTO EYES AS BLUE AND MYSTERIOUS AS THE SEA..."

"WHEN SHE SPOKE, HER VOICE HAD THE SLIGHTEST TOUCH OF A FOREIGN ACCENT..."

THANK YOU! YOU SEE, I CANNOT WALK! IT IS A PROBLEM, BUT I DECIDED NOT TO LET IT PREVENT ME FROM LEAVING MY NATIVE COUNTRY TO ENTER YOUR COLLEGE!

SHE'S A PARALYSIS VICTIM! BUT THIS COURAGEOUS GIRL HASN'T LET IT STOP HER FROM GETTING AN EDUCATION!

"SUDDENLY, SHE NOTICED THE MELTED RUBBER TIRES..."

HMM!

UH-OH! HOW CAN I EXPLAIN THEM WITHOUT MAKING HER SUSPECT MY *SUPERMAN* IDENTITY?

"THEN SHE SMILED AT ME, AND I HAD THE STRANGE SENSATION THAT HER EYES SEEMED TO BE LOOKING RIGHT INTO MY MIND!"

THE SPEED OF THE WHEELS MUST HAVE CREATED SO MUCH FRICTION HEAT THAT THE RUBBER MELTED! THAT COULD EXPLAIN IT, COULDN'T IT?

SHE SAID THAT ALMOST AS IF -- AS IF WE *BOTH* KNEW IT ISN'T TRUE! BUT, OF COURSE, THAT'S IMPOSSIBLE!

"I WAS STILL THINKING OF HER WHEN OUR BIOLOGY CLASS ADJOINED LATER TO THE COLLEGE *"ARK"*-- A FLOATING AQUARIUM ANCHORED NEAR THE SEA SHORE..."

HER NAME IS LORI LEMARIS, SHE SAID! A LOVELY NAME FOR A LOVELY GIRL!

②

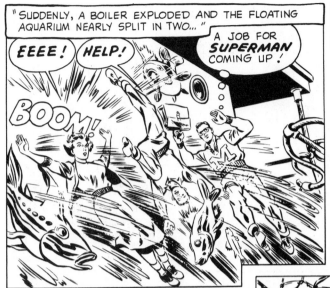

"SUDDENLY, A BOILER EXPLODED AND THE FLOATING AQUARIUM NEARLY SPLIT IN TWO..."

EEEE!

HELP!

A JOB FOR *SUPERMAN* COMING UP!

BOOM!

"EVERYONE JUMPED INTO THE WATER AND SWAM TO SHORE A FEW YARDS AWAY--SO I WAS UNOBSERVED AS I DIVED TO AN UNDERWATER CAVERN ..."

I'M GLAD I MADE A HABIT OF CARRYING MY SUPER-COSTUME IN MY SCHOOL BRIEFCASE!

"THEN I BECAME AN UNDERWATER "COWBOY", HERDING TOGETHER ALL THE FISH THAT HAD ESCAPED FROM THE AQUARIUM..."

GIT ALONG, LITTLE DOGIE!

NOW I'LL WEAVE THESE LONG STRANDS OF SEA WEED INTO A NET "CAGE" ABOUT THE SPECIMENS UNTIL THE AQUARIUM IS REPAIRED AND READY TO STOCK THEM AGAIN!

"SUDDENLY, I SAW A FAMILIAR STUDENT--A STUDENT NOW IN TERRIBLE DANGER!"

LORI--IN THE GRIP OF A GIANT OCTOPUS!

"EVEN AS I SHOT FORWARD, I WAS AMAZED TO SEE THAT LORI WAS NOT FRIGHTENED, BUT CALMLY REGARDING THE CREATURE..."

HER LIPS ARE MOVING! IF I DIDN'T KNOW BETTER, I'D ALMOST BELIEVE SHE WAS TALKING TO THE OCTOPUS!

245

"SUDDENLY, TO MY ASTONISHMENT, THE OCTOPUS SLID HIS TENTACLES FROM HER AND PLACIDLY SWAM AWAY.'"

GREAT SCOTT! IT'S LEFT HER UNHARMED!

YOU'RE LUCKY YOU WEREN'T HURT! I'M STILL WONDERING WHY THE OCTOPUS LEFT YOU SO SUDDENLY!

WELL, *SUPERMAN*... HE PROBABLY SAW YOU STREAKING NEAR AND WAS FRIGHTENED AWAY!

"AS DAYS SPED BY, I BECAME INTRIGUED WITH THIS MYSTERIOUS GIRL AND DATED HER STEADILY, MEETING HER AT THE SCHOOL SODA SHOP... "

CLARK, BEING WITH YOU HAS BEEN WONDERFUL, BUT IT'S GETTING LATE! I MUST BE HOME BY EIGHT O'CLOCK!

WHY DOES SHE ALWAYS HAVE TO BE HOME EVERY NIGHT BY EIGHT, I WONDER?

" I THOUGHT OF LORI CONSTANTLY NOW -- IN OUR ASTRONOMY CLASS, I DAY-DREAMED OF IMPRESSING HER BY ACTUALLY FLYING HER TO THE PLANETS IN MY *SUPERMAN* IDENTITY... "

"IN OUR ART CLASS, I DAY-DREAMED OF SCULPING MT. EVEREST IN HER IMAGE TO PROVE MY LOVE FOR HER... "

" IN OUR MUSIC CLASS, I DAY-DREAMED OF FLYING A GREAT ORCHESTRA AROUND THE WORLD, SO ALL WOULD HEAR A LOVE SONG I'D WRITE FOR HER... "

LORI, LORI IS MY LOVE

"LATER, I MET LORI, TOOK HER TO A ROMANTIC SPOT--AND PROPOSED.'"

LORI--I LOVE YOU; WILL YOU MARRY ME? BEFORE YOU GIVE ME YOUR ANSWER, I MUST TELL YOU THE TRUTH ABOUT MYSELF...

YOU DON'T HAVE TO TELL ME, CLARK--I'VE KNOWN FROM THE VERY BEGINNING THAT *YOU ARE SUPERMAN!*

Y-YOU KNEW? BUT HOW...?

THAT'S NOT IMPORTANT! WHAT IS IMPORTANT IS THAT ALTHOUGH I LOVE YOU, I CAN NEVER MARRY YOU!

BUT--IF IT'S BECAUSE OF YOUR LEGS, THAT DOESN'T MATTER TO ME! AFTER ALL, I'M *SUPERMAN!* I'LL SEARCH THE UNIVERSE FOR A CURE THAT CAN MAKE YOU WALK AGAIN!

PLEASE, DON'T QUESTION ME ANYMORE! NOW I REALLY HAVE TO GO! I MUST BE HOME BY EIGHT!

WHY CAN'T SHE MARRY ME? AND WHY DOES SHE ALWAYS HAVE TO LEAVE ME AT EIGHT? DOES SHE GO TO MEET ANOTHER MAN?

"I'M AFRAID I LET MY JEALOUSY GET THE BETTER OF ME--AND LATER USED MY X-RAY VISION TO LOOK INTO HER TRAILER HOUSE OFF THE CAMPUS..."

LORI REPORTING! I LEAVE FOR HOME TONIGHT! MY MISSION IN AMERICA IS COMPLETE!

THIS IS WHY SHE RETURNS AT EIGHT-- TO MAKE SECRET RADIO REPORTS! HER "MISSION", SHE SAID! IS IT POSSIBLE LORI IS A FOREIGN AGENT--A SPY?

I LOVE LORI--BUT I LOVE MY COUNTRY, TOO! IF SHE IS AN ENEMY, SHE MAY BE AFTER SECRET DATA ON THE SECRET SCIENTIFIC RESEARCH BEING DONE AT THIS COLLEGE! I MUST SEARCH HER ROOM FOR EVIDENCE WHEN SHE GOES OUT TO DINNER!

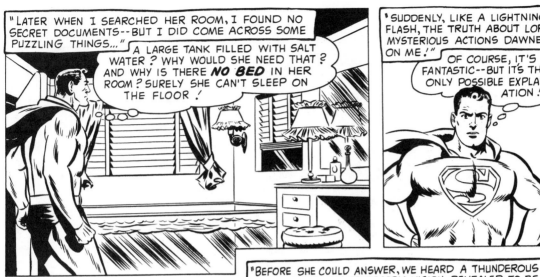

"LATER WHEN I SEARCHED HER ROOM, I FOUND NO SECRET DOCUMENTS--BUT I DID COME ACROSS SOME PUZZLING THINGS..."

A LARGE TANK FILLED WITH SALT WATER? WHY WOULD SHE NEED THAT? AND WHY IS THERE **NO BED** IN HER ROOM? SURELY SHE CAN'T SLEEP ON THE FLOOR!

'SUDDENLY, LIKE A LIGHTNING FLASH, THE TRUTH ABOUT LORI'S MYSTERIOUS ACTIONS DAWNED ON ME!'

OF COURSE, IT'S FANTASTIC--BUT IT'S THE ONLY POSSIBLE EXPLANATION!

"LATER, I CONFRONTED LORI, BUT BEFORE I COULD SAY A WORD SHE LOOKED AT ME WITH THOSE EYES THAT SEEMED TO LOOK RIGHT INTO MY MIND..."

SO YOU'VE GUESSED THE TRUTH ABOUT ME, HAVEN'T YOU, **SUPERMAN?**

YES--BUT HOW...?

"BEFORE SHE COULD ANSWER, WE HEARD A THUNDEROUS ROAR, WHICH MY TELESCOPIC VISION REVEALED TO BE CAUSED BY A SUDDEN DISASTER.'"

SUPERMAN, WHAT IS IT?

ROOAA-RR

THE STATE DAM HAS BURST! THERE ARE HOMES IN THE VALLEY! I'VE GOT TO STOP THE FLOOD AS SWIFTLY AS POSSIBLE!

WAIT, **SUPERMAN!** I CAN BE OF USE! I WANT TO DO WHAT I CAN TO REPAY THE PEOPLE HERE WHO HAVE BEEN SO KIND TO ME!

I UNDERSTAND! ALL RIGHT, LORI!

⑦

"I SUPPOSE IT WOULD HAVE SEEMED CRAZY TO ANYONE ELSE! AFTER ALL, WHAT COULD A PARALYZED GIRL DO TO HELP **ME** ON A MISSION REQUIRING SUPER-POWERS!"

"THE JOB DONE, I FLEW LORI TO HER TRAILER HOME AND EXPLAINED HOW I'D GUESSED THE TRUTH ABOUT HER... "

WHEN I SAW NO BED HERE, THE FANTASTIC THOUGHT OCCURRED TO ME THAT YOU DIDN'T NEED ONE-- BECAUSE YOU SLEPT IN THAT SALT WATER TANK! I KNEW ONLY A *MERMAID* COULD DO THAT!

IT'S TRUE... I'M A CREATURE OF THE SEA--

...TO REMAIN IN PERFECT HEALTH, MY BODY MUST BE IMMERSED IN SALT WATER AT LEAST TEN HOURS A DAY-- THAT'S WHY I HAD TO RETURN HERE EVERY NIGHT AT EIGHT! YOU SEE-- MY HOME IS THE SUNKEN ISLAND KNOWN AS ATLANTIS!

I GUESSED THAT FAST--

JUST AS I GUESSED-- THAT OCTOPUS DIDN'T HARM YOU BECAUSE YOU "TALKED" TO IT!

YES, I PROJECTED MY THOUGHT- WAVES TO IT, BECAUSE "TALKING" IS IMPOSSIBLE UNDERWATER, WE SEA-PEOPLE HAVE MASTERED THE *ART OF READING MINDS!* TELEPATHY ENABLED ME TO LEARN YOUR SECRET IDENTITY!

ORIGINALLY, MY PEOPLE LIVED ON ANCIENT *ATLANTIS,* AND WHEN OUR SCIENTISTS LEARNED OUR ISLAND WAS SINKING INTO THE SEA, THEY CONSTRUCTED A HUGE GLASS DOME... "

DO NOT LOSE HEART! ATLANTIS HAS SUNK--BUT ATLANTIS IS NOT DEAD! THE DOME SHALL KEEP OUT THE SEA!

"THEN, ONE DAY, OUR SCIENTISTS FOUND A WAY TO CONVERT US INTO A RACE OF MERMEN AND MERMAIDS--AND SO WE TRULY BECAME A NEW RACE UNDER THE SEA!"

SMASH THE DOME! WE DO NOT NEED IT ANY LONGER! FROM NOW ON THE SEA IS OUR HOME!

BUT ONCE EVERY HUNDRED YEARS, ONE OF US IS CHOSEN TO RETURN TO THE UPPER WORLD TO LEARN OF THE SURFACE PEOPLE'S PROGRESS! THIS TIME I WAS CHOSEN, AND THOUGH I LOVE YOU, I MUST NOW RETURN TO MY PEOPLE!

YES, LORI--I-I UNDERSTAND! I'LL CARRY YOU TO THE SEA NOW...

SUPERGIRL

As we all know, **SUPERMAN** arrived on Earth in a space rocket long ago, when he was superbaby! The **MAN OF STEEL** has always thought he was the sole survivor of the tragic catastrophe that destroyed his home world, **KRYPTON**! But fate has many strange twists! And the happiest event in **SUPERMAN'S** lonely life occurs one day, which will astound and delight all fans of **SUPERMAN** too! For this is not an ordinary tale of **SUPERMAN**, but the launching of a new member of our "SUPER FAMILY!" So, without further ado, we take pride in introducing...

The SUPERGIRL *from* KRYPTON!

GREAT GUNS! I SEEM TO SEE A YOUNGSTER FLYING, DRESSED IN A SUPER-COSTUME! IT... UH... MUST BE AN ILLUSION!

LOOK AGAIN, **SUPERMAN**! IT'S ME... **SUPERGIRL**! AND I'M REAL!

ONE DAY IN **METROPOLIS** WHERE CLARK KENT, WHO IS SECRETLY **SUPERMAN**, WORKS AS A REPORTER FOR THE **DAILY PLANET**...

MY SUPER-HEARING PICKED UP A ROARING SOUND FAR OUT OF TOWN! I'LL CHECK WHAT IT IS WITH MY TELESCOPIC VISION!

RRRRRRRR RRRRR RRR!

GREAT GUNS! A GUIDED MISSILE IS ABOUT TO CRASH! THERE'S A HUMAN PASSENGER IN IT! THIS IS A JOB FOR **SUPERMAN**!

RRRRRRRR RRR RRRRR RR RRRRR RR!

SWIFTLY, CLARK SHEDS HIS OUTER GARMENTS TO REVEAL HIS OTHER DYNAMIC COSTUME!

LUCKILY, NOBODY ELSE IS IN THE OFFICE AT THE MOMENT! BUT HAVE I TIME TO REACH THE ROCKET? IT'LL SMASH IN SECONDS!

DESPITE HIS SUPER-SPEED, THE **MAN OF STEEL** IS TOO LATE!

IT...IT CAME AT GREATER SPEED THAN ANY ROCKET KNOWN ON EARTH BEFORE! IN FACT, IT REMINDS ME OF THE ROCKET THAT BROUGHT ME TO EARTH THIS SAME WAY, WHEN I WAS **SUPERBABY** YEARS AGO!

I SURVIVED MY CRASH BECAUSE I CAME FROM **KRYPTON**, A WORLD OF SUPER-GRAVITY! THAT GAVE ME SUPER-POWERS AND INVULNERABILITY IN EARTH'S LESSER GRAVITATION! BUT WHOEVER WAS IN THIS ROCKET WON'T COME OUT ALIVE!

YOU'RE DUE FOR A SUPER-SHOCK, **SUPERMAN!**

DON'T WORRY, **SUPERMAN!** I'M ALIVE WITHOUT A SCRATCH!

GREAT SCOTT, A YOUNG GIRL, UNHARMED! BUT...BUT THAT MEANS YOU'RE **INVULNERABLE** LIKE ME!

WHY NOT, **SUPERMAN?** I'M ALSO FROM THE PLANET **KRYPTON!**

THAT'S IMPOSSIBLE! **I** WAS THE ONLY SURVIVOR WHEN **KRYPTON** EXPLODED LONG AGO! BESIDES, YOU WEREN'T EVEN BORN AT THE TIME!

TO ADD TO THE MYSTERY, WHY ARE YOU WEARING A SUPER-COSTUME LIKE MINE? HOW DID YOU KNOW MY NAME? HOW CAN YOU SPEAK THE EARTH LANGUAGE SO WELL? AND... AND...??

BAFFLED, **SUPERMAN?** LET ME TELL YOU MY STORY, AS MY PARENTS TOLD IT TO ME! WHEN **KRYPTON** BLEW UP, **YOU** WERE NOT THE ONLY ONE TO ESCAPE ALIVE...

2

"BY SHEER LUCK, A LARGE CHUNK OF THE PLANET WAS HURLED AWAY INTACT, WITH PEOPLE ON IT..."

OUR STREET OF HOMES IS BEING FLUNG FREE INTO SPACE, SAVING US FROM THE CONCUSSION THAT WIPED OUT ALL OTHERS!

"AMONG THE PITIFUL FEW SURVIVORS WAS A SCIENTIST, ZOR-EL..."

FORTUNATELY, A LARGE BUBBLE OF AIR CAME ALONG WITH THIS CHUNK! ALSO, THIS FOOD MACHINE IS STILL WORKING! WE CAN STAY ALIVE INDEFINITELY!

"BUT THEIR JOY WAS SHORT-LIVED, FOR, WHEN NIGHT FELL..."

OHH... I FEEL WEAK!

GREAT STARS! THE GROUND IS GLOWING GREEN! THE NUCLEAR EXPLOSION CONVERTED OUR SHATTERED PLANET INTO KRYPTONITE, AN ELEMENT WHOSE RADIATIONS CAN POISON AND DESTROY US IN TIME!

"BUT LUCKILY, ZOR-EL HAD A ROLL OF SHEET METAL IN HIS LAB, AND..."

THAT'S LEAD, WHICH STOPS ALL RADIATIONS! COVER ALL THE GROUND AROUND OUR HOMES! IT WILL ALLOW US TO SURVIVE, SAFE FROM THE KRYPTONITE RAYS!

"LIFE SETTLED DOWN FOR THE KRYPTON REFUGEES AND, SOME YEARS LATER, ZOR-EL TOOK A WIFE AND A DAUGHTER WAS BORN TO THEM....ME!"

IT'S TIME FOR KARA'S BOTTLE, DEAR!

OUR CHILD CAN GROW UP SAFELY AS LONG AS THE LEADEN SHIELD UNDER OUR COMMUNITY WARDS OFF THOSE KRYPTONITE RADIATIONS!

"BUT FATE PLAYED A CRUEL TRICK, WHEN I HAD GROWN INTO GIRLHOOD..."

INTO THE HOUSE, KARA! A METEOR FLOCK IS SMASHING HOLES IN THE LEADEN SHIELD, RELEASING KRYPTONITE RADIATIONS! WE ARE ALL DOOMED... =CHOKE!=

3

"DESPERATELY, MY FATHER RACED AGAINST TIME IN HIS LAB, CONSTRUCTING A SPACE ROCKET!"

WE HAVE A MONTH BEFORE **KRYPTONITE** RADIATIONS SLOWLY POISON THE AIR! BUT BEFORE THAT FATAL HOUR, THIS ROCKET WILL SEND OUR DAUGHTER TO ANOTHER WORLD!

BUT WHICH WORLD? I'LL USE THE **SUPER-SPACE TELESCOPE** TO FIND SOME CIVILIZED WORLD WHERE **KARA** CAN GROW UP SAFELY!

"EXAMINING MANY PLANETS, MY MOTHER SPIED A STARTLING PHENOMENON ON ONE PARTICULAR WORLD..."

LOOK, MOTHER! WHO IS THAT FLYING MAN?

I...I DON'T KNOW, DEAR! BUT THAT IS A CIVILIZED WORLD! I'LL PICK UP THEIR BROADCASTS WITH OUR SPACE RADIO, AND DECIPHER THEIR LANGUAGE!

"IT WAS EARTH, OF COURSE, AND AFTER LEARNING THEIR LANGUAGE, MY MOTHER HEARD A PROGRAM HONORING THEIR MOST FAMOUS HERO!"

THE CITY OF **METROPOLIS** PAYS TRIBUTE TODAY TO **SUPER-MAN** WHO ORIGINALLY CAME FROM THE PLANET **KRYPTON!** HE GAINED HIS SUPER-POWERS IN EARTH'S LESSER GRAVITY!

THEN YOU TOO WOULD HAVE SUPER-POWERS ON EARTH, **KARA!** WE'LL SEND YOU THERE TO MEET **SUPERMAN**, WHO IS ONE OF OUR PEOPLE!

10,000 LBS.

"MY MOTHER ALSO MADE ME A SPECIAL COSTUME..."

I'LL MAKE IT LIKE **SUPERMAN'S** SUIT SO HE'LL KNOW YOU FOR A **KRYPTON** GIRL! I CAN CUT AND SEW IT HERE, BUT ON EARTH IT WILL BECOME INDESTRUCTIBLE **SUPER-CLOTH!**

THE SPACE ROCKET IS FINISHED, TOO! HURRY! THE **KRYPTONITE** RADIATIONS ARE FILLING THE AIR LIKE POISON!

"BARELY IN TIME, I WAS SHOT FREE OF MY DOOMED PEOPLE!"

WE HAVE AIMED THE ROCKET FOR EARTH! FAREWELL, **KARA**...⸨GASP!⸩

MY FATHER... MOTHER... ALL THE PEOPLE ARE DYING! I'M AN **ORPHAN** OF SPACE NOW... ⸨SOB!⸩

4

As the tragic story of **KARA**, the girl from **KRYPTON**, ends...

YES, I KNOW IT WAS HEARTBREAKING, KARA! I WAS ORPHANED FROM MY PARENTS THE SAME WAY! AS A BABY, I WAS ALSO SHOT AWAY IN A SPACE ROCKET BY MY FATHER, **JOR-EL**!

JOR-EL? WHY MY FATHER'S NAME WAS **ZOR-EL**, YOUR FATHER'S **BROTHER**!

GREAT SCOTT! THEN YOU'RE MY-- **COUSIN**!

This is perhaps the happiest moment in **SUPERMAN'S** life, to find he has a long-lost living relative from his native world!

WE MAY BE ORPHANS, BUT WE HAVE EACH OTHER NOW! I'LL TAKE CARE OF YOU LIKE A BIG BROTHER, COUSIN KARA!

THANKS, COUSIN **SUPERMAN**!... ≡CHOKE!≡ YOU MEAN I'LL COME AND LIVE WITH YOU?

HMM...NO! THAT WOULDN'T WORK! YOU SEE, I'VE ADOPTED A SECRET IDENTITY ON EARTH WHICH MIGHT BE JEOPARDIZED! BUT I HAVE A GREAT IDEA FOR YOUR FUTURE LIFE! FIRST, LET'S SEE IF YOU CAN FLY!

I...I CAN! I HAVE SUPER-POWERS JUST LIKE YOU DO, COUSIN!

I JUST WANTED TO MAKE SURE! IN MY YOUTH IN SMALLVILLE, I WAS HONORED AS **SUPER-BOY**! YOU TOO CAN GAIN FAME AS **SUPER-GIRL**, THE **GIRL OF STEEL**!

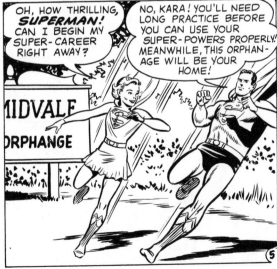

OH, HOW THRILLING, **SUPERMAN**! CAN I BEGIN MY SUPER-CAREER RIGHT AWAY?

NO, KARA! YOU'LL NEED LONG PRACTICE BEFORE YOU CAN USE YOUR SUPER-POWERS PROPERLY! MEANWHILE, THIS ORPHANAGE WILL BE YOUR HOME!

MIDVALE ORPHANGE

⑤

AFTER SUPERMAN LEAVES...

ER-- I'M SORRY, LINDA, BUT THE ORPHANAGE IS OVERCROWDED AND TH IS THE ONLY ROOM WE HAVE! I'LL HELP YOU TIDY IT UP...

NO, MISS HART! I'LL DO IT MYSELF!

WHEN ALONE...

NO ONE WILL SEE ME USE MY SUPER-POWERS, WITH THE DOOR CLOSED! I'LL BEND THE IRON LEG OF MY COT STRAIGHT! THAT PROVES I HAVE SUPER-STRENGTH TOO, JUST LIKE MY COUSIN SUPERMAN!

WHEN WE WATCHED THROUGH THE SUPER-TELESCOPE, MY MOTHER AND I SAW ALL OF SUPERMAN'S POWERS DISPLAYED! SUPER-BREATH IS HANDY, TOO, TO DUST OUT MY ROOM IN ONE BIG BLOW!

NOW THE HEAT OF MY X-RAY VISION WILL FUSE THIS CRACKED MIRROR SMOOTH AGAIN!

ALSO I CAN USE X-RAY VISION THROUGH THE WALLS TO SEE THE OTHER ORPHANS HERE! HOPE I CAN MAKE FRIENDS WITH THEM ALL! THIS WILL BE MY HOME FROM NOW ON, ON THE PLANET EARTH!

LIGHT'S OUT, CHILDREN! TIME FOR BED! GOOD-NIGHT!

HMM...WHILE EVERY-ONE'S ASLEEP, IT'S MY CHANCE TO CHANGE TO SUPERGIRL AND LOOK OVER MY NEW HOME TOWN! NOBODY WILL SEE ME IN THE DARK, SO I'M NOT DISOBEYING SUPERMAN!

SOON, *SUPERGIRL* IS ON A SECRET "PATROL" OF MIDVALE!

MIDVALE IS A PRETTY LITTLE TOWN! I LIKE IT ALREADY! MAYBE I CAN STILL DO SUPER-DEEDS FOR WORTHY PEOPLE WITHOUT BEING SEEN, LIKE A SORT OF "GUARDIAN ANGEL!"

PRESENTLY, AT A MOVIE THEATRE...

NOW SHOWING
OLD TIME FILMS... HISTORY OF SUPERBOY IN SMALLVILLE!

WHY, THAT MOVIE IS ABOUT *SUPERMAN* WHEN HE WAS MY AGE! I'M PROUD OF THE FAME AND HONOR MY COUSIN HAS EARNED ALL HIS LIFE!

WILL I SOMEDAY DO AS GOOD A JOB IN MIDVALE, AS *SUPERGIRL?* WHAT WILL THE FUTURE BRING FOR ME?

MIDVALE ORPHANAGE

IF YOU WANT TO FIND OUT, READERS, YOU CAN! *SUPERGIRL'S* ADVENTURES WILL CONTINUE REGULARLY HEREAFTER IN *ACTION COMICS*, ALONG WITH THE DOINGS OF HER FAMOUS COUSIN, *SUPERMAN!* SEE THE NEXT ISSUE FOR ANOTHER THRILLING STORY ABOUT THIS *GIRL OF STEEL*, A BRAND-NEW MEMBER OF OUR *SUPER-FAMILY* ALONG WITH *SUPERBOY* AND *SUPERMAN!*

The End

SCIENTISTS WATCH BREATHLESSLY ONE DAY, AS THE ARMY LAUNCHES A NEW ROCKET...

AMONG THE CREW, BY SPECIAL APPOINTMENT, ARE CLARK KENT AND LOIS LANE, REPORTERS OF THE *DAILY PLANET*...

WE HARDLY FEEL ANY DISCOMFORT FROM THE HIGH SPEED IN THESE ANTI-SHOCK SEATS! ISN'T IT THRILLING, CLARK?

WE'RE MAKING HISTORY, LOIS! LOOK BEHIND... ONLY CAMERAS HAVE SEEN THAT SIGHT BEFORE!

..THREE.. ..TWO.. ..ONE.. FIRE!

THERE GOES *THE COLUMBUS*, THE FIRST EXPERIMENTAL SPACESHIP WITH HUMANS ABOARD!

AT THE HEIGHT OF 200 MILES, AWESOME SPACE SCENES UNFOLD...

WE'RE ABOVE EARTH'S ATMOSPHERE IN BLACK SPACE, WHERE THE STARS SHINE IN THE *DAYTIME!*

LATER, ANOTHER MOMENTOUS MILESTONE IS PASSED...

10,000 MILES FROM EARTH! WE'VE BROKEN ALL ROCKET RECORDS! HOORAY!

BUT... BUT LOOK! THOSE TEST ANIMALS BROUGHT ALONG BY THE SCIENTISTS... WHY ARE THEY WHIRLING MADLY?

A MORE AMAZING MYSTERY ARISES!

GREAT GUNS! A FLYING SAUCER FROM OUTER SPACE IS FOLLOWING US, SHOOTING STRANGE RAYS! WHO CAN IT BE?

AS CLARK KENT, WHO IS SECRETLY *SUPERMAN*, PROBES INTO THE UNKNOWN CRAFT WITH HIS X-RAY VISION...

DID THE EARTHLINGS DARE TO SEND A SHIP TO STOP ME, *BRAINIAC*, MASTER OF SUPER-SCIENTIFIC FORCES? WE'LL SHOW THEM, KOKO! THE NEXT RAY I SHOOT OUT WILL DO FAR WORSE THAN MAKE ANIMALS DANCE MADLY! HA, HA!

AN ENEMY FROM SOME ALIEN PLANET!

As a ray from the strange craft jolts THE COLUMBUS...

OH, IF ONLY SUPERMAN WERE HERE!

I AM... BUT I'D BE REVEALING MY SECRET IDENTITY IF I SUDDENLY APPEARED IN THIS SHIP! HMM... I'LL USE THIS AND GET OUT...

SPACE LUNG FOR EMERGENCY ESCAPE

After Clark dons the device and exits through the emergency escape hatch...

POOR CLARK-- HE'S SO AFRAID, HE'S JUMPING BACK TO EARTH!

I'LL PRETEND TO ZOOM BACK TO EARTH, PROPELLED BY THE BUILT-IN SUPERSONIC JETS!

Once out of sight, timid Clark changes to powerful SUPERMAN!

THEY'LL ASSUME CLARK REACHED EARTH AND SENT SUPERMAN TO THE RESCUE. I'LL SPEED BACK AND CAPTURE THAT SINISTER ALIEN!

But incredibly, when SUPERMAN tries to smash into the flying saucer...

OOF! I... I ONLY REBOUNDED FROM AN INVISIBLE WALL!

EARTHLING FOOL! NOTHING IN THE UNIVERSE CAN PENETRATE THE ULTRA-FORCE BARRIER THAT SURROUNDS MY SHIP! HA, HA!

Unable to invade the impenetrable craft, the MAN OF STEEL changes tactics!

I'LL SHOVE THE EARTH ROCKET AHEAD AT SUPER-SPEED, SO THAT IT WILL BE OUT OF HARM'S WAY! GOT TO GO FASTER... FASTER...!

SUPERMAN WINS THE DEADLY RACE!

WHEW! WE'RE OUT OF RANGE OF HIS DESTRUCTIVE RAYS!

DON'T WORRY ABOUT THEM, KOKO! WE HAVE OTHER BUSINESS TO DO ON EARTH NOW!

WHAT IS *BRAINIAC'S* EVIL PLAN? AIR HOSES ALL CONNECTED... THE BOTTLES ARE READY! ONE IS ALREADY FILLED! NOW WE'LL FILL THE OTHERS, EH, KOKO? HA, HA!

WE ARE HOVERING OVER EARTH! NOW TO USE THE HYPER-BOMBSIGHT...

AH, I HAVE THE FIRST EARTH CITY-- PARIS--IN THE CROSS-HAIRS! I PRESS THE BUTTON AND...

BELOW, CITIZENS OF PARIS OBSERVE A BAFFLING PHENOMENON!

SACRE BLEU! WHAT IS THAT CONE OF PECULIAR RAYS STRIKING THE WHOLE CITY?

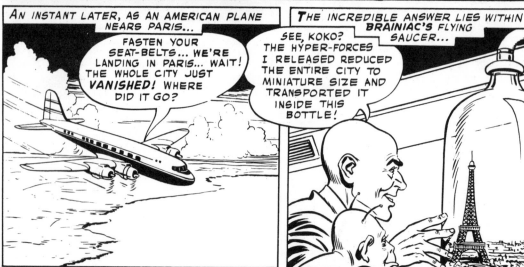

AN INSTANT LATER, AS AN AMERICAN PLANE NEARS PARIS...

FASTEN YOUR SEAT-BELTS... WE'RE LANDING IN PARIS... WAIT! THE WHOLE CITY JUST *VANISHED!* WHERE DID IT GO?

THE INCREDIBLE ANSWER LIES WITHIN *BRAINIAC'S* FLYING SAUCER...

SEE, KOKO? THE HYPER-FORCES I RELEASED REDUCED THE ENTIRE CITY TO MINIATURE SIZE AND TRANSPORTED IT INSIDE THIS BOTTLE!

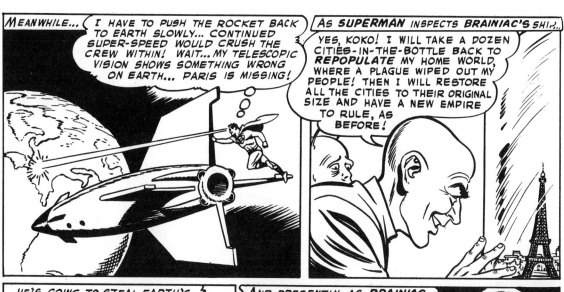

MEANWHILE... I HAVE TO PUSH THE ROCKET BACK TO EARTH SLOWLY... CONTINUED SUPER-SPEED WOULD CRUSH THE CREW WITHIN! WAIT... MY TELESCOPIC VISION SHOWS SOMETHING WRONG ON EARTH... PARIS IS MISSING!

AS SUPERMAN INSPECTS BRAINIAC'S SHIP...

YES, KOKO! I WILL TAKE A DOZEN CITIES-IN-THE-BOTTLE BACK TO REPOPULATE MY HOME WORLD, WHERE A PLAGUE WIPED OUT MY PEOPLE! THEN I WILL RESTORE ALL THE CITIES TO THEIR ORIGINAL SIZE AND HAVE A NEW EMPIRE TO RULE, AS BEFORE!

HE'S GOING TO STEAL EARTH'S GREATEST CITIES! YET I CAN'T STOP HIM AS LONG AS HIS SHIP IS PROTECTED BY THAT ULTRA-FORCE BARRIER! I'LL JUST HAVE TO STAND BY... AND WATCH HELPLESSLY...

AND PRESENTLY, AS BRAINIAC CONTINUES HIS RAID OF EARTH BY STEALING THE CITY OF ROME!...

ONE AFTER ANOTHER, THE WORLD'S GREATEST CITIES BECOME TOY VILLAGES IN BOTTLES!

AN OXYGEN SUPPLY KEEPS THE TINY PEOPLE ALIVE! AREN'T THEY CUTE, KOKO? BUT LET ME EXAMINE THAT BRIDGE IN THIS CITY THEY CALL NEW YORK!

LATER, WHEN **THE COLUMBUS** REACHES EARTH UNDER ITS OWN POWER...

I'LL RUSH TO THE OFFICE AND GET OUT THE STORY OF **SUPERMAN'S** DUEL WITH THAT EVIL ALIEN!

COLUMBUS

BUT IF **SUPERMAN** IS GONE, HOW CAN **CLARK KENT** GREET LOIS AT THE **DAILY PLANET**?

YOU'RE BACK FROM SPACE, LOIS! WHAT HAPPENED AFTER I... ER... SENT **SUPERMAN** TO SAVE THE ROCKET SHIP?

YOU WON'T BELIEVE IT, CLARK, BUT **SUPERMAN** WAS DEFEATED BY THE ALIEN AND... **GOODNESS!** WHAT'S THAT RAY STRIKING THE CITY?

DAILY PLANE

IN THE WINK OF AN EYE, METROPOLIS MEETS THE SAME FATE AS ITS SISTER CITIES!...

ANOTHER MINIATURE CITY, KOKO! BACK ON MY DESOLATE WORLD, HYPER-FORCES WILL RESTORE IT TO NORMAL SIZE... TO JOIN MY NEW EMPIRE! HA!

AS **BRAINIAC** THRUSTS HIS TWEEZERS DOWN INTO THE MODEL-SIZED METROPOLIS...

THE ALIEN REDUCED US TO **TOM THUMB** SIZE! AND... AND FOR ONCE, **SUPERMAN** ISN'T HERE TO PROTECT US!

THAT'S WHAT **YOU** THINK, LOIS!

SOON, AS CLARK CHANGES IN SECRET...

I ONLY **PRETENDED** TO FLEE AFTER THE BATTLE...TO FOOL **BRAINIAC**! I SECRETLY CIRCLED BACK THROUGH SPACE TO METROPOLIS, WHICH WAS SURE TO BECOME A CITY-IN-A-BOTTLE, TOO! THIS WAS MY ONLY WAY TO GET **INSIDE** THE ALIEN'S SHIP, PAST HIS **ULTRA-FORCE BARRIER**!

AT THAT MOMENT...

COME, KOKO! WE'D BETTER CHECK THE BOTTLE WHICH IMPRISONS OUR PRIZE CITY! THIS SUPER-HARD METAL STOPPER WILL SEAL UP METROPOLIS SO NONE OF ITS TINY INHABITANTS CAN ESCAPE!

HE CORKED IT... BEFORE I WAS ABLE TO FLY OUT!

270

SUDDENLY, SUPERMAN THINKS OF A SUPER-STRATEGY...

HMM... THIS CHART, AND TWO OTHER THINGS IN YOUR CITY, MAY SAVE US! I WANT YOUR MOST POWERFUL ROCKET! AND A CERTAIN ANIMAL FROM THE ZOO!

CAN YOU GUESS WHAT ANIMAL SUPERMAN TAKES ALONG IN THE ROCKET, LATER?

I LOST MY FLYING ABILITY, BUT THIS ROCKET WILL GET ME UP TO THE METAL CORK OF THIS GIANT BOTTLE!

SUPERMAN PURPOSELY RAMS THE ROCKET'S NOSE INTO THE UNDERSIDE OF THE CORK, AND THEN...

NOW TO LET THE METAL-EATING MOLE FEAST HIS WAY UP THROUGH THE CORK! HE'LL BURROW A TUNNEL BIG ENOUGH FOR ME TO CLIMB THROUGH!

THE INGENIOUS PLAN WORKS!..

NOW THAT I'M OUTSIDE THE BOTTLE, I'M FREE OF THE KRYPTON-GRAVITY WITHIN THE BOTTLE! MY SUPER-POWERS RETURNED! I CAN FLY TO THE CONTROL PANEL AND USE KIMDA'S OPERATIONAL CHART!

WITH NO INTERFERENCE FROM THE SLEEPING ALIEN, THE MOTE OF STEEL PUNCHES THE CORRECT BUTTONS... IN A SPECIAL WAY!

MY FINGER'S TOO SMALL... BUT THIS IS USING MY HEAD! EACH BUTTON I PRESS MAKES A CITY REAPPEAR BACK ON EARTH IN NORMAL SIZE, UNHARMED!

LOOK! METROPOLIS SUDDENLY RETURNED, AS MYSTERIOUSLY AS IT VANISHED YESTERDAY!

BUT TRANSMITTING THE EARTH CITIES BACK DRAINS THE BATTERIES OF THEIR COSMIC-POWER, AND *SUPERMAN* MEETS A TRAGIC DILEMMA!

ONLY ONE CHARGE OF HYPER-FORCES LEFT... ENOUGH TO RESTORE THE *KRYPTON* CITY TO NORMAL SIZE OR ME... BUT NOT *BOTH!*

20

0

UNSELFISHLY, *SUPERMAN* IS READY TO SACRIFICE HIMSELF!

WELL, I'M ONLY *ONE* MAN! THE HYPER-RAY CAN SAVE A *MILLION* PEOPLE IN THE *KRYPTON* CITY, ALLOWING THEM TO LIVE ON EARTH! I'LL PRESS THE BUTTON THAT WILL LIBERATE THEM!

BUT BEFORE HE REACHES THE BUTTON...

THE... THE RAY STRUCK ME... I'M REGAINING NORMAL SIZE SWIFTLY! HMM... THAT TINY ROCKET "PUNCHED" THE BUTTON AHEAD OF ME!

SUPERMAN CATCHES THE ROCKET IN HIS PALM AND...

IT'S I, KIMDA! I FLEW THE ROCKET OUT OF THE HOLE IN THE CORK TO PUNCH THE BUTTON, KNOWING ONLY ONE CHARGE WOULD BE LEFT! WE COULD NOT LET EARTH BE DEPRIVED OF ITS GREAT SUPER-HERO!

YOU SACRIFICED YOUR PEOPLE FOR *ME!* I'M GRATEFUL-- BUT YOUR CITY MUST FOREVER REMAIN TINY NOW!

PRESENTLY...

LET *BRAINIAC'S* SHIP FLY ON! WHEN HE AWAKENS, HE WILL HAVE NO STOLEN CITIES! LET HIM LIVE ON HIS DESOLATE WORLD... *ALONE*... A CRUEL KING WITHOUT A KINGDOM!

FINALLY, AT THE NORTH POLE IN SUPERMAN'S FORTRESS OF SOLITUDE...

THE MINIATURE *KRYPTON* CITY WILL KEEP SAFELY HERE! PERHAPS I'LL FIND A WAY TO RESTORE IT TO NORMAL SIZE... AND LIVE WITH MY PEOPLE AGAIN... SOMEDAY! WHO KNOWS?...

THE END

ONE FALL DAY, IN SMALLVILLE, **SUPERBOY** DECIDES TO CALL ON A RECENT NEWCOMER TO THE RURAL TOWN...

THAT MUST BE HIM... THE CURLY-HAIRED YOUTH DRIVING THAT TRACTOR! I'D LIKE TO GET ACQUAINTED!

BUT SUDDENLY...

¿GASP!: A **K-KRYPTONITE** METEOR! IT WILL...KILL ME...!

WHEN THE PLANET **KRYPTON** EXPLODED, YEARS AGO, INSTANTS AFTER THE INFANT **SUPERBOY** ESCAPED THE DOOMED PLANET IN A ROCKET SHIP, ATOMIC FISSION TRANSFORMED THE PLANET'S BROKEN FRAGMENTS INTO **KRYPTONITE**...

...WHOSE RADIATIONS ARE DEADLY TO **SUPERBOY**...!

OH-HHH! THE PAIN...!

HOLD ON, **SUPERBOY!** I'LL GET RID OF THE METEOR!

SMASHED OVER THE CLIFF'S EDGE BY THE TRACTOR, THE GREEN METEOR BOUNCES DOWN INTO A GULLY, AND SINKS IN QUICKSAND...

KER-PLOP!

SAFELY BEYOND REACH OF THE METEOR'S BALEFUL RADIATIONS, **SUPERBOY** SWIFTLY RECOVERS...

I OWE MY LIFE TO YOU! WHAT'S YOUR NAME?

LEX! LEX **LUTHOR!** MEETING YOU, **SUPERBOY**, IS ABOUT THE MOST THRILLING THING THAT EVER HAPPENED TO ME!

Panel 1:
DO YOU LIKE SURPRISES? FOLLOW ME!

I WONDER WHAT HE IS GOING TO SHOW ME!

Panel 2:
INSIDE *LUTHOR'S* BARN...

GREAT SCOTT! PICTURES OF ME... AND *SUPERBOY* TROPHIES...EVERYWHERE!

I HAVE HERO-WORSHIPPED YOU FOR YEARS! TO ME, YOU'RE THE GREATEST BOY IN THE WORLD!

THIS GIRDER BENT BY *SUPERBOY* AROUND AN ESCAPING GIANT GORILLA.

ROCK WITH *SUPERBOY'S* FIST IMPRINT IN IT.

Panel 3:
GOLLY, I'M REALLY TOUCHED!...WHAT ARE ALL THESE SCIENTIFIC LAB GADGETS DOING HERE?

I AM A FARM-BOY NOW, *SUPERBOY,* BUT MY SECRET AMBITION IS TO BECOME THE WORLD'S GREATEST SCIENTIST! I'D LIKE TO BECOME AS FAMOUS AS YOU!

Panel 4:
SHORTLY...

AND NOW IT'S MY TURN TO SURPRISE YOU! YOU SAVED MY LIFE, AND I WANT TO EXPRESS MY GRATITUDE!

WHAT IN THE WORLD ARE YOU DOING WITH THAT ABANDONED JUNK?

Panel 5:
FOR ONE MINUTE THE *BOY OF STEEL* WORKS AT SUPER-SPEED, THEN...

¿GASP!¿ IT'S... MAGIC! YOU'VE CONSTRUCTED A MODERN EXPERIMENTAL LABORATORY OUT OF THAT JUNK!

BE BACK IN A FLASH!

Panel 6:
SOON, SUPERBOY RETURNS... AND AFTER AMAZINGLY SWIFT ACTIVITY...

I'VE GIVEN YOU RARE CHEMICALS, SOME STILL UNKNOWN, WHICH I BURROWED OUT OF THE GROUND, AT SUPER-SPEED! ALSO, I TRANSFERRED EVERYTHING HERE, FROM YOUR OLD LAB!

BOY, WHAT A PAL!

3

THIS LABORATORY, AND MY SUCCESSFUL EXPERIMENT, WOULD NEVER HAVE BEEN POSSIBLE, IF NOT FOR *SUPERBOY!* SOMEHOW, I'VE GOT TO REPAY HIM! BUT HOW...??

AND THEN, A FATEFUL DECISION...

I'VE GOT IT! I WILL INVENT A *KRYPTONITE ANTIDOTE* WHICH WILL PROTECT *SUPERBOY* FOREVER FROM THE DREAD MENACE OF *KRYPTONITE* METEORS!

EAGERLY, YOUNG *LUTHOR* BEGINS CONSTRUCTING A STRANGE MECHANISM...

FIRST I'LL BUILD A GIANT CLAW-ARM OF METAL, MADE OUT OF SOME OF THE HEAVY EQUIPMENT *SUPERBOY* INSTALLED IN THE LABORATORY!

SOON...

HA, HA, HA! HOW *EASILY* I PLUCK THE *KRYPTONITE METEOR* FROM OUT OF THE *QUICK-SAND'S* DEPTHS WITH THIS GIANT CLAW!

AFTERWARD...

THERE, I'VE GOT THE FEW CHIPS I NEED! NOW TO DROP THE METEOR BACK INTO THE QUICKSAND, SO IT CAN NEVER HARM *SUPERBOY* AGAIN!

CLUNK! CLUNK!

SHORTLY, *LUTHOR'S* CLEVER BRAIN COMES TO GRIPS WITH A NEAR-IMPOSSIBLE TASK, IN HIS LABORATORY...

I'VE GROUND DOWN THE *KRYPTONITE* CHIPS INTO A FINE DUST... AND *BLENDED* IT WITH A LIQUEFIED FORM OF THE PROTO-PLASMIC LIFE I CREATED! I MUST NOT-- *I WILL NOT*--FAIL!

5

SHORTLY BEFORE DAWN, IN THE LABORATORY'S ALCOVE...

SUCCESS! I SUCCEEDED IN CREATING THE KRYPTONITE ANTIDOTE!... OOPS!!

≷COUGH≷...≷COUGH≷...

THAT CHEMICAL FLASK I OVERTURNED HAS SET THE LAB AFIRE! FUMES... SMOKE... RADIATION!

ACID

WHAT GOOD LUCK! SUPERBOY IS FLYING BY ON PATROL!

HELP, SUPERBOY! HELP!!

SWIFTLY, THE BOY OF STEEL HURTLES DOWN INTO ACTION...

LUTHOR'S INSIDE THAT FLAMING ALCOVE! I'LL EXTINGUISH THE BLAZE WITH A MIGHTY SUPER-PUFF OF BREATH!

AS THE FLAMES VANISH, SUPERBOY ENTERS THE DAMAGED ALCOVE, EXPECTING LUTHOR'S THANKS, BUT...

YOU RAT! YOUR PUFF OF SUPER-BREATH BLEW AN ACID BOTTLE AGAINST THE ANTIDOTE BOTTLE! THEY BROKE, AND THEIR CONTENTS DESTROYED THE FORMULA FOR MY GREAT DISCOVERY! NOT ONLY THAT-- THE GAS FUMES MADE MY HAIR FALL OUT! I'M BALD!

BUT...IT WAS AN ACCIDENT...!

DON'T LIE! YOU WERE JEALOUS OF MY GENIUS! SO YOU DELIBERATELY BROKE THOSE BOTTLES AND DESTROYED MY FORMULA WHICH WAS THE RESULT OF THOUSANDS OF EXPERIMENTS! YOU KNEW I COULD NEVER DUPLICATE THIS FORMULA AGAIN!

6

THE FIRE DESTROYED THE ONLY EXISTING SAMPLE OF MY PROTOPLASMIC DISCOVERY! I WILL NEVER BE ABLE TO DISCOVER IT AGAIN!

AND THE FUMES MADE YOUR HAIR FALL OUT! WHAT A TRAGEDY! I - I'M... SORRY...

SORRY!... WILL THAT BRING BACK MY DISCOVERY? WILL BEING SORRY BRING BACK MY HAIR?!!

PLEASE... IF YOU WOULD JUST GIVE ME A CLUE TO THE FORMULA... THEN MAYBE I CAN HELP YOU REDISCOVER IT!

LIAR! WHY DON'T YOU ADMIT YOU DELIBERATELY RUINED ME BECAUSE YOU'RE JEALOUS! YOU WERE AFRAID MY GENIUS WOULD MAKE ME MORE FAMOUS THAN YOU!

AFTER THE WAY YOU SAVED MY LIFE? I WOULDN'T HARM YOU, AND YOU KNOW IT!

SUDDENLY, LUTHOR OBSERVES...

THAT TUBE UP THERE... IT SURVIVED THE FIRE, AND A TINY BIT OF PROTOPLASM IS STILL INSIDE! I'LL USE IT TO BE REVENGED ON SUPERBOY!

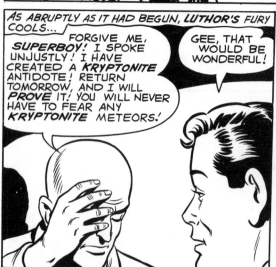

As ABRUPTLY AS IT HAD BEGUN, LUTHOR'S FURY COOLS...

FORGIVE ME, SUPERBOY! I SPOKE UNJUSTLY! I HAVE CREATED A KRYPTONITE ANTIDOTE! RETURN TOMORROW, AND I WILL PROVE IT! YOU WILL NEVER HAVE TO FEAR ANY KRYPTONITE METEORS!

GEE, THAT WOULD BE WONDERFUL!

BUT AFTER THE BOY OF STEEL DEPARTS, LUTHOR DROPS HIS FRIENDLY POSE...

I HATE HIM, I HATE HIM!! HOW COULD I EVER HAVE HERO-WORSHIPPED THAT SUPER-RAT?!! I'LL DESTROY EVERY PICTURE, EVERY TROPHY OF HIM!

7

SUPERBOY WILL REGRET THE DAY HE DECIDED TO STEAL THE GLORY OF LUTHOR!

WRATHFULLY, LUTHOR EXTRACTS THE TINY REMNANT OF HIS GREAT DISCOVERY...

I WILL USE THIS TINY SPECK OF PROTOPLASM TO MAKE SUPERBOY REGRET THE DAY HE DECIDED TO THWART MY GENIUS!

...AS THE PROTOPLASMIC MARVEL IS BLENDED WITH A VARIETY OF LIQUID CHEMICALS...

NO MORE KRYPTONITE ANTIDOTE WILL EVER BE MADE... SINCE THE LAST SPECK OF THE MIRACLE PROTOPLASM IS HERE IN THIS FLASK!

NEXT MORNING...

LUTHOR, I BROUGHT THIS SPACE-GLOBE SO YOU MAY WITNESS THE SUCCESS, OR FAILURE, OF THE KRYPTONITE ANTIDOTE WHEN I TEST IT IN OUTER SPACE!

DRINK! THEN YOU AND I SHALL SEE FOR OURSELVES HOW YOU NEED NO LONGER FEAR KRYPTONITE METEORS!

AFTER SUPERBOY DOWNS THE POTION, LUTHOR ENTERS THE SPACE-GLOBE, THEN...UP THEY STREAK...UP...UP...INTO OUTER SPACE...

A KRYPTONITE METEOR SWARM, DEAD AHEAD! I... CAN'T HELP FEELING NERVOUS! THE LIVES OF BOTH LUTHOR AND I DEPEND ON WHETHER HIS ANTIDOTE REALLY WORKS!

SOON... AS SUPERBOY EXPERTLY WHIZZES IN AND OUT AMONG THE DEADLY METEORS...

IT WORKS! I FEEL NORMAL! I AM IMMUNE TO KRYPTONITE!

THE FOOL! DOES SUPERBOY REALLY THINK, AFTER WHAT HE HAS DONE TO ME, THAT I WOULD HELP HIM??

8

UNEXPECTEDLY, OUT OF THE COSMOS, WHIZZES SUPERBOY'S CANINE PAL, KRYPTO!

...SUPERBOY ISN'T BOTHERED BY THOSE KRYPTONITE METEORS! THEY MUST BE MADE OF FOOL'S KRYPTONITE, WHICH LOOKS EXACTLY LIKE KRYPTONITE, BUT IS HARMLESS!

BUT... ::GROAN:: THE PAINS... AWFUL! I'M CLEARING OUT! HE MAY BE INVULNERABLE TO KRYPTONITE, BUT I'M NOT! PHOOIE!

HA, HA! EVIDENTLY SUPERBOY DOESN'T SEE KRYPTO WHIZZING AWAY! GOOD! THAT SUPERDOG WON'T BE AROUND TO HELP HIS MASTER!

AND AS SUPERBOY RETURNS LUTHOR TO EARTH, AGAIN...

GOLLY, I'M IMMUNE TO KRYPTONITE, FOREVER! I'M TERRIBLY GRATEFUL TO YOU, LEX!

DON'T BE, YOU RAT! I PLACED SOME CRYSTALS IN THE ANTIDOTE THAT MADE ITS EFFECTS ON YOU ONLY TEMPORARY! IT WILL WEAR OFF SOON!

YOU COULD HAVE HAD LIFE-LONG IMMUNITY TO KRYPTONITE, IF YOU HADN'T BECOME JEALOUS OF ME, AND SOUGHT TO CRUSH MY GREATNESS!

LUTHOR FOOLED ME COMPLETELY! I REALLY THOUGHT HE STILL WANTED TO BE FRIENDS...

DO YOUR WORST! YOU'LL SEE! I'LL STILL BECOME MORE ADMIRED, AND MORE FAMOUS THAN YOU!

YOU WON'T BELIEVE THIS, LUTHOR, BUT I ONLY WISH SUCCESS FOR YOU!

IT'S UNFORTUNATE LUTHOR'S FATHER, A TRAVELING SALESMAN, IS RARELY HOME. HIS SON NEEDS A FATHER'S GUIDANCE...

WEEKS LATER, LUTHOR APPROACHES SMALLVILLE'S MAYOR WITH A STARTLING PROPOSITION...

HMMM. YOUR FANTASTIC IDEA MIGHT WORK AT THAT, LUTHOR! I'LL ASK THE CITY COUNCIL TO ORDER CONSTRUCTION AT ONCE...

MY WEATHER-TOWER WILL KEEP SMALLVILLE, AND ITS OUTSKIRTS, WARM AS TOAST, THIS WINTER!

9

TRUE TO **LUTHOR'S** PROMISE, HIS **WEATHER-TOWER** TRANSFORMS THE SUN'S RAYS INTO SOLAR-ENERGY, GENTLY HEATING SMALLVILLE DESPITE THE RAVAGES OF WINTER...

AMAZING! THERE ISN'T A SPECK OF SNOW IN SMALLVILLE, AND SUMMER CROPS ARE STILL GROWING! YET OTHER COMMUNITIES ARE SNOWED IN!

PROUDLY, YOUNG **LUTHOR** ENJOYS THE SWEET TASTE OF SUCCESS...

LUTHOR, YOUR **WEATHER-TOWER** IS A BLESSING TO OUR COMMUNITY! YOU'RE WONDERFUL!

HA, HA! AND I HAVE EVEN MORE STARTLING DISCOVERIES UP MY SLEEVE!

MAYBE **LUTHOR** **WILL** BECOME MORE FAMOUS THAN ME, AT THAT! GOOD FOR HIM!

BUT ONE DAY, IN THE KENT HOME, AS THE FAMILY DINES...

GOOD GRIEF! MA AND PA KENT ARE KEELING OVER! IT'S SUDDENLY BECOME STIFLING HOT FOR THEM! I'D BETTER CHECK WITH MY TELESCOPIC, X-RAY VISION AND SEE WHAT GIVES!

WHAT HE SEES PROMPTS CLARK TO CHANGE TO HIS SECRET IDENTITY AS THE **BOY OF STEEL**, AND FLASH INTO ACTION AT SUPER-SPEED...

SOMETHING'S GONE WRONG WITH THE TOWER MECHANISM, TURNING IT INTO A TERRIBLE HEAT-RAY! THE ENTIRE TOWN MAY BURN TO A CRISP, UNLESS I ACT!

THERE! A BLAST OF MY SUPER-COLD BREATH HAS CAUSED THE TOWER TO FREEZE AND BREAK! BUT NOW, THE TOP OF THE TOWER IS FALLING TOWARD INNOCENT BYSTANDERS!

PUFF!

A SUPER-SWOOP, AND...

CAUGHT IT! THE BYSTANDERS ARE SAFE! NOW TO EXTINGUISH SOME FIRES, THEN REJOIN MA AND PA!

FROM AN OVERNIGHT HERO, *LUTHOR* BECOMES AN OVERNIGHT HEEL...

GREAT SCIENTIST, BUNK! YOU ALMOST BURNT DOWN THE WHOLE TOWN!

THE INGRATES!... *SUPERBOY* PROBABLY CAUSED THE TOWER'S TROUBLES, THE JEALOUS RAT!

INFURIATED AT THE BLOW TO HIS PRIDE, *LUTHOR* WORKS ON A NEW PROJECT FOR MANY MONTHS! THEN, ONE DAY...

AH... WHAT *SEEDS*! THERE HAS NEVER BEEN ANY THING LIKE THEM BEFORE ON *EARTH*!

...AND AS SPRING ARRIVES...

YOU'RE GIVING THESE SEEDS AWAY, FREE, LEX?

YES, LANA, TO EVERYONE! TELL YOUR FATHER TO PLANT THEM RIGHT AWAY, AND FRUIT-TREES WILL SPRING INTO EXISTENCE BY MORNING!

EVERYONE SHARES IN *LUTHOR'S LATEST* DISCOVERY...

TAKE THESE MIRACLE-SEEDS AND PLANT THEM *NOW*, MR. WADE, IF YOU WANT TO SEE A MIRACLE HAPPEN *TOMORROW*!

I DUNNO! WE FOLKS STILL HAVEN'T FOR-GOTTEN ABOUT THAT *WEATHER-TOWER* O' YOURS! BUT I'LL TAKE A CHANCE AND PLANT 'EM! WHAT HAVE I GOT TO LOSE?

NEXT MORNING...

≶GASP!≷ THE SEEDS GREW INTO TREES, OVER-NIGHT, JUST AS *LUTHOR* SAID THEY WOULD! ISN'T IT FANTASTIC, CLARK?

IT SURE IS!

THE WHOLE TOWN, AND COUNTRYSIDE, IS FLABBERGASTED...FOR THE SAME MIRACLE OCCURS EVERYWHERE...

I CAN'T BELIEVE IT! THOSE CHERRY AND PEAR TREES WEREN'T THERE, YESTERDAY!

HE'S A *MAGICIAN*, THAT'S WHAT *LUTHOR* IS!

11

BUT THAT NIGHT...

IT'S RAINING HARD OUT-SIDE--*GREAT GUNS!* WHAT'S THAT LOUD RIPPING, SMASHING NOISE!?

BRR-RRHM

IT MAY BE A JOB FOR *SUPERBOY,* SON!

CHANGING IDENTITIES, *SUPERBOY* HURTLES OUT THROUGH HIS HOME'S SECRET TUNNEL, AND DIS-COVERS...

OH, NO! THE RAIN AFFECTED THE CHEMICALS IN *LUTHOR'S* TREES, CAUSING THEM TO GROW INTO *GIANTS!* HOUSES AND BARNS ARE BEING SMASHED!

FLYING LOW, *SUPERBOY* RIPS MAMMOTH TREES OUT OF THE GROUND AND HURLS THEM SEAWARD, AT GREAT SPEED...

IN A FEW MORE MINUTES, THE TOWN OF SMALLVILLE WOULD HAVE BEEN CRUSHED TO A PULP BY THESE GIANT TREES!

THEN, EXPERTLY, *SUPERBOY'S* X-RAY VISION SCORCHES ANY OF *LUTHOR'S* SURVIVING SEEDS OUT OF EXISTENCE...

LUTHOR'S TO BLAME... YET I FEEL SORRY FOR HIM! HE DIDN'T INTEND TO MAKE TROUBLE! HIS ONLY CRIME WAS CARE-LESSNESS!

ONCE AGAIN, *LUTHOR* SUFFERS THE TOWN'S DISDAIN...

YOU'RE A MENACE, *LUTHOR!* FROM NOW ON, KEEP YOUR DISCOVERIES TO YOURSELF!

THANK GOODNESS FOR *SUPERBOY,* OR WE'D HAVE BEEN KILLED BY *LUTHOR'S* "KINDNESS"!

SIZZLING WITH FURY, *LUTHOR* ONCE MORE HAULS THE *KRYPTONITE* METEOR OUT OF ITS DEEP QUICKSAND HOME...

I NEED YOU AGAIN!

12

AND WHEN *SUPERBOY* CALLS TO OFFER HIS REGRETS...

KEEP YOUR PHONEY SYMPATHY, *SUPER-BOY!* I KNEW YOU'D COME HERE TO GLOAT, AND I'M READY! SEE WHAT IS BEHIND THIS RISING LEAD SECTION OF THE WALL?

A... *KRYPTONITE TRAP!!!*

AND AS THE *BOY OF STEEL'S* BODY IS WRACKED BY UNBEARABLE PAIN...

DIE... SLOWLY... PAINFULLY! IN THIS BOTTLE ARE THE LAST FEW DROPS OF *KRYPTONITE* ANTIDOTE THAT REMAIN... SALVAGED FOR A MOMENT SUCH AS THIS...! YOU CAN'T HAVE IT !!

THE... INHUMAN DEVIL...!

DESPERATELY, *SUPERBOY* USES THE VERY LAST OUNCE OF HIS VACUUM-BREATH TO DRAW THE BOTTLE OUT OF *LUTHOR'S* HAND SO THAT IT FALLS AND SMASHES AGAINST *SUPERBOY'S* STEEL-HARD MOUTH...

TRICKED!!!

AND AS THE PRECIOUS DROPS DRAIN DOWN INTO HIS THROAT, AND *SUPERBOY'S* AWESOME POWERS RETURN...

THE ANTIDOTE'S EFFECT WILL SOON WEAR OFF, AND YOU WILL NEVER GET THE ANTIDOTE AGAIN! GO AHEAD, JAIL ME!

NO! YOU SAVED MY LIFE ONCE! NOW WE'RE EVEN! I OWE YOU NOTHING!

FOR YOUR OWN SAKE, I HOPE YOU WILL STRAIGHTEN OUT YOUR THINKING AND USE YOUR BRILLIANT MIND TO HELP HUMANITY AS I DO!

DON'T WORRY ABOUT ME, *SUPERBOY!* I'LL BECOME EVEN MORE FAMOUS THAN YOU! AND I'LL DESTROY YOU, TOO!

13

STRANGE! I JUST REALIZED THAT *LEX LUTHOR* HAS THE SAME INITIALS AS *LANA LANG!* *LL!* -- WILL *LUTHOR* BECOME A GREAT SCIENTIST? OR... A CRIMINAL?

UNFORTUNATELY, AS WE ALL KNOW, *LUTHOR* GREW UP TO BECOME *SUPERMAN'S* ARCH-ENEMY, AND ONE OF THE MOST DASTARDLY CRIMINALS IN THE HISTORY OF CRIME !

SUPERMAN

PENCILS:
CURT SWAN
INKS:
GEORGE KLEIN

SUPERMAN, PREPARE TO DIE! YOU'LL NEVER BE ABLE TO FIGHT OFF THIS AUTOMATON BLOODHOUND WITHOUT YOUR SUPER-POWERS!

PART I

SINCE THE DAYS, YEARS AGO, WHEN, AS SUPERBOY, HE WAS LIVING IN SMALLVILLE, THE GREATEST ENEMY OF THE MAN OF STEEL HAS BEEN LEX LUTHOR! AGAIN AND AGAIN, SUPERMAN HAS THWARTED LUTHOR WHEN THE LATTER USED HIS SCIENTIFIC GENIUS FOR CRIMINAL PURPOSES! BUT NOW FATE BRINGS A DAY WHEN SUPERMAN, WITHOUT HIS MIGHTY SUPER-POWERS, MUST MEET HIS GREAT FOE IN A MAN-TO-MAN STRUGGLE —

The SHOWDOWN BETWEEN LUTHOR and SUPERMAN!

IN A BLEAK PRISON CELL SITS A MAN WITH ONE OF THE MOST BRILLIANT MINDS OF THE AGE!

I'M LOCKED UP IN THIS CAGE, BUT **HE** ROVES THE WHOLE WORLD! HE... **SUPERMAN**...THE MAN WHO PUT ME HERE BECAUSE HE'S REALLY JEALOUS OF MY SCIENTIFIC GENIUS, WHICH I USE FOR CRIME!

IT'S TIME THE LONG FEUD BETWEEN **SUPERMAN** AND ME WAS SETTLED, ONE WAY OR ANOTHER! I'M GOING TO HAVE IT OUT WITH HIM, ONCE AND FOR ALL!

A FEW WEEKS LATER,. IN THE PRISON-SHOP...

YES, OUR BIGGEST STAMPING PRESS HAS BROKEN DOWN!

I'LL REPORT THIS TO THE TEMPORARY WARDEN!

MY SECRET SABOTAGE CAUSED IT TO BREAK DOWN... THE FIRST STEP TOWARD MY SHOWDOWN WITH **SUPERMAN!**

TO A DISMAYED OFFICIAL, **LUTHOR** MAKES AN OFFER!

YOU SAY YOU CAN REBUILD THE PRESS? BY ALL MEANS, **LUTHOR**, GO AHEAD... WE NEED IT BADLY!

I'LL MAKE IT WORK BETTER THAN EVER!

IT'S WHY I WAITED TILL THE REGULAR WARDEN WAS ON VACATION... **HE** WOULD NEVER TRUST ME TO WORK WITH MACHINERY, KNOWING MY ABILITIES! BUT HIS TEMPORARY SUBSTITUTE DOESN'T SUSPECT!

DAYS OF INTENSIVE WORK FOLLOW, AND THEN...

IT DOESN'T LOOK LIKE THE SAME MACHINE AT ALL! ARE YOU SURE IT WILL WORK?

ABSOLUTELY! I'LL MAKE THE FINAL ADJUSTMENTS INSIDE IT, AND THEN GIVE YOU A DEMONSTRATION!

THE DEMONSTRATION IS A FEARFUL ONE!

HA, HA! HOW DOES THIS IMPRESS YOU?

HE'S MADE IT INTO A STEEL GIANT THAT'S SMASHING OUT THROUGH THE WALL! GUARDS!

②

BUT NO GUARDS OR WALLS OR WEAPONS CAN STOP THE STEEL COLOSSUS!

OUR BULLETS JUST BOUNCE OFF IT!

AND *LUTHOR'S* HEADING IT OFF THE ROAD SO OUR CARS CAN'T FOLLOW!

AS NIGHT FALLS, HOURS LATER, *LUTHOR* ABANDONS HIS ESCAPE-MACHINE AND REACHES HIS GOAL!

THEY CAN NEVER FIND ME IN THIS SECRET HIDEOUT I PREPARED LONG AGO! IT'S LEAD-LINED, SO NOT EVEN *SUPERMAN'S* VISION CAN LOCATE IT!

I'M FREE NOW TO START THE CAMPAIGN THAT WILL BRING ABOUT A FINAL SHOWDOWN BATTLE BETWEEN *SUPERMAN* AND MYSELF! IT WON'T TAKE LONG TO DEVISE A BROADCASTER-INTERRUPTOR SUCH AS I'LL NEED!

A FEW NIGHTS LATER, AS *METROPOLIS'* FAMILIES WATCH A POPULAR WESTERN TV SERIES...

TAKE OFF THAT SHERIFF'S BADGE AND I'LL FIGHT YOU MAN-TO-MAN... IF YOU DARE!

I'M TAKING OFF THE BADGE... COME ON!

SUDDENLY, THE BROADCAST IS INTERRUPTED AND A GRIM FACE APPEARS!

SUPERMAN HAS NEVER YET DARED MEET *ME*, *LUTHOR*, MAN-TO-MAN, ON EVEN TERMS! I CHALLENGE HIM TO MEET ME IN A FAIR FIGHT, WITHOUT HIS SUPER-POWERS TO HELP HIM!

3

AND THE NEXT MORNING, AT THE **METROPOLIS DAILY PLANET**, REPORTERS LOIS LANE AND JIMMY OLSEN ARE INDIGNANT WHEN **LUTHOR** INTERRUPTS ANOTHER TELECAST!

LUTHOR SPEAKING! NOTICE, EVERYBODY, THAT IN THIS HEAVYWEIGHT BOUT, THE FIGHTERS ARE **EVENLY MATCHED!** BUT SUPER-MAN IS AFRAID TO MEET **ME** ON EVEN TERMS!

THAT DETESTABLE **LUTHOR** IS JUST NEEDLING **SUPERMAN** FOR HIS OWN PURPOSES... **SUPERMAN** WILL IGNORE HIS CHALLENGE!

BUT REPORTER CLARK KENT, WHO IS SECRETLY **SUPERMAN**, THINKS DIFFERENTLY!

IF MY CAREER AS **SUPERMAN** IS TO CONTINUE, I MUST ACCEPT HIS CHALLENGE! IF PEOPLE THOUGHT THAT I WAS AFRAID TO MEET HIM WITHOUT MY SUPER-POWERS, THEY MIGHT LOSE FAITH IN ME AS A DEFENDER OF THE WEAK AND OPPRESSED!

AND SOON, SPEAKING FROM STATION METV...

LUTHOR, WHEREVER YOU ARE, I ACCEPT YOUR CHALLENGE TO BATTLE YOU WITHOUT MY SUPER-POWERS! MEET ME ON MOUNT KOMO TOMORROW AND I GUARANTEE SAFE-CONDUCT!

AT LAST!

NEXT DAY, HIGH ON A BARREN PEAK, A FEUD THAT BEGAN MANY YEARS AGO IN **SMALLVILLE** REACHES ITS CLIMAX!

ON A WORLD LIKE **KRYPTON**, WHICH HAS A RED SUN, I'D HAVE NO SUPER-POWERS! I'LL BUILD A SPACE-SHIP THAT WILL TAKE US TO A SIMILAR PLANET IN A SOLAR SYSTEM WHICH REVOLVES AROUND A RED SUN!

IF YOU WIN THERE AND BEST ME, I'LL RETURN WITH YOU, AND SERVE OUT MY TIME IN PRISON! BUT IF I WIN, I'LL LEAVE YOU ON THAT WORLD AND RETURN ALONE!

SWIFTLY, THE **MAN OF STEEL** FORGES METAL AND CONSTRUCTS A FAST SPACE-SHIP!

I'LL HAVE NO SUPER-POWERS OR ABILITY TO FLY ON THE WORLD I'VE SELECTED FOR OUR BATTLE-GROUND... WITHOUT THIS SHIP, I WON'T BE ABLE TO RETURN!

OH, **SUPERMAN**, DON'T LET YOUR PRIDE PUSH YOU INTO THIS! **LUTHOR** CAN BE DANGEROUS AS A COBRA AND I'VE GOT A FATAL PREMONITION ABOUT THIS!

SOON, OUT FROM EARTH TOWARD A FAR RED STAR, SPEEDS A CRAFT CONTAINING THE TWO DEADLY ENEMIES!

THERE GOES THE SHIP WITH **SUPERMAN** AND **LUTHOR** IN IT... THE WHOLE WORLD IS ROOTING FOR **SUPERMAN** TO WIN!

WHAT WILL HAPPEN OUT THERE?

NOBODY, NOT EVEN **SUPERMAN** OR **LUTHOR**, DREAMS OF WHAT FATE HAS IN STORE! ④

SOON, THE SHIP LANDS ON A DESERT-LIKE WORLD AND, AFTER BUILDING A CRUDE RING OUT OF PETRIFIED LOGS...

THE GRAVITY ON THIS PLANET IS GREATER THAN EARTH'S, BUT THOSE "GRAVITY SHOES" I MADE GIVE YOU EXACTLY THE SAME POWERS OF WALKING THAT I HAVE ON THIS *KRYPTON*-LIKE WORLD!

I SUPER-COMPRESSED MY CLARK KENT CLOTHES AND HID THEM IN THE POUCH OF MY CAPE WHEN I WENT BACK INTO THE SHIP FOR THE SHOES!

THAT'S GOOD! I'VE WAITED A LONG TIME...

...FOR THIS MOMENT! HOW DO YOU LIKE BEING ON THE RECEIVING END FOR A CHANGE?

OOF!

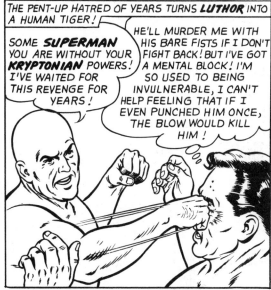

THE PENT-UP HATRED OF YEARS TURNS *LUTHOR* INTO A HUMAN TIGER!

SOME *SUPERMAN* YOU ARE WITHOUT YOUR *KRYPTONIAN* POWERS! I'VE WAITED FOR THIS REVENGE FOR YEARS!

HE'LL MURDER ME WITH HIS BARE FISTS IF I DON'T FIGHT BACK! BUT I'VE GOT A MENTAL BLOCK! I'M SO USED TO BEING INVULNERABLE, I CAN'T HELP FEELING THAT IF I EVEN PUNCHED HIM ONCE, THE BLOW WOULD KILL HIM!

NEXT MOMENT...

HA! I GAVE YOU A BLACK EYE, AND NOW I'M GOING TO GIVE YOU THE BEATING OF YOUR LIFE!

OOF...

WHAT A FOOL I WAS TO ACCEPT *LUTHOR'S* CHALLENGE TO FIGHT HIM *MAN-TO-MAN!*

⑤

BUT SUDDENLY, *SUPERMAN'S* INSTINCT FOR SELF-DEFENSE MAKES HIM FORGET HIS MENTAL BLOCK, AND HE MAKES A THRILLING COMEBACK!

NOW FOR THE FINISH ...AWK!

I NEVER DARED HIT YOU HARD, WHEN I HAD SUPER-STRENGTH, BECAUSE I KNEW THAT EVEN ONE BLOW WOULD KILL YOU, BUT NOW THAT WE'RE EVENLY MATCHED... IT'S A PLEASURE!

WHEW, HE NEARLY HAD ME! THIS IS ONLY THE FIRST ROUND... BUT I'LL GET A LITTLE WATER FROM THE SHIP TO REVIVE HIM!

BUT WHEN **SUPERMAN** RETURNS WITH THE WATER...

HE REVIVED...AND HAS GONE INTO THAT WEIRD CACTUS FOREST! I'LL FOLLOW AND HAVE IT OUT WITH HIM, BUT IF HE'S AS CUNNING AS USUAL, I'LL HAVE TO BEWARE OF CLEVER TRAPS!

ALREADY, **LUTHOR** IS SETTING UP A DEADLY AMBUSH!

HERE IN THE CACTUS FOREST, I CAN PLAY CAT-AND-MOUSE WITH HIM! HE'LL FOLLOW MY TRACKS...AND IF THIS GROWTH-POWDER I HAD CONCEALED IN MY BELT BUCKLE DOESN'T FINISH HIM, MY OTHER SCIENTIFIC TRICKS WILL!

AND **SUPERMAN** FOLLOWING, SUDDENLY FINDS HIMSELF IN TERRIBLE PERIL!

LUTHOR HAS USED SOME GROWTH-STIMULATOR TO MAKE THESE CACTI GROW SUPER-FAST! THEY'LL CRUSH ME BETWEEN THEIR SPINES IN A MOMENT...I CAN'T JUMP HIGH ENOUGH TO ESCAPE THEM! WAIT..., I REMEMBER, BACK ON **KRYPTON**...

...WHEN I WAS SMALL, MY FATHER SHOWED ME A NATURE-FILM ABOUT **KRYPTON'S SCARLET JUNGLE**!...

YES, **KAL-EL**, MY SON, THOSE ARE THE STRANGE MOVING FORESTS! WHEN THEY ADVANCE IN THEIR YEARLY MIGRATION, THE ONLY SAFETY IS **UNDER** THEM, IN TUNNELS, UNTIL THEY'VE PASSED!

IF THIS TYPE OF VEGETATION IS SIMILAR TO **KRYPTON'S**, THEN THE ONLY WAY OF ESCAPE IS **DOWNWARD**, LIKE THOSE KRYPTONIAN TUNNELS! CAN'T USE MY HANDS TO DRILL, BUT IF I CAN DIG A FOXHOLE IN TIME WITH THIS SHARP STONE...

THE CACTI ARE CRUSHING **EACH OTHER** TO DEATH BY THEIR WILD GROWTH! MY KRYPTONIAN TRICK SAVED ME... AND WHEN I'VE TUNNELED OUT OF HERE I CAN SEARCH FOR **LUTHOR!**

BUT, ON LOW, ROCKY HILLS JUST BEYOND THE CACTUS FOREST, THE WILY **LUTHOR** REACHES FOR ANOTHER SECRET WEAPON CONCEALED ON HIS PERSON...

HA! **SUPERMAN** THINKS I CAN'T SEE HIM STEALING THROUGH THE FOREST... BUT I'LL CATCH HIM WITH THIS ROD I HID IN MY LEAD-LINED SHIRT POCKET, ALONG WITH OTHER GIMMICKS I INVENTED!

77587

THIS ROD IS A "THERMAL DETECTOR" THAT'S SENSITIVE TO HIS **BODY-HEAT!**... AH...ITS NEEDLE IS POINTING TO HIS EXACT LOCATION!

THIS BOULDER IS AIMED AT HIS EXACT POSITION!

AND DOOM CRASHES TOWARD **SUPERMAN**, FROM ABOVE!

IN THESE CACTI, I CAN'T DODGE THAT HUGE BOULDER IN TIME...BUT THIS SMALLER ROCK, IF I THROW IT RIGHT, MAY DEFLECT IT UPWARD!

7

THAT WAS CLOSE! BUT HOW COULD *LUTHOR*, UP THERE WHERE HE CAN'T SEE ME, KNOW EXACTLY WHERE I AM?

A QUICK MIND DEDUCES THE ONLY POSSIBLE ANSWER!

HE MUST BE USING A THERMAL-DETECTOR TO SPOT MY BODY-HEAT! BUT THIS TINY, SMOKELESS *FIRE* I MADE, OF DRIED CACTUS-TWIGS, WILL FOOL THE DETECTOR, AND WHILE THE DETECTOR POINTS AT THE FIRE'S HEAT, I'LL CIRCLE AROUND *LUTHOR* FROM BEHIND!

THE FIRE IS TRICKING HIM...WHILE HE ROLLS MORE BOULDERS TOWARD IT, I'LL GET BEHIND HIM! THIS WIND IS BLOWING UP SAND AND WILL MAKE IT DIFFICULT FOR HIM TO SEE ME!

BUT THE RISING WIND *IS* AN OMEN OF A DREAD DANGER ON THIS DESERT WORLD! AS IT BECOMES A GALE...

A TERRIFIC SAND-STORM! I CAN'T SEE...CAN HARDLY BREATHE...HAVE TO GET BACK TO THE SHIP, IF I CAN FIND IT...

AS THE MIGHTY SAND-STORM REACHES ITS HEIGHT, *SUPERMAN* WANDERS... LOST!

I'VE WANDERED FOR HOURS AND CAN'T FIND THE SHIP! WITHOUT MY SUPER-STRENGTH I'M TIRING FAST, AND WITHOUT MY X-RAY VISION, I CAN'T SEE WHERE I AM! BUT I...HAVE TO KEEP GOING...

DRIVEN BY STORM, EXHAUSTED, TORMENTED BY THIRST, THE MAN WHO WAS ONCE THE MIGHTIEST OF ALL MEN STUMBLES ON!

IF I DON'T FIND SHELTER AND WATER SOON... I'LL DIE! *LUTHOR* WILL HAVE THE LAST LAUGH ON ME!

AND *SUPERMAN'S* ARCH-ENEMY, CROUCHING FROM THE STORM'S FURY AMID SHELTERING ROCKS, PLOTS TO MAKE HIS DOOM CERTAIN!

WITHOUT HIS SUPER-POWERS, *SUPERMAN* WILL PERISH IN THIS STORM! WHEN THE STORM ABATES, I'LL FIND HIM DEAD! THEN I'LL BURY HIM!

END PART I (8)

SUPERMAN

REG. U.S. PAT. OFF.

HURRAH FOR GREAT **LUTHOR**... HE'S CONQUERING THE EVIL **SUPERMAN**!

OUR HERO, **LUTHOR**, IS UNBEATABLE!

PART II

FAR IN THE UNIVERSE, ACROSS THE WASTES OF A DYING, DESERT WORLD, **SUPERMAN** AND **LUTHOR** HAVE CARRIED THEIR GREAT FEUD! NOW, AS THEIR TITANIC STRUGGLE DRAWS TO ITS CONCLUSION, EVEN THE **MAN OF STEEL**, WHO NOW HAS NO SUPER-POWERS, IS STUNNED BY THE STRANGE, UNEXPECTED END OF...

The SUPER-DUEL!

N-267

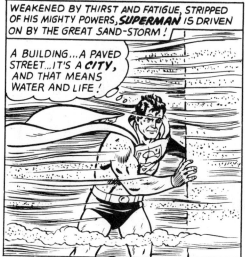

WEAKENED BY THIRST AND FATIGUE, STRIPPED OF HIS MIGHTY POWERS, **SUPERMAN** IS DRIVEN ON BY THE GREAT SAND-STORM!

A BUILDING...A PAVED STREET...IT'S A **CITY**, AND THAT MEANS WATER AND LIFE!

BUT QUICKLY, COMES TRAGIC DISAPPOINTMENT!

THIS CITY LOOKS MUCH LIKE THE CITIES OF PERISHED **KRYPTON**! BUT...IT'S DESERTED ...**DEAD**!

THIS WAS ONCE A GREAT FOUNTAIN, BUT IT'S DRY NOW! THERE'S NO WATER IN THIS PLACE! I CAN'T SEARCH ANY FARTHER... EVERYTHING'S GETTING BLURRED...

IN HIS DELIRIUM, IT SEEMS TO **SUPERMAN** THAT THIS HALF-FAMILIAR CITY IS THE WORLD OF HIS BIRTH!

WHY, I'M BACK ON **KRYPTON!** IT'S JUST AS I REMEMBERED IT!

THERE'S MY FATHER AND MOTHER ...**JOR-EL** AND **LARA!** THEY'RE STILL ALIVE!...OH, NO -- MY HAND WENT THROUGH THEM...IT'S ALL AN **HALLUCINATION** CAUSED BY MY DELIRIUM...

SUDDENLY, ACROSS THE WEIRD SPECTERS CONJURED UP BY HIS FEVERED DELIRIUM, MOVE **REAL** FIGURES!

THOSE STRANGE BEASTS OF THIS DESERT WORLD... THEY'VE EVOLVED TO CARRY **WATER** IN THEIR BIG HOLLOW HORNS! THEY MUST GO LONG DISTANCES FOR WATER, DIP IT UP, AND CARRY IT THAT WAY!

IF THEY RUN AWAY, I'M LOST! BUT THEY SEEM FRIENDLY, ALMOST TAME...THEY MUST HAVE ONCE BEEN DOMESTICATED BY MAN, AND AREN'T AFRAID!

I CAN DRAW UP WATER WITH THIS HOLLOW REED...AND I NEVER KNEW HOW DELICIOUS WATER IS, TILL NOW! I WON'T TAKE TOO MUCH FROM THEM... JUST ENOUGH TO KEEP ME GOING UNTIL I CAN FIND MORE...

2

BUT FIRST, I'VE GOT TO REST! I'LL NEED ALL MY STRENGTH WHEN I GO BACK TO MEET **LUTHOR** IN COMBAT AGAIN!

BUT NOW THAT THE STORM IS OVER, **LUTHOR** EMERGES FROM HIS ROCK SHELTER AND SETS FORTH IN GRIM SEARCH OF **SUPERMAN**!

SUPERMAN SURELY PERISHED IN THE STORM, BUT I WON'T BE CERTAIN I'VE WON OUR DUEL UNTIL I FIND HIS BODY! HMM... THE STORM BLEW AWAY HIS TRACKS, BUT I'LL TRY THIS DIRECTION...

FATE LEADS **LUTHOR**, NOT IN THE WAY THAT **SUPERMAN** WENT, BUT IN A DIFFERENT DIRECTION!

I THOUGHT THIS WHOLE DESERT WORLD WAS DEAD, BUT THERE ARE PEOPLE IN THAT CITY! I'LL TRY TO FIND OUT IF THEY'VE SEEN **SUPERMAN**!

THIS UNDERGROUND WATER BURSTING UP IN A BIG FOUNTAIN MUST BE THEIR ONLY WATER-SUPPLY! BUT THEY CAN'T UNDERSTAND MY QUESTIONS! I'LL HAVE TO HUNT THE CITY FOR **SUPERMAN**!

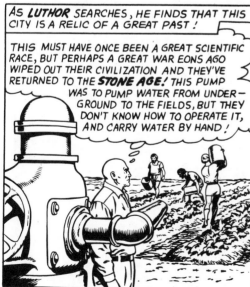

AS **LUTHOR** SEARCHES, HE FINDS THAT THIS CITY IS A RELIC OF A GREAT PAST!

THIS MUST HAVE ONCE BEEN A GREAT SCIENTIFIC RACE, BUT PERHAPS A GREAT WAR EONS AGO WIPED OUT THEIR CIVILIZATION AND THEY'VE RETURNED TO THE **STONE AGE**! THIS PUMP WAS TO PUMP WATER FROM UNDER-GROUND TO THE FIELDS, BUT THEY DON'T KNOW HOW TO OPERATE IT, AND CARRY WATER BY HAND!

SUDDENLY, AN ALARM OF TERROR!

DORULG!

DORULG!

THOSE MONSTROUS BIRDS WILL RAVAGE THEIR CROPS...AND THEY SEEM TO HAVE NO WAY TO REPEL THEM! HMM... MAYBE THERE'S A WAY, RIGHT HERE AT HAND!

3

USING HIS GREAT SCIENTIFIC ABILITIES, **LUTHOR** WORKS FAST!

I'VE GOT ONLY A FEW MOMENTS TO ALTER THE PUMP AND ITS PIPES, AND THEN GET IT GOING! THE RADIUM BATTERY WHICH ONCE WORKED IT SHOULD STILL HAVE POWER!

SOON, THE ALTERED PUMP BECOMES A MIGHTY WEAPON!

AS THE MENACE IS REPELLED, **LUTHOR**, FOR THE FIRST TIME IN HIS LIFE, FINDS HIMSELF A POPULAR HERO!

THEY'RE GRATEFUL THAT I SAVED THEIR CROPS... THEY DON'T KNOW I ONLY DID IT SO THEY'LL HELP ME FIND **SUPERMAN!**

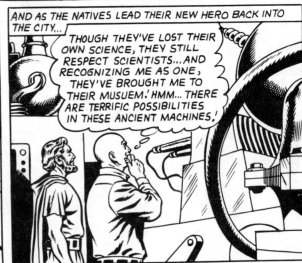

AND AS THE NATIVES LEAD THEIR NEW HERO BACK INTO THE CITY...

THOUGH THEY'VE LOST THEIR OWN SCIENCE, THEY STILL RESPECT SCIENTISTS... AND RECOGNIZING ME AS ONE, THEY'VE BROUGHT ME TO THEIR MUSUEM! HMM... THERE ARE TERRIFIC POSSIBILITIES IN THESE ANCIENT MACHINES!

IN THE NEXT FEW HOURS, **LUTHOR** USES ONE OF THE STRANGE MACHINES FOR **LEARNING!**

THIS **LESSON MACHINE,** USED TO TEACH CHILDREN LONG AGO, IS TEACHING ME THEIR LANGUAGE WITH SUPER-SPEED! THAT'LL ENABLE ME TO TELL THESE PEOPLE I MUST FIND **SUPERMAN!**

SHORTLY, A GRATEFUL PEOPLE HONOR **LUTHOR!**

YOU ARE A WISE MAN, LIKE OUR FOREFATHERS ... YOU WILL USE THE ANCIENT WISDOM WE HAVE FORGOTTEN TO HELP US, GREAT **LUTHOR!**

IT'S STRANGE... I NEVER HAD A CROWD CHEER ME BEFORE, AND I RATHER LIKE IT!

HURRAH FOR **LUTHOR!**

HURRAH!

4

YES, SHORTAGE OF **WATER** IS OUR GREATEST PROBLEM...THIS FOUNTAIN IS OUR ONLY SOURCE.!

FROM MY STUDY OF IT, I FEAR THIS FOUNTAIN MAY SOON FAIL! BUT I RECALL SEEING A MACHINE IN YOUR MUSEUM WHICH MAY HELP ME PROVIDE ANOTHER SOURCE OF WATER!

SUPERMAN CAN WAIT TILL I'VE DONE THAT!

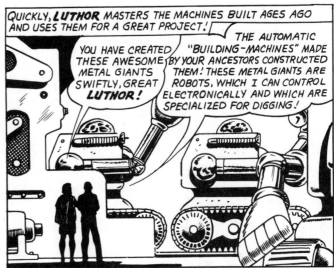

QUICKLY, **LUTHOR** MASTERS THE MACHINES BUILT AGES AGO AND USES THEM FOR A GREAT PROJECT!

YOU HAVE CREATED THESE AWESOME METAL GIANTS SWIFTLY, GREAT **LUTHOR**!

THE AUTOMATIC "BUILDING-MACHINES" MADE BY YOUR ANCESTORS CONSTRUCTED THEM! THESE METAL GIANTS ARE ROBOTS, WHICH I CAN CONTROL ELECTRONICALLY AND WHICH ARE SPECIALIZED FOR DIGGING!

I'M USING THE ROBOTS TO DIG DEEP UNDERGROUND UNTIL THEY FIND MORE WATER!

WE KNOW THAT YOU WILL SUCCEED, YOUR WISDOM IS SO GREAT!

BUT AS HOURS PASS...

THE ROBOTS CAN'T FIND ANY OTHER SOURCE OF WATER IN THIS PLANET...YET I CAN'T LET THESE PEOPLE DOWN WHEN THEY THINK I'M A HERO!

SUDDENLY, **LUTHOR** IS SHARPLY RECALLED TO THE GREAT FEUD THAT BROUGHT HIM HERE!

I FOUND YOUR *TRACKS* WHEN I RETURNED TO THE SHIP AND TRAILED YOU HERE, **LUTHOR**...WE CAN FINISH OUR FIGHT NOW!

IS THIS STRANGER YOUR FRIEND, GREAT **LUTHOR**?

NO, HE'S MY ENEMY!

IF HE'S THE ENEMY OF OUR GREAT HERO, HE MUST BE EVIL...WE WILL KILL HIM!

NO, LET GO OF HIM! I HAVE VOWED TO FIGHT HIM ON EVEN TERMS, IN SINGLE COMBAT!

5

TO KEEP US ON EVEN TERMS, I'LL HAVE THESE PEOPLE SHOW YOU A SET OF THEIR ANCIENT INVENTIONS! YOU CAN STUDY THEM TONIGHT, AND FIGURE OUT HOW TO USE THEM...AS I'LL USE MY SET AGAINST YOU!

AGREED! WE'LL DUEL TOMORROW!

BUT WHEN *SUPERMAN* HAS LEARNED THE LANGUAGE BY THE TEACHING-MACHINE, AND HAS STUDIED THE MACHINES...

THESE ANCIENT INVENTIONS *DO* HAVE TERRIFIC POWERS...AND *LUTHOR* IS A GREAT SCIENTIST AND WILL KNOW HOW TO MAKE WEAPONS OUT OF THEM! I'VE GOT TO PREPARE TO MEET HIM...

WHILE *SUPERMAN* STUDIES, *LUTHOR'S* PLAN TO HELP THE NATIVES GETS A SET-BACK!

MY ROBOTS COULD FIND NO OTHER WATER THAN THE WANING SUPPLY THAT FEEDS THE FOUNTAIN! IT'LL DISAPPOINT THESE PEOPLE TERRIBLY... I WON'T TELL THEM TILL AFTER MY DUEL WITH *SUPERMAN!*

NEXT DAY, IN AN ANCIENT ARENA, *LUTHOR* FACES *SUPERMAN* FOR A FINAL SHOWDOWN!

CRUSH YOUR EVIL ENEMY, GREAT *LUTHOR!* WE'RE ALL CHEERING FOR YOU!

FOR THE FIRST TIME, THERE'S NOT ONE PERSON ROOTING FOR *ME* IN A FIGHT! ON THIS WORLD, I'M A VILLAIN AND *LUTHOR* IS A HERO!

LUTHOR BEGINS THE DUEL BY SELECTING A UNIQUE DEVICE FROM HIS STOCKPILE OF WEAPONS!

THAT'S AN ANTI—GRAVITY TORNADO HE'S RELEASED AT ME! I'LL COUNTER IT FAST BY CREATING A *BIGGER* ONE WITH THE SAME TYPE INSTRUMENT!

6

AS **SUPERMAN** IS WHIRLED AROUND BY THE MINIATURE TORNADO...

I MANAGED TO PUSH THE CONTROL BUTTON THAT ENERGIZES MY INSTRUMENT TO FULL POWER... HOPE IT WORKS!

HA! OUR HERO, **LUTHOR**, IS TOO MUCH FOR HIM!

NEXT MOMENT, **LUTHOR** IS SUDDENLY THREATENED BY THE SAME TORNADO MENACE HE RELEASED AT **SUPERMAN!**

IT'S SO BIG NOW IT'LL ENGULF **ME**, TOO, IN A MOMENT. I MUST TURN IT OFF!

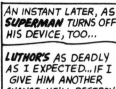

AN INSTANT LATER, AS **SUPERMAN** TURNS OFF HIS DEVICE, TOO...

LUTHOR'S AS DEADLY AS I EXPECTED... IF I GIVE HIM ANOTHER CHANCE, HE'LL DESTROY ME! I'VE GOT TO ACT THE MOMENT I HIT THE GROUND!

ACTING SWIFTLY, THE **MAN OF STEEL** STRIKES OUT!

THESE TINY "SHOOTING SUNS," ONCE USED FOR ILLUMINATION, SHOULD STOP YOU!

ON THE CONTRARY, I'LL STOP **THEM** WITH THIS RING— PROJECTOR WHICH SPREADS OUT A WALL OF DARK FORCE THAT NO HEAT, LIGHT OR ENERGY CAN PASS!

THE MIGHTY DUEL GOES ON, UNTIL **LUTHOR** UNLEASHES A FINAL AND TERRIBLE WEAPON!

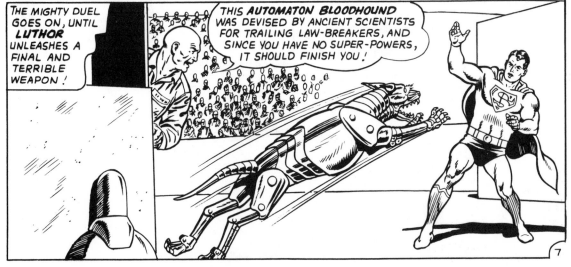

THIS **AUTOMATON BLOODHOUND** WAS DEVISED BY ANCIENT SCIENTISTS FOR TRAILING LAW-BREAKERS, AND SINCE YOU HAVE NO SUPER-POWERS, IT SHOULD FINISH YOU!

7

ITS STRENGTH IS TREMENDOUS..., AND IF ITS JAWS REACH MY THROAT, IT'S ALL OVER! IT MUST BE POWERED BY A SELF-CONTAINED BATTERY... IF MY HANDS CAN ONLY FIND THE CONTROL PANEL...

NEXT MOMENT, AS HE RIPS OUT THE CONTROL WIRES...

THAT DEACTIVATES THE THING!

YOUR CLEVERNESS HAS SAVED YOU SO FAR, BUT I CAN STILL USE MY BARE *HANDS*!

WEAKENED BY HIS BATTLE WITH THE TERRIBLE BLOODHOUND, **SUPERMAN** FEELS FATALLY OUT-MATCHED!

LUTHOR IS WINNING! HURRAH! AND WHEN HE'S WON, HE'LL FIND US MORE WATER AS HE PROMISED!

THEY DON'T KNOW YET THAT I *CAN'T* FIND THEM WATER...

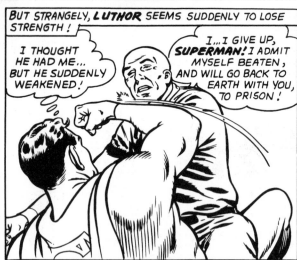

BUT STRANGELY, **LUTHOR** SEEMS SUDDENLY TO LOSE STRENGTH!

I THOUGHT HE HAD ME... BUT HE SUDDENLY WEAKENED!

I...I GIVE UP, **SUPERMAN**! I ADMIT MYSELF BEATEN, AND WILL GO BACK TO EARTH WITH YOU, TO PRISON!

AND AS VICTOR AND VANQUISHED DEPART...

YOU WON'T FORGET YOUR PROMISE TO GET US WATER, GREAT **LUTHOR**?

NO... I WON'T FORGET, MY FRIENDS! ...I'LL DO IT!

AS THEIR SPACE SHIP LEAVES THE SOLAR SYSTEM WITH A RED SUN AND ENTERS ONE WITH A YELLOW ORB, **SUPERMAN** REGAINS ALL HIS POWERS!

I CAN'T GET THEM WATER, BUT WITH YOUR POWERS, **YOU** COULD! THERE'S AN *ICY* PLANET JUST AHEAD! YOU COULD THROW VAST MASSES OF ICE BACK TO THAT DESERT WORLD!

IT WOULD HELP THOSE PEOPLE AND I'LL DO IT... EVEN IF THEY DID THINK ME A VILLAIN!

8

FASTER THAN A SPEEDING BULLET!

MORE POWERFUL THAN A LOCOMOTIVE!

ABLE TO LEAP TALL BUILDINGS AT A SINGLE BOUND!

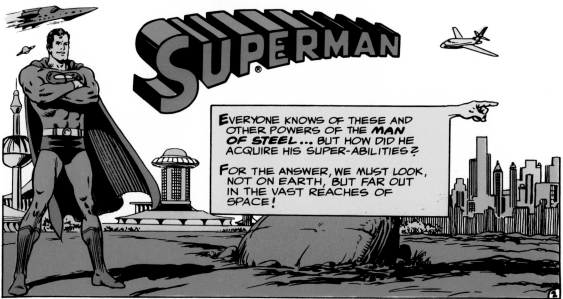

SUPERMAN

EVERYONE KNOWS OF THESE AND OTHER POWERS OF THE **MAN OF STEEL** ... BUT HOW DID HE ACQUIRE HIS SUPER-ABILITIES?

FOR THE ANSWER, WE MUST LOOK, NOT ON EARTH, BUT FAR OUT IN THE VAST REACHES OF SPACE!

YEARS AGO, THE GIANT PLANET *KRYPTON* REVOLVED AROUND A GREAT *RED SUN*...

KRYPTON WAS INHABITED BY A HIGHLY INTELLIGENT CIVILIZATION. AMONG ITS FOREMOST CITIZENS WERE SCIENTIST *JOR-EL* AND HIS WIFE, *LARA*...

I'M WORRIED ABOUT OUR SON, *KAL-EL*!

I KNOW...HE'S OVER A YEAR OLD AND HE HASN'T STARTED *READING* YET!

THE SCIENTISTS OF *KRYPTON* HAD STUDIED MANY DISTANT WORLDS, INCLUDING *EARTH*...

YES, I CALCULATE THAT A *KRYPTONIAN* ON THE TINY PLANET *EARTH* WOULD HAVE TREMENDOUS STRENGTH BECAUSE OF ITS LIGHTER GRAVITY!

AND THE GREATER ENERGY OF ITS *YELLOW SUN* WOULD GIVE HIM OTHER FANTASTIC POWERS!

BUT THE TIME CAME WHEN *KRYPTON* WAS SHAKEN BY MYSTERIOUS RUMBLINGS...

ANOTHER *GROUND-QUAKE!*

THERE HAVE BEEN SIMILAR ONES ALL OVER THE PLANET!

IN THE *HALL OF WISDOM*, THE RULING *SCIENCE COUNCIL* AWAITED AN ANNOUNCEMENT FROM ONE OF ITS MEMBERS...

WHAT DO YOU SUPPOSE HE HAS ON HIS MIND?

WE'LL SOON KNOW...HERE HE COMES!

FELLOW SCIENTISTS, *KRYPTON IS DOOMED!*

ANGER AND FRUSTRATION MINGLED IN **JOR-EL'S** MIND AS HE HURRIED HOME...

THOSE IDIOTS CAN STAY HERE AND DIE...

BUT I MUST CONTINUE MY ROCKET EXPERIMENTS... BUILD A SHIP TO TAKE ME AND MY FAMILY TO EARTH!

LARA WAITED ANXIOUSLY, AND WHEN **JOR-EL** ARRIVED...

I CAN SEE IT... THEY STILL WON'T BELIEVE YOU!

I THOUGHT THE QUAKES WOULD CONVINCE THEM, BUT THEY DON'T **WANT** TO BELIEVE THE TRUTH!

THE FOOLS! THEIR BLINDNESS WILL DOOM **BILLIONS!**

MONTHS PASSED, AS **JOR-EL** WORKED FURIOUSLY. AND THEN, ONE TERRIBLE DAY... THE END CAME!...

IN MINUTES, MIGHTY STRUCTURES CRUMBLED, AS TRANSIT TUBES WERE RIPPED ASUNDER!...

AND IN **JOR-EL'S** HOME...

LARA, QUICK... BRING **KAL** TO THE SPACE-SHIP MODEL!

311

GOOD-BYE, SON...

...AND GOOD LUCK!

HOLD ON, *LARA*... IN MOMENTS, *KRYPTON* WILL EXPLODE!

BUT *KAL* IS SO LITTLE! I HOPE HE FINDS A GOOD HOME ON *EARTH*!

THEN, AS NATURE'S FURY GATHERED FOR ONE FINAL CATACLYSMIC BLAST...

7

KAL-EL'S PITIFULLY SMALL SPACE-SHIP ROCKETED OUTWARD FROM THE LAST DEATH-THROES OF THE EXPLODING PLANET...

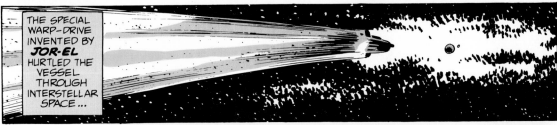

THE SPECIAL WARP-DRIVE INVENTED BY JOR-EL HURTLED THE VESSEL THROUGH INTERSTELLAR SPACE...

...UNTIL IT APPROACHED ITS DES-TINATION, THE PLANET EARTH!...

IT CIRCLED THIS WORLD...

THEN, AT LAST, IT PLUNGED TO THE SURFACE...

JONATHAN, LOOK... WHAT'S THAT THING THAT JUST CRASHED?

DON'T KNOW! LET'S TAKE A LOOK!

LOADING THE ROCKET ON THEIR PICK-UP TRUCK, JONATHAN AND MARTHA KENT DROVE TOWARD *SMALLVILLE*...

SMALLVILLE POP. 1009.

COUNTY ORPHANAGE

SHOULD WE TELL THEM HOW WE FOUND THE BABY, JONATHAN?

NO! WE'LL JUST SAY WE FOUND AN ABANDONED CHILD!

THEN WE'LL HIDE THE ROCKET!

SOON, IN THE OFFICE OF THE DIRECTOR OF THE ORPHANAGE...

WE'D LIKE TO ADOPT THE BABY, IF POSSIBLE!

WE INVESTIGATE ALL APPLICANTS CAREFULLY! WE'LL LET YOU KNOW, MRS. KENT!

SOON, THE ORPHANED INFANT DISPLAYED AMAZING ABILITIES...

GREAT SCOTT! HOW ON EARTH...?

I STARTED TO LIFT HIM...BUT *HE* LIFTED *ME* INSTEAD!

315

AND ANOTHER TIME...

I'VE LOST MY RING! WHERE COULD IT BE?

IT'S BEHIND THE LITTLE CHEST, MA!

WHY, HERE IT IS! BUT HOW DID YOU KNOW?

I JUST... SAW IT... AS IF I HAD X-RAY EYES!

ANOTHER POWER! FANTASTIC!

SOON, CLARK ADOPTED HIS SUPERBOY IDENTITY AND ACHIEVED WORLDWIDE FAME, BUT THEN HIS MOTHER DIED. AS HIS FATHER LAY ILL OF THE SAME DISEASE...

DAD...

NOT MUCH TIME!

NURSE, PLEASE LEAVE US ALONE!

NO ONE ON EARTH HAS POWERS EQUAL TO YOURS, CLARK! YOU'VE USED THEM WELL AS SUPERBOY!

BUT THERE MAY BE EVEN GREATER NEED FOR YOUR POWERS WHEN YOU'RE A MAN! YOU MUST USE THEM WISELY!-- FOR GOOD!

I WILL, PA... I SWEAR IT!

GOOD, SON... NEVER FORGET... YOUR VOW...

HE--HE'S GONE! I'M THE MIGHTIEST BEING ON EARTH...

...YET ALL MY SUPER-POWERS COULDN'T SAVE HIM!

13

319

MOST OF THE PEOPLE DIDN'T EAT THAT CAKE. THEY SAVED IT AS A SOUVENIR. THERE ARE HUNDREDS OF PIECES STILL IN *SMALLVILLE*...

SUPERBOY'S CAKE

AFTER GRADUATING FROM *METROPOLIS UNIVERSITY*, CLARK GOT A JOB AS A REPORTER ON THE *DAILY PLANET*...

LOIS LANE... JIMMY OLSEN... AND OUR EDITOR, *PERRY WHITE*...

...ALL FINE PEOPLE... AND GOOD FRIENDS!

ALSO, THIS JOB GIVES ME ACCESS TO NEWS OF CRIMES *IMMEDIATELY*-- SO I CAN ACT SWIFTLY AS *SUPERMAN*!

AT LAST, TO REWARD HIM FOR HIS SUPER-DEEDS, A GRATEFUL WORLD HONORED *SUPERMAN* IN A UNIQUE WAY...

THE MEMBER NATIONS OF THE *U.N.* HAVE VOTED YOU HONORARY CITIZENSHIP IN ALL THEIR COUNTRIES!

THANK YOU, SIR... AND ALL THE MEMBERS! I'LL TRY TO DESERVE THIS HONOR!

AND EVERY DAY, AS THE AWED CITIZENS OF *METROPOLIS* GAZE UP TO SEE A RED-AND-BLUE FORM STREAKING THROUGH THE SKY...

LOOK! UP IN THE SKY!

IT'S A *BIRD!*

IT'S A *PLANE!*

IT'S *SUPERMAN!*

THE END.

15

A SPLIT-SECOND LATER...

THIS ANTENNA SHOULD DO THE TRICK!

RIPPPPPP

WOW! SUPERMAN USED THE ANTENNA TO *SPEAR* THE GIANT GLOBE!

HIS SUPER-AIM GUIDED IT TOWARD THAT EMPTY LOT!

WHAT AN ARM!

THEN, IN A NEARBY ALLEY...

NOW TO SWITCH TO MY CLARK KENT IDENTITY...TO KEEP THAT APPOINTMENT WITH MY NEW BOSS, MORGAN EDGE, HEAD OF GALAXY BROADCASTING!

SOON, IN THE BIG-WHEEL'S SWANK SUITE...

THE *PLANET* IS A GREAT SHEET, BUT FACE IT, KENT-- NEWSPAPERS ARE *OUTDATED!* WE'RE CHANGING THINGS!

Y-YOU MEAN...I'M F-FIRED?

NOT AT ALL! WE'RE GOING TO DO A RE-TREAD JOB ON YOU, FRIEND.

STEP INTO MY PRIVATE ELEVATOR, WHILE I FILL YOU IN!

THE NEWS MOVES FAST NOWADAYS! HEADLINES CAN'T WAIT! OUR MILLIONS OF TV VIEWERS WANT THEIR NEWS STORIES *HOT OFF THE GRIDDLE!*

SO, I'M MAKING *YOU* THE *FIRST ROVING TV REPORTER* IN METRO-POLIS!

2

I'M GIVING YOU THIS *ROLLING NEWSROOM*...A SOUPED-UP MOBILE TV STUDIO...TO HELP YOU COVER HOT NEWS STORIES WHENEVER AND WHEREVER THEY BREAK!

WOW! NOW THERE'S A *FREAKY SET* OF WHEELS!

WCBS GALAXY BROADCASTING SYSTEM

YOU CAN TRANSMIT ANY SCOOP, LIVE, TO OUR ENTIRE TV NETWORK. TELEPHOTO LENSES, REMOTE PICK-UP MICROPHONES, RADAR... THERE'S ENOUGH ADVANCED EQUIPMENT TO MAKE YOU A *SUPER-REPORTER!*

NATURALLY!

AFTER EDGE LEAVES...

ME, A *TV REPORTER!* I'LL GET AROUND EASIER NOW, BUT I'LL STILL MISS THE *PLANET!*

...I'LL MISS THE *THUNDER OF THOSE PRESSES*...

...THE *SMELL* OF PRINTERS' INK!

BUT TIMES CHANGE...AND EVEN *SUPERMAN* HAS TO CHANGE ALONG WITH THEM!

WHAT I NEED IS A *BIG STORY* TO GET ME OFF THE LAUNCHING PAD!

TOMORROW SEASIDE FOLK & ROCK FESTIVAL

STARS OF THE WORLD OF ROCK

THE Ding-a-Lings
The SODA POPS
PORKY and the HAMLETS
THE ASTRONAUTS

HEY, *THERE'S AN ANGLE!* THOSE ROCK FESTIVALS ARE THE BIG THING NOW! A LIVE TELECAST OF THIS EVENT WOULD BE *TERRIFIC* FOR A STARTER!

GALA

AND SO, NEXT DAY AT THE FESTIVAL SITE...

YES, FOLKS, WOODSTOCK SET THE PACE! OUR NATION'S YOUTH IS FLOCKING TO ROCK FESTIVALS LIKE *THIS* ONE AT *SEASIDE!* JEEPS.... JALOPIES, THEY'RE USING *EVERYTHING* BUT POGO STICKS TO GET HERE!

AND THIS IS *CY HORKIN*, PRODUCER OF ROCK FESTS ACROSS THE COUNTRY. CY WAS A SCIENCE PROFESSOR AT CENTRAL UNIVERSITY UNTIL HE LEFT THREE YEARS AGO--

--BECAUSE OF A FACULTY DISPUTE!

ROCK MUSIC IS MY BAG NOW! IT BRINGS KIDS TOGETHER, TURNS THEM ON! DIG ALL THOSE BEAUTIFUL FANS WHO TRAVELED *THOUSANDS OF MILES* TO MAKE THIS SCENE!

YOU MUST BE PROUD, CY!

BY THE WAY, KENT, YOU *CAN'T* BROADCAST THE MUSIC! I SOLD THE MUSIC RIGHTS TO A RECORD COMPANY!

OKAY, I'LL JUST TELE-CAST THE PICTURES AND MY COMMENTARY FROM *INSIDE* MY SOUND-PROOF TRUCK!

SOON, THE BASH IS GOING FULL BLAST...

PIN-UP BABY, YOU BLOW MY MIND!

PIN-UP BABY, GONNA LEAVE YOU BEHIND!

4

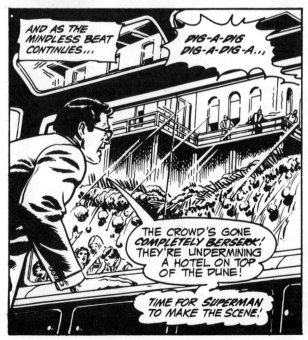

WOW! SUPERMAN AIRLIFTED OUR HOTEL JUST IN TIME!

NOT A BAD SUPER-FEAT, IF I DO SAY SO MYSELF... AND THE TV AUDIENCE IS FOLLOWING MY ACTION ON THE AUTOMATED CAMERA!

BUT HOW DO I TURN OFF THOSE KOOKS BELOW?

DIG-A-DIG-A-DIG-A...

ABRUPTLY, AS THE MUSIC ENDS...

HUH? WHAT HAPPENED? WHY WERE WE DIGGING HERE?

THERE WAS SOMETHING ABOUT THAT MUSIC...

MAN, I COULD HAVE DUG A HOLE TO CHINA!

MEANWHILE, AFTER SUPERMAN RETURNS AND SWITCHES TO CLARK...

WHAT CAUSED THE WEIRD EFFECT OF THAT MUSIC ON YOUR AUDIENCE, CY? IT WOULD'VE BEEN A DISASTER IF SUPERMAN HADN'T SHOWN UP!

GUESS THAT TUNE CAME ON TOO STRONG! CALL IT ROCK POWER! HA-HA!

LATER, IN MORGAN EDGE'S OFFICE...

ROCK POWER IS RIGHT! HALF THE COUNTRY WATCHED THAT ON OUR NETWORK! AND SUPERMAN'S STUNT WAS THE SHOW-STOPPER!

BUT I STILL KEEP WONDERING, MR. EDGE, WHAT MADE THAT AUDIENCE GO BERSERK?

FORGET IT, KENT! STAY WITH THOSE ROCK FESTIVALS ON YOUR NEWSCASTS! THEY'RE SWEEPING THE COUNTRY BY STORM!

WHATEVER YOU SAY... HORKIN IS PUTTING ON ANOTHER JAM-BOREE AT STONE MOUNTAIN NEXT WEEK! I'LL COVER IT!

6

THEY'VE BLOWN THEIR MINDS! THEY'RE FIGHTING PITCHED BATTLES FOR SODA POP AND CANTEENS OF WATER!

DRINK, BABY, DRINK IT DOWN!

I'VE GOT TO DO SOMETHING BEFORE THEY KILL EACH OTHER! THERE'S NO OTHER WAY BUT THE OLD SUPERMAN ROUTINE!

LIKE A MIGHTY SUPERSONIC DRILL, THE MAN OF STEEL BORES INTO THE EARTH AGAIN, AND YET AGAIN...

LIKE WOW! SUPERMAN IS RELEASING GEYSERS OF WATER FROM UNDERGROUND STREAMS!

DRINK, BABY, DRINK! WE'VE GOT ALL WE NEED NOW!

SUDDENLY, THE MUSIC STOPS...

I CUT OFF THE AMPLIFIERS WHEN I SAW WHAT WAS GOING ON! HAS EVERYONE GONE CRACKERS?

SEARCH ME, HORKIN! UNDER THESE BUCKETS, YOU DON'T HEAR ANYTHING BUT THE BEAT! WE NEVER TURNED ON ANYONE THIS WAY BEFORE!

HUH? WHAT GIVES? A MINUTE AGO, I WAS READY TO DRINK A RESERVOIR! NOW I CAN'T SWALLOW ANOTHER DROP!

I INHALED ENOUGH TO FLOAT THE QUEEN ELIZABETH!

8

LATER, AFTER *SUPERMAN* RESUMES HIS ROLE OF CLARK...

THAT'S *TWICE* I'VE SEEN YOUR AUDIENCE FLIP THAT WAY, CY! HOW DO YOU EXPLAIN IT?

BECAUSE THAT *ROCK BEAT* HITS THEM WHERE THEY *LIVE*, KENT! MAYBE THAT'S WHY MY FESTS ARE SO POPULAR!

HORKIN COULD BE RIGHT, FOLKS! FANS FLOCK TO HIS FESTIVALS BECAUSE THE MUSIC TURNS THEM ON!

BUT IF CLARK ONLY KNEW WHAT WAS HAPPENING IN A HIDDEN CUBICLE, BACKSTAGE...

HA! IT WAS THIS *ELECTRONIC BRAIN* THAT REALLY SPARKED THE RIOTS! HOOKED INTO THE SOUND SYSTEM, IT CONVERTS THE LYRICS OF ANY SONG INTO AN *IRRESISTIBLE COMMAND* AFFECTING ANYONE LISTENING TO THE *AMPLIFIED MUSIC!*

WHILE THESE EARPHONES PROTECTED *ME*, THE AUDIENCE WAS *FORCED* TO "DRINK" ON COMMAND! THEY ACTED LIKE LEMMINGS, THE RODENTS WHICH DROWN THEMSELVES, COMPELLED BY SOME MYSTERIOUS COMMAND OF NATURE!

THAT'S *TWICE, SUPERMAN* INTERFERED WITH MY TESTS! BUT I'VE PROVED THAT THE *LEMMING EFFECT* WORKS! WITH IT, I CAN BRAINWASH A CROWD,...AND FORCE THEM TO COMMIT THE CRIME OF THE CENTURY!

DAYS LATER, IN HIS ARCTIC FORTRESS...

CY HORKIN WOULDN'T LET CLARK BROADCAST THE MUSIC... BUT I TAPED SOME OF IT SECRETLY FOR ANALYSIS!

HM! MY SONIC ANALYZERS GIVE NO CLUE TO THE AUDIENCE'S WEIRD REACTION!

DRINK, BABY! DRINK IT DOWN!

SUDDENLY...

OH, NO! THAT TAPE RECORDER MUST HAVE BEEN DEFECTIVE! IT SHORT-CIRCUITED, AND RUINED THE TAPE!

FFFZZZZAAAPP

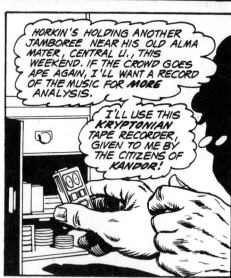

HORKIN'S HOLDING ANOTHER JAMBOREE NEAR HIS OLD ALMA MATER, CENTRAL U., THIS WEEKEND. IF THE CROWD GOES APE AGAIN, I'LL WANT A RECORD OF THE MUSIC FOR MORE ANALYSIS.

I'LL USE THIS KRYPTONIAN TAPE RECORDER, GIVEN TO ME BY THE CITIZENS OF KANDOR!

KANDOR... ONCE A MIGHTY CITY OF MY NATIVE PLANET KRYPTON... BEFORE IT WAS DESTROYED! KANDOR WAS SHRUNKEN INTO THAT BOTTLE BY THE EVIL COMPUTER, BRAINIAC!

SOME DAY, I'LL FIND A WAY TO ENLARGE THE CITY AND MY KINSMEN TO NORMAL SIZE!

BUT, AS EARTH'S GUARDIAN, I HAVE OTHER PROBLEMS RIGHT NOW... LIKE SOLVING THE PUZZLE OF THOSE MOBS WHO GO HAYWIRE AT HORKIN'S PERFORMANCES!

332

YOUR SUPER-BRAIN COULDN'T BE CONTROLLED! YOU ONLY *PRETENDED* TO BE AFFECTED SO WE'D FOLLOW *YOU* AND DEMOLISH THAT ELECTRONIC BRAIN!

A GOOD GUESS!

ACTUALLY, I DIDN'T KNOW HOW THEIR MINDS WERE BEING CONTROLLED UNTIL MOMENTS AGO!

"MY BRAIN IS IMMUNE TO OUTSIDE CONTROL! BUT THEN I LISTENED TO THE *KRYPTONIAN* TAPE RECORDER. AMPLIFIED THROUGH *KRYPTONIAN* ELECTRONICS, THOSE LYRICS BRAINWASHED ME AS EASILY AS IF I WERE AN ORDINARY MORTAL!"

"BUT WHILE WRECKING THAT ABANDONED SUBURB, A FALLING TIMBER KNOCKED MY EARPHONE LOOSE, AND..."

WHAT WAS *THERE* ABOUT THAT MUSIC THAT FORCED ME TO DESTROY?

AHA! MY TELESCOPIC VISION JUST SPOTTED THE RAT IN THE WOODPILE!

AS *SUPERMAN* ENDS HIS BRIEF REVERIE...

HAND OVER THAT HEEL, SUPERMAN! WE'LL ZONK HIM BUT GOOD!

NO! YOU'RE LETTING YOUR ANGER CONTROL YOU...ACTING WITHOUT THOUGHT! BEWARE OF THE *LEMMING EFFECT!*

EVEN *THIS* RAT DESERVES A FAIR TRIAL!

AND SO, WEEKS LATER...

SUPERMAN, MAKE THEM TURN IT OFF! PLEASE, DON'T LET THEM TORTURE ME LIKE THIS!

SORRY, HORKIN, BUT IT SEEMS ALL THE OTHER PRISONERS *LIKE* ROCK MUSIC!

The End

14

AS ROVING TV REPORTER CLARK KENT HEARS A NEWS BULLETIN IN HIS MOBILE TV VAN...

CALLING *SUPERMAN!* SOLAR FURNACE AT *LOOKOUT MOUNTAIN* OUT OF CONTROL! SCIENTISTS FEAR CATASTROPHE!

THERE'S MY CUE AGAIN!

AT SUPER-SPEED, HE FLASHES TO THE SCENE...

SUPERMAN

OUR EXPERIMENTAL SOLAR POWER GENERATOR EXPLODED! *DO SOMETHING, SUPERMAN...* BEFORE THE CHAIN REACTION IGNITES THE ATMOSPHERE AND *TURNS EARTH INTO A BALL OF FLAME!*

B-920

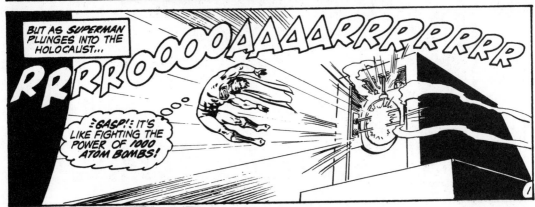

BUT AS *SUPERMAN* PLUNGES INTO THE HOLOCAUST...

RRRROOOOAAAARRRRRRR

:GASP!: IT'S LIKE FIGHTING THE POWER OF *1000* ATOM BOMBS!

337

BUT A STARTLING MOMENT LATER...

ULP! MY X-RAY VISION SHOWS A GENUINE "CONTINENTAL" DOLLAR IN WASHINGTON'S POCKET!

LINCOLN'S CARRYING TWO TICKETS TO THE FORD THEATER...

AND CUSTER'S WEARING BUCKSKINS INSTEAD OF A UNIFORM, JUST AS HISTORY SAID HE DID. THESE MEN ARE THE MCCOY!

FORD THEATER

AND WHAT ARE YOU?... SOME KIND OF CIRCUS PERFORMER? A TRAPEZE ARTIST?

THEY CALL ME SUPERMAN!... I'LL EXPLAIN! YOU SEE I HAVE STRANGE POWERS...ABILITIES BEYOND THOSE OF ORDINARY MORTALS!

STRANGE POWERS? THE POOR DEVIL'S TAKEN LEAVE OF HIS SENSES!

I'LL TELL YOU ABOUT THEM LATER. RIGHT NOW, WE'VE GOT TO FIND OUR WAY OUT OF HERE!

LOOKS LIKE WE'RE IMPRISONED BY A FORCE-FIELD...POSSIBLY THE WORK OF SOME ALIEN INVADERS! BUT I'LL BREAK THROUGH WITH MY SUPER-STRENGTH!

FORCE-FIELD? ALIEN INVADERS? SUPER-STRENGTH?

WHAMMO!

SO MUCH FOR HIS SUPER-HUMAN POWERS! HA-HA!

IN THE NEXT MOMENT...

THE WALL WEAKENED! *I'M BREAKING THROUGH!*

ULP! IT WAS A MISTAKE TO BRING *SUPERMAN* OUT OF THE PAST! HIS SUPER-HUMAN POWERS ARE *IMPOSSIBLE* TO CONTROL!

ALL RIGHT, FRIEND, WHAT'S THE PITCH?

WELCOME TO THE *24TH CENTURY HISTORICAL FOUNDATION!* OUR CHRONO-SELECTOR BROUGHT YOU HERE WITH THE OTHER GREAT HEROES BECAUSE YOU WERE THE *LAST MIGHTY SUPERMAN* OF YOUR ERA!

THE *LAST SUPERMAN ??* IN MY ERA, I AM THE *ONE AND ONLY MAN OF STEEL!*

THE MEMORY BLACKOUT EFFECT! POOR FELLOW!.... SOME OF YOUR MEMORY CELLS WERE ERASED!

PUT ON A CEREBRO-HELMET! A HISTORY TAPE RECORDS THE TRAGIC EVENTS IN YOUR PAST WHICH YOUR BRAIN WAS PRO-GRAMMED TO *FORGET!*

THIS I'VE GOT TO SEE!

"BACK IN THE MIDDLE OF THE 20TH CENTURY, AN INFANT NAMED KAL-EL WAS ROCKETED TO EARTH JUST AS HIS NATIVE PLANET, KRYPTON, EXPLODED!"

I'LL NEVER FORGET THAT GHASTLY DAY!

NATURALLY, YOU DON'T REMEMBER! ALL INCIDENTS REFERRING TO YOUR *REINCARNATIONS* WERE *ERASED* FROM YOUR BRAIN CELLS TO PRESERVE YOUR SELF-CONFIDENCE!

HOWEVER, I HAVE *FINAL PROOF!* COME THIS WAY!

OUR HISTORICAL FOUNDATION WAS BUILT ON THE SITE OF THE OLD RESEARCH INSTITUTE WHICH RECONSTRUCTED YOUR BODY *TWICE! THIS CRYPT WAS YOUR FINAL RESTING PLACE!*

AND IN THE MACABRE DEPTHS OF THE MAUSOLEUM...

THESE ARE THE REMAINS OF *SUPERMAN I!*

SUPERMAN I

SUPERMAN II

AND IN THIS JAR, *SUPERMAN II* IS PRESERVED FOREVER!

AND NOW, THE *PROOF* YOU'VE BEEN ASKING FOR! DO YOU WANT TO SEE IT?

SUPERMAN III

NO! NO! NO!... I-I BELIEVE YOU! HOW COULD I BEAR TO LOOK AT MY *OWN DEAD BODY!*?

BUT YOU DIED A *SUPER-HERO!* SEE, CENTURIES AFTERWARD, WE HONOR YOUR MEMORY WITH THIS MEDAL-- GRANTED ONLY FOR THE *GREATEST COURAGE!*

WEAR IT! YOU EARNED IT A THOUSAND TIMES OVER ON YOUR *FINAL MISSION!*

HOW IRONIC! ACCEPTING A *POSTHUMOUS REWARD...* FOR THE FEAT WHICH KILLED ME!

AS THEY LEAVE THE CRYPT, SUDDENLY...

BLEEP! BLEEP!

THAT SIGNAL...IT'S A VISI-CAST NEWS BULLETIN!

ATTENTION ALL RESCUE SERVICES! THIS IS AN *EMERGENCY ALERT!*

AN ARCHAEOLOGICAL EXPEDITION SEEKING A LOST CIVILIZATION UNDER THE GREENLAND ICE-CAP HAS BEEN BURIED IN AN ICE-QUAKE! FIFTY MEN ARE TRAPPED!

THEY DON'T KNOW IT, BUT THEY'RE PAGING *SUPERMAN!*

DON'T WORRY! I'LL SAVE THEM!... UP...UP AND AWAY!

SUPERMAN'S LEGENDARY CALL TO ACTION! IT HASN'T BEEN HEARD IN *CENTURIES!*

SPLIT-SECONDS LATER, A MILE BENEATH THE ICE-CAP...

WHAMMMO

NO...IT'S A SUPER-BEING... BORING THROUGH THE ICE TO RESCUE US....A *SUPERMAN!*

WH-WHAT IS IT... ANOTHER QUAKE?

KRRRUNNNCHH

KAPPOWWW

BUT SUPERMAN DIED CENTURIES AGO!

10

SOON, BACK AT THE *HISTORICAL FOUNDATION*...

HE NOT ONLY RESCUED THE EXPEDITION, BUT UNCOVERED THE *LOST CIVILIZATION!*

NOW WE *KNOW* WHAT IT MEANS TO HAVE A *SUPERMAN* AS EARTH'S GUARDIAN!

PRESENTLY...

SUPERMAN... HOW CAN WE THANK YOU?

BY ANSWERING *ONE* QUESTION!... FIRST TELL ME IF I HAVE IT FIGURED RIGHT!

LINCOLN IS HEADED FOR THE THEATER WHERE HE'LL BE *ASSASSINATED!* CUSTER IS BOUND FOR HIS FAMOUS *"LAST STAND"!* AND WASHINGTON IS ABOUT TO DIE OF *PNEUMONIA!*

CORRECT! WE SELECTED EACH HERO AT THE *END* OF HIS CAREER!

THEN WHAT ABOUT *ME?* TELL ME...*HOW* AM I SUPPOSED TO DIE?

IF YOU MUST KNOW...ACCORDING TO HISTORY, YOU WILL PERISH WHEN YOU SAVE THE EARTH FROM A CATASTROPHIC EXPLOSION CAUSED BY A NEW FORM OF ENERGY!

SUDDENLY...

THE ALARM! *TIME'S UP!* YOU MUST GO BACK INTO THE FORCE-FIELD! YOU AND THE OTHERS MUST BE RETURNED INTO THE PAST!

BEEP BEEP BEEP

NO! WHY SHOULD I GO *TO DIE?* I'M STAYING *HERE!*

345

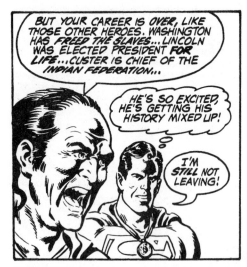

BUT YOUR CAREER IS *OVER,* LIKE THOSE OTHER HEROES. WASHINGTON HAS *FREED THE SLAVES...* LINCOLN WAS ELECTED PRESIDENT *FOR LIFE...* CUSTER IS CHIEF OF THE *INDIAN FEDERATION...*

HE'S SO EXCITED, HE'S GETTING HIS HISTORY MIXED UP!

I'M *STILL NOT* LEAVING!

LISTEN!... THE SECOND AND *FINAL* WARNING!

OO EEEEE EEEEE

HOW WOOOO WWWW

BY THE NATURAL LAWS OF TIME AND SPACE, YOU *MUST* RETURN TO YOUR *PLACE* IN THE PAST... *OR OUR UNIVERSE WILL BE DESTROYED!*

WHILE YOU AND THE OTHERS ARE HERE, THE TIME-FLOW HAS STOPPED COMPLETELY IN YOUR ERA! BACK THERE, HISTORY CAN'T GO ON WITHOUT YOU! IT'S DAMMED UP LIKE A RAGING RIVER!

THE FEEDBACK OF SPATIO-TEMPORAL FORCES IS BUILDING UP TO *CATASTROPHE!* IF THE PAST HAS CEASED, THERE CAN BE NO PRESENT! ALREADY OUR WORLD'S BEGINNING TO *DISSOLVE INTO PURE ENERGY!*

GO BACK... OR *BILLIONS* WILL DIE!

THE BLOOD OF COUNTLESS PEOPLE WOULD BE ON MY HANDS! I MUST RETURN... *THOUGH IT MEANS MY LIFE!*

HE'S LEAVING... THERE'S STILL TIME TO ACTIVATE THE RETRO-CIRCUIT!

12

BUT ON HIS RETURN TO EARTH...

I DON'T UNDERSTAND! I'M STILL ALIVE! BUT THIS MISSION WAS SUPPOSED TO MEAN MY DEATH! THE RECORDS OF THE 24TH CENTURY PROVED IT! I EVEN SAW MY OWN TOMB!

MY DEATH MADE ME A HERO IN THE FUTURE. THIS MEDALLION PROVES IT!

HOLD IT! MY MICROSCOPIC VISION INDICATES THERE'S NO METAL LIKE THIS ON EARTH!

AND THAT TWISTED HISTORY THEY WERE SPOUTING... ABOUT WASHINGTON FREEING THE SLAVES... AND LINCOLN ELECTED PRESIDENT FOR LIFE...

THERE'S ONLY ONE WAY IT ADDS UP!

YES, I WAS IN THE FUTURE-- THE FUTURE OF A PARALLEL WORLD... A WORLD LIKE OUR OWN, BUT IN ANOTHER DIMENSION!

"IT'S LIKE AN IMAGE OF OUR UNIVERSE, SEEN IN A WARPED MIRROR. EACH HERO OF OUR WORLD HAS A DUPLICATE IN THE PARALLEL EXISTENCE. BUT THEIR LIVES AND FATES DIFFER!"

"THAT EXPERIMENTAL CHRONO-SELECTOR WARPED THE FORCES OF TIME AND SPACE SO BADLY, IT TORE AN OPENING IN *OUR* WORLD AND ACCIDENTALLY PULLED ME INTO *THEIR* FUTURE INSTEAD OF THEIR *SUPERMAN III*!"

LATER, AS *SUPERMAN* SWITCHES TO CLARK...

WASHINGTON... AND THE OTHERS I MET... WERE THEY FROM *OUR* HISTORY OR FROM THE HISTORY OF THAT *TWIN EARTH*? I'LL *NEVER* KNOW!

WHATEVER THE ANSWER, IT'S *GREAT* TO BE ALIVE AND WELL... BACK IN...

...MY OWN ERA... IN MY OWN WORLD!

BUT SOMEWHERE, IN ANOTHER CORNER OF TIME AND SPACE, MY *DOUBLE,* *SUPERMAN III,* LIES DEAD-- A HERO *ENSHRINED* FOREVER!

The End.

SUPERMAN

ROCKETED AS A BABY FROM THE EXPLODING PLANET KRYPTON, KAL-EL GREW TO MANHOOD ON EARTH--WHOSE YELLOW SUN AND LIGHTER GRAVITY GAVE HIM FANTASTIC SUPER-POWERS! IN THE CITY OF METROPOLIS, HE POSES AS MILD-MANNERED NEWSMAN CLARK KENT--BUT BATTLES EVIL ALL OVER EARTH-- AND BEYOND AS ...

Created by
JERRY SIEGEL &
JOE SHUSTER

...AND THANKS TO SUPERMAN, THE QUEEN DORY WAS PULLED AWAY FROM THE KILLER TYPHOON INTACT-- WITHOUT A SINGLE CASUALTY AMONG THE LINER'S PASSENGERS...

...THOUGH THERE WERE A NUMBER OF REPORTS OF SEA-SICKNESS BY THE TIME THE MAN OF STEEL TOWED THE VESSEL INTO PORT!

WHEN A MAN HAS JOURNEYED TO DISTANT PLANETS AND STRANGE DIMENSIONS, FACED WEAPONS OF THE FUTURE AND SORCERY OF THE PAST, IT TAKES A LOT TO SURPRISE HIM! BUT "SURPRISE" IS A MILD WORD FOR THE SENSATION SUPERMAN FEELS WHEN FACED WITH ...

S-3328

The MIRACULOUS RETURN of JONATHAN KENT!

WRITER: CARY BATES
LETTERER: MILT SNAPINN
PENCILLER: CURT SWAN
COLORIST: GENE D'ANGELO
INKER: FRANK CHIARAMONTE
EDITOR: JULIUS SCHWARTZ

6:59 P.M. -- SIGN-OFF TIME FOR THE WGBS 6 O'CLOCK NEWS...

...AND SO, ON THURSDAY, MARCH 6TH, 1980...THIS IS LANA LANG --

--AND CLARK KENT, FOR WGBS-- HOPING YOUR NEWS ISN'T BAD NEWS! THANK YOU AND GOOD NIGHT!

GREAT JOB! SEE YOU BOTH TOMORROW--SAME TIME, SAME STATION!

WITH CORN LIKE THAT, MR. JOSH COYLE, I CAN SEE WHY YOU'RE STAYING INSIDE YOUR DIRECTOR'S BOOTH TONIGHT!

AND AS ONE OF THE CO-ANCHORS IS ABOUT TO MAKE A QUIET EXIT...

CRIME IN THE CITY HAS BEEN ON THE UPSWING LATELY! MIGHT BE A GOOD IDEA IF I WORKED IN SOME EXTRA PATROL-TIME TONIGHT!

♪ OH, CLA-RK... ♪

...HOPE YOU HAVEN'T MADE PLANS THIS EVENING, LUV-- BECAUSE THERE'S A TABLE FOR THREE WAITING FOR US AT MARCEL'S!

ER... I SORT OF HAD PLANS, LANA --

--DID YOU SAY A TABLE FOR THREE?

UH-HUH! BUT DON'T EXPECT ME TO TELL YOU WHO'S GOING TO JOIN US! MY MYSTERY GUEST HASN'T SEEN YOU IN A LONG TIME -- AND WANTS TO SURPRISE YOU!

LANA LOOKS DELIGHTED WITH HERSELF... I MIGHT AS WELL FORGET ABOUT THINKING UP A WAY TO BACK OUT OF HER INVITATION!

NO MATTER WHAT MY EXCUSE MIGHT BE... IT WOULDN'T MATTER! WHEN LANA DECIDES SHE'S GOING TO HAVE HER WAY-- SHE'LL TAKE NOTHING LESS THAN YES FOR AN ANSWER!

OH, TAXI!

I'D THINK YOU'D AT LEAST BE A BIT *CURIOUS* ABOUT WHO'S WAITING FOR US INSIDE! AREN'T YOU EVEN GOING TO ASK FOR ONE ITTY-BITTY HINT?

GOSH, *NO!* I WOULDN'T WANT *ANYTHING* TO SPOIL THE SURPRISE!

MARCEL'S

;YAWN; I HAVEN'T EVEN BOTHERED TO CHECK OUT THE TABLE *IN ADVANCE* WITH *SUPER-VISION!*

GUESS I'M JUST NOT IN THE *MOOD* FOR *INTRIGUE* TONIGHT!

BON SOIR, ANDRÉ!

GOOD EVENING, MLLE. LANG! YOUR OTHER *GUEST* HAS ALREADY *ARRIVED!*

YES, ANDRÉ, I *SEE* HIM!

WELL, CLARK--CARE TO MAKE A LAST-SECOND GUESS?

ODD... THE *BACK* OF THAT MAN'S *HEAD* LOOKS VERY *FAMILIAR!*

WELL, HERE HE IS, CLARK--MY *MYSTERY GUEST!* I'M *SURE* HE NEEDS NO *INTRODUCTION!*

GREAT *SCOTT!* IF I DIDN'T *KNOW BETTER*--I'D *SWEAR* I'M STANDING FACE-TO-FACE WITH MY *FOSTER FATHER*--JONATHAN KENT!

IT SURE IS *SWELL* TO SEE YOU AGAIN, *SON!*

OH, I KNOW--WE KEEP UP MORE THAN OUR SHARE OF *LETTERS* AND *PHONE CALLS*... BUT THEY CAN'T COMPARE TO THE *REAL THING!*

3

FOR A FLEETING INSTANT, THE SHOCK AND THE PRESENT FADE FROM CLARK'S MIND--AS HE RECALLS A TRAGIC DAY FROM SMALLVILLE AND THE PAST....

FIRST *MOM KENT* A FEW DAYS AGO....AND NOW *DAD!* EVEN WITH MY *SUPER-POWERS*, I COULDN'T *SAVE* THEM!

IF YOU'LL NOTICE, THE *LADY* HAS TAKEN HER *SEAT!* LET'S *SETTLE DOWN* FOR A *GREAT EVENING!*

IF THIS WAS *YOUR* IDEA, LANA...*CONGRATULATE* YOURSELF. EVEN *STEVE LOMBARD* COULDN'T HAVE COME UP WITH A SICKER, MORE *TASTELESS* PRACTICAL JOKE!

NOW....CLARK--THIS GET-TOGETHER WAS *MY* IDEA! I CALLED LANA THIS AFTERNOON, SOON AS THE TRAIN FROM *SMALLVILLE* PULLED INTO *METRO-CENTRAL STATION!*

GREAT SUNS! ACCORDING TO MY *SUPER-HEARING*, LANA'S STEADY PULSE-BEAT INDICATES SHE *REALLY BELIEVES* THIS IS *JONATHAN KENT!*

"...BUT LANA SHOULD KNOW BETTER, TOO--SHE GREW UP NEXT DOOR TO US IN *SMALLVILLE*."

"...AND SHE WAS STANDING BESIDE ME AT MY *PARENTS' FUNERAL*--A FEW WEEKS BEFORE WE BOTH LEFT FOR *COLLEGE!*"

WHOEVER THIS *IMPOSTOR* IS--HE MUST HAVE SOME SORT OF *HYPNOTIC CONTROL* OVER LANA! IT'S THE ONLY THING THAT MAKES SENSE!

I HOPE YOU DIDN'T MIND ME *ORDERING* FOR YOU, SON? YOUR LETTERS MENTIONED THAT *BOEUF BOURGUIGNON* IS YOUR *FAVORITE* DISH THESE DAYS...

...AND LANA ASSURES ME THE BOURGUIGNON THEY SERVE IS *FIRST RATE!*

I PROPOSE A *TOAST*-- TO *FATHER-AND-SON REUNIONS!*

THE OLD COOT HAS DONE HIS *HOMEWORK* ON ME.... BUT I'LL *EXPOSE* HIM BEFORE THE WAITER BRINGS OUR *HORS D'OEUVRES!*

AT THAT VERY MOMENT, SEVERAL BLOCKS AWAY...

CAREFUL, HUBERT-- THERE'S ONE OF THOSE AWFUL PANHANDLERS ASKING FOR A HANDOUT!

I'LL AVOID HIM, ANDREA!

HI, THERE--MY NAME'S STARSHINE...AND I'M TRYIN' TO RUSTLE UP SOME BREAD FOR A TICKET TO L.A.!

CAN YOU SPARE ANY CHANGE, MAN?

YOU WANT SOME "BREAD"... YOU WANT A TICKET TO L.A.... THEN GO GET A JOB!

"STARSHINE" MY CLAVICLE! WHEN ARE THESE SHIFTLESS HIPPIES GOING TO LEARN NOBODY GETS A FREE RIDE IN THIS LIFE?

OKY-DOKY, YOU TWO! I TRIED DEALIN' WITH YOU THE NICE WAY!

NOW I'M GONNA HAVE TO BE NOT-SO-NICE!

BOTH OF YOU... GIVE ME ALL YOUR VALUABLES...

...OOO PLEASE!

EEEK! MY JEWELRY! MY MINK!

MY WATCH... MY WALLET-- FLYING INTO HIS HANDS!

5

THANKS TO YOUR GENEROSITY, I CAN NOW AFFORD A FIRST-CLASS SEAT ON A JETLINER!

DON'T WORRY ABOUT ME HAVIN' A GUILT-TRIP, YOU TWO--I KNOW YOU FOLKS KEEP YOUR INSURANCE PAID UP!

STAY COOL-- AND HAVE A NICE NIGHT!

WHY, THAT IMPUDENT UPSTART! DON'T JUST STAND THERE, HUBERT--GO AFTER HIM!

WITH MY HIGH BLOOD-PRESSURE? I'M CALLING THE POLICE!

WHILE AT THE RESTAURANT...

...YES, INDEED... THOSE WERE THE DAYS! I'M SURE "PA" CAN NEVER FORGET THE TIME YOU AND I BROUGHT THAT INJURED RABBIT HOME, LANA-- REMEMBER?

LIKE IT WAS YESTERDAY, CLARK--EVEN THOUGH WE WERE ONLY TEN YEARS OLD AT THE TIME!

MARCEL'S

INJURED RABBIT...? YOU WERE ONLY TEN, YOU SAY...?

SURELY THAT COULDN'T HAVE SLIPPED YOUR MIND, MR. KENT?

NOW I HAVE HIM! THERE'S NO WAY THIS IMPOSTOR COULD HAVE POSSIBLY RESEARCHED SOMETHING SO OBSCURE!

AH, YES... NOW IT'S COMING BACK TO ME!

THAT RABBIT-- WHICH CLARK NAMED... "MR. MICKEY", AS I RECALL--HAPPENED TO BE A MRS.-- AND MORE THAN READY TO DELIVER!

THAT MONTH OUR GARAGE BECAME A NURSERY FOR SIX BABY BUNNIES!

YOU WERE SO SWEET ABOUT IT, MR. KENT! YOU EVEN BUILT A LITTLE PEN FOR THEM TO PLAY IN!

; SLURP ; HOW COULD HE HAVE POSSIBLY KNOWN?

ONCE AGAIN, LANA'S PULSE-BEAT PROVES SHE'S NOT IN CAHOOTS WITH HIM ON THIS!

6

NEARBY, AT A 24 HOURS-A-DAY BANK...

HEY, MAN-- I'M NOT LOOKIN' FOR A HASSLE!

I KNOW-- YOU CAME IN LOOKING FOR A HANDOUT! YOU MIGHT THINK ASKING A BANK GUARD IF HE CAN SPARE ANY CHANGE IS A REAL LAUGH-RIOT --

ALL NIGHT METRO-CARD DEPOSIT AND WITHDRAWAL

--BUT WE DON'T "DIG" YOUR KIND OF "ANIMAL HOUSE" HUMOR!

ONE MORE PIECE OF ADVICE, PUNK-- GO TAKE A BATH!

I TRIED... I REALLY TRIED THAT TIME... BUT EVEN ON MY BEST BEHAVIOR, THEY TREAT ME LIKE DIRT!

PLOP

SO NOW IT'S INSTANT-KARMA TIME! THOSE TURKEYS ARE GONNA GET BACK THE KIND OF TREATMENT THEY DESERVE!

HEAR ME, METRO-BANK! GIVE ME ALL YOUR MONEY--

...PLE-ASE!

AND BETWEEN THE MAIN COURSE AND DESSERT --CLARK KENT'S ASTONISHMENT MOUNTS WITH EVERY HEARTBEAT...

I'M SEEING THE IMPOSSIBLE WITH MY OWN MICROSCOPIC VISION --AND I STILL CAN'T BELIEVE MY SUPER-EYES!

THOSE ARE DEFINITELY PA KENT'S FINGERPRINTS! I'D RECOGNIZE THEM ANYWHERE-- THERE'S NO MISTAKE!

CAN I REALLY BE SITTING ACROSS FROM --A LIVING, BREATHING GHOST?

ANDRÉ, MON CHER-- WHAT'S ALL THE COMMOTION, OUTSIDE?

PERHAPS ANOTHER GRAY LIBERATION MARCH, MLLE. LANG! THE SENIOR CITIZENS IN THE AREA HAVE BEEN MOST VOCAL OF LATE IN THEIR PROTESTS OVER AGE DISCRIMINATION!

7

YOU HAVE *SOMETHING* AGAINST *GRAY LIB,* SIR?

OH, *NON,* MONSIEUR! SOME OF OUR BEST PATRONS ARE... UH...*OLDER TYPES!*

GREAT SUNS! MY X-RAY VISION REVEALS THE COMMOTION IS A FANTASTIC *BANK ROBBERY* TWO BLOCKS AWAY!

I'VE GOT TO COME UP WITH AN *INSTANT EXCUSE* TO LEAVE THE TABLE.... WITHOUT REKINDLING LANA'S OLD *SUSPICIONS!*

I KNOW WHAT I'LL DO --

MR. KENT,,, IS ANYTHING *WRONG* --?

UHH...,IT'S JUST MY ULCER KICKING UP A LITTLE! I GUESS THE BEEF BOURGUIGNON WAS TOO RICH FOR ME!

I TAKE PILLS TO RELIEVE THE PAIN,,, BUT --

--I'M ALL OUT! SON, I GOT THIS *PRE-SCRIPTION* FILLED AT THAT *DRUG STORE* DOWN THE STREET ON MY LAST VISIT! WOULD YOU *MIND...?*

NOT AT ALL, DAD! I'LL GET IT *REFILLED* FOR YOU!

I-I CAN'T *BELIEVE* THIS IS REALLY HAPPENING! IT COULDN'T BE MERE *COINCIDENCE* --

THE REPORTER MAKES A SWIFT EXIT-- HIS FACE ONLY PARTIALLY MASKING THE STARK AND UTTER ASTONISHMENT NOW CHILLING EVERY INCH OF HIS *SUPER-SPINE...*

THIS PRESCRIPTION IS *AUTHENTIC*,,, BUT IT WAS ORIGINALLY FILLED OUT IN *SMALLVILLE*-- OVER *TWENTY* YEARS AGO!

MY MICROSCOPIC VISION JUST *CONFIRMED* THE AGE OF THE YELLOWED LABEL!

BACK IN THE OLD DAYS-- EVEN AFTER DAD KENT'S ULCER CLEARED UP, HE ALWAYS CARRIED THIS EMPTY *PILL BOTTLE* AROUND-- IN CASE I NEEDED A QUICK *EXCUSE* TO *LEAVE* AND SWITCH TO *SUPERBOY!*

AFTERWARD I'D BRING IT BACK "*FILLED*" WITH *HARMLESS SUGAR PILLS!*

ONLY *NOW* IT'S A JOB FOR *SUPERMAN!* HE MUST'VE *READ* THE SUDDEN *CONCERN* ON MY FACE AND FIGURED I NEEDED TO *GET AWAY*-- JUST LIKE *OLD TIMES!*

I HAD WORKED OUT AN EXCUSE OF MY OWN, BUT I'M STILL A *BOY* TO PA-- GREAT *KRYPTON*-- WHAT AM I *SAYING*?

10

NEXT MOMENT, AS INVISIBLE TWIN BEAMS OF TELESCOPIC VISION SHOOT OUT OF THE BOAT AND BEYOND THE HORIZON...

THE COAST OF CHINA IS 200 MILES FROM HERE....AND AT A SLOW BOAT'S SPEED, IT'LL TAKE A FULL DAY TO REACH PORT!

BUT NOT IF I CAN HELP IT ALONG!

AND AFTER SUPERMAN APOLOGIZES* FOR HIS UNANNOUNCED ARRIVAL -- AND ASKS HIS HOSTS THEIR DESTINATION...

I'M ASSUMING THAT ONCE WE REACH CHINA--I'LL HAVE FULFILLED THE COMMAND...AND BE FREE TO FLY HOME!

*CHINESE IS ONE OF THOUSANDS OF EARTHLY AND INTERPLANETARY LANGUAGES AT SUPERMAN'S COMMAND!--JULIE

WITH A STEADY STREAM OF SUPER-BREATH FILLING THE SAILS -- WE'LL BE SIGHTING LAND SHORTLY!

是回寒冽

用我奔捉

WHAT A WEIRD DAY THIS HAS BEEN!

FIRST I MEET A 70-YEAR-OLD MAN WHO PROFESSES TO BE MY FOSTER FATHER --

--AND THEN I FIND MYSELF PITTED AGAINST A FELLOW WHO HAS THE POWER TO SEND ME HURTLING HALF-WAY AROUND THE WORLD...JUST BY OPENING HIS MOUTH!

YES, SIR... SOME DAY!

ONCE IN CHINA, SUPERMAN TAKES OFF AGAIN WITH A GIGANTIC LEAP ALL THE WAY BACK TO METROPOLIS...

...AND THEN--LIKE MAGIC--THE MONEY WAS BACK IN THE BANK... JUST LIKE THE KID TOLD US IT WOULD BE!

WHEN WE GRABBED HIM, HE MUTTERED SOMETHING UNDER HIS BREATH AND LEFT US EMPTY-HANDED!

YOU CAN SEE THE REPLAY ON THE ELEVEN O'CLOCK WGBS NEWS! LANA LANG AND HER CAMERAMAN ARRIVED JUST IN TIME TO CATCH THIS STARSHINE CHARACTER PULLING HIS VANISHING ACT!

THAT'S SOME CONSOLATION, AT LEAST! LANA MUST'VE LEFT MARCEL'S IN A HURRY...

...THE MOMENT SHE FOUND OUT THERE WAS A BIG STORY BREAKING JUST DOWN THE STREET--

--WHICH SAVED MY FATH--ER...THE OLD MAN THE TROUBLE OF EXPLAINING WHY CLARK TOOK SO LONG WITH HIS PRESCRIPTION!

AFTER AN X-RAY VISION SCAN OF THE POSH RESTAURANT TWO BLOCKS AWAY...

NO SIGN OF HIM IN MARCEL'S! HE MUST'VE PAID THE CHECK AND LEFT!

NO TELLING WHERE HE MIGHT TURN UP NEXT! BUT WHEN AND IF HE DOES, I'LL BE READY...

MARCEL'S

...WITH UNDENIABLE PROOF THAT THE "JONATHAN KENT" WHO'S DISRUPTED MY LIFE IS NOTHING BUT A BALD-PATED PHONEY!

AND NOW... A HURRY-UP TRIP TO...

"...THE SMALLVILLE CEMETERY!"

SMALLVILLE CEMETERY

ORPHEUM

SMALLVILLE ORPHEUM

I COULD HAVE DONE THIS FROM THE AIR WITH MY TELESCOPIC VISION... BUT IT WAS TIME FOR ME TO PAY MY RESPECTS TO MA AND PA KENT ANYWAY!

SOMETHING NO ONE MUST EVER SEE SUPERMAN DOING!

J. CAPP

BUT WHEN CLARK REACHES A CERTAIN OF SECTION OF THE CEMETERY...

N-NO! GOOD LORD-- NO!

THERE SHOULD BE TWO GRAVES HERE! JONATHAN WAS LAID TO REST NEXT TO HIS WIFE, MARTHA!

IS THE WHOLE WORLD GOING INSANE... OR JUST ME?

MARTHA CLARK KENT

AND A MILE DOWN THE ROAD--321 MAPLE STREET--THE HOUSE WHERE SUPERBOY GREW TO EXTRAORDINARY MANHOOD...

CHIEF PARKER SHOULD BE STAYING HERE-- TAKING CARE OF THE HOUSE, AS HE HAS SINCE HIS RETIREMENT FROM THE POLICE FORCE!

BUT THERE'S NO SIGN OF HIS BELONGINGS-- WHILE PA KENT'S ARE HERE, AS THOUGH HE'S BEEN USING THEM RECENTLY!

J. KENT

ALL THESE LETTERS... POSTMARKED METROPOLIS AND DATING BACK A DECADE, ADDRESSED TO JONATHAN KENT!

IT'S NOT ETHICAL TO READ OTHER PEOPLE'S MAIL,... BUT THAT PRINCIPLE HARDLY APPLIES HERE--

--SINCE EVERY LETTER APPEARS TO BE FROM ME... WRITTEN IN MY OWN HANDWRITING... FILLED WITH PERSONAL DETAILS ONLY I COULD'VE PUT DOWN ON PAPER!

April 7, 1975

Dear Dad,
Sorry I couldn't stop by last weekend, but there was an emergency JLA meeting.

NOT ONLY CAN'T I UNDERSTAND WHAT'S GOING ON,... I CAN'T EVEN BEGIN TO RATIONALIZE WHY THIS HAS HAPPENED...OR HOW!

YET THE EVIDENCE ADDS UP TO THE SAME MIRACULOUS CONCLUSION--

--MY FATHER IS ALIVE,...AND WELL ...AND STILL LIVING IN SMALLVILLE!!

14

AND SPEAKING OF JONATHAN KENT--BACK IN METROPOLIS...

'SCUSE ME, COULD YOU GIVE ME DIRECTIONS? I'M LOOKING FOR 344 CLINTON STREET... THAT'S WHERE MY SON LIVES!

YA HEAR THE MAN, JIGGER? HE WANTS TO VISIT HIS SON!

GOL-LEE! I'M ALL CHOKED UP!

W-WHAT ARE YOU DOING?

WE'RE GONNA GIVE YOU DIRECTIONS, POPS--'CEPT THERE'S GONNA BE A FEE INVOLVED!

STEP INTO OUR "OFFICE"!

AS FOR 344 CLINTON-- YOU'RE LEANING AGAINST THE BACK OF IT!

NOW PAY UP! HAND OVER YOUR WALLET!

NOTHING DOING! YOU HOOLIGANS DON'T FRIGHTEN ME!

SUDDENLY...

WHAT THE HEY--?

WHERE'D THAT WIND COME FROM?

WHOOOOSHHH

"WIND" MY EYE...

...THAT WAS A LIFE-SAVING BLAST OF SUPER-BREATH!

S-S-S-SUPERMAN!

MY...MY...I DIDN'T KNOW YOU GUYS STUTTERED!

16

AND, ON THE THIRD FLOOR OF 344 CLINTON STREET--APARTMENT 3-D--THE RESIDENCE OF CLARK KENT...

IT WAS *LUCKY* FOR *ME* YOU DECIDED TO FLY *HOME* WHEN YOU *DID*, SON! I GUESS I DIDN'T ACT VERY *SMART* WITH THOSE *MUGGERS*...

...BUT LOW-LIFES LIKE THOSE TWO ALWAYS *DID* RILE ME SOMETHING *FIERCE!*

SON... ARE YOU *FEELING* OKAY?

344 CLINT

YOU'RE STANDING THERE WITH THE ODDEST SMILE...

IT'S *HIM*...IT'S REALLY *HIM!* THERE'S NOT A SHRED OF DOUBT LEFT IN MY MIND ANY MORE!

WHAT'S WRONG WITH THAT? CAN'T A *SUPER*-SON BE HAPPY TO SEE HIS FATHER?

WELCOME TO *METROPOLIS*, PA! I MAY BE A LITTLE *CONFUSED* RIGHT NOW... BUT I'M SO VERY *GLAD* YOU AND I ARE *TOGETHER* AGAIN!

ME, TOO, CLARK... ME, TOO!

AT THAT VERY MOMENT, JUST OUTSIDE THE CITY LIMITS --A SANDY-HAIRED YOUNG MAN SHOUTS A STRANGE PROCLAMATION INTO THE AIR...

LISTEN UP, METROPOLIS-- I'M TALKING TO ALL YOU *OVER-THIRTY* TYPES!

THIS IS *STARSHINE* SPEAKING... THE *SUPREME RULER* OF THE *YOUTH GENERATION!*

YOU *ADULTS* HAVE *HASSLED* US FOR THE *LAST* TIME-- NOW I'M TAKING COMMAND OF THE CITY!

EVERYONE OVER THIRTY-- GET OUT OF METROPOLIS AND STAY OUT--

"--PLEASE!"

THERE YOU HAVE IT, READER! A YOUNG MAN WHO POSSESSES THE EXTRAORDINARY POWER TO HAVE HIS EVERY COMMAND OBEYED! AND AN ELDERLY MAN WHO INEXPLICABLY SEEMS TO HAVE DEFIED DEATH!

TWO INCREDIBLE PUZZLES WITH *ONE* UNIMAGINABLE ANSWER! BE HERE NEXT ISSUE FOR --

"THE SECRET WORLD OF JONATHAN KENT!"

ROCKETED AS A BABY FROM THE EXPLODING PLANET *KRYPTON*, *KAL-EL* GREW TO MANHOOD ON *EARTH*-- WHOSE YELLOW SUN AND LIGHTER GRAVITY GAVE HIM FANTASTIC *SUPER-POWERS!* IN THE CITY OF *METROPOLIS*, HE POSES AS MILD-MANNERED NEWSMAN *CLARK KENT*-- BUT BATTLES EVIL ALL OVER *EARTH*--AND *BEYOND*--AS...

SUPERMAN

Created by
JERRY SIEGEL &
JOE SHUSTER

JONATHAN KENT, KINDLY FOSTER-FATHER TO *CLARK* (*SUPERBOY*) *KENT*, TRAGICALLY *DIED* MANY YEARS AGO... AND WAS *BURIED* NEXT TO HIS WIFE, MARTHA KENT-- *TRUE* OR *FALSE?*

CLARK (*SUPERMAN*) KENT AND HIS FOSTER-FATHER, *JONATHAN KENT*, STOP BY *MARTHA KENT'S* GRAVE TO PAY THEIR RESPECTS! THE TIME IS *1980*... AND *JONATHAN KENT* IS NOW A SPRY *70*-YEAR-OLD WIDOWER WHO NEVER REMARRIED-- *TRUE* OR *FALSE?*

THE *ASTONISHING ANSWER* IS REVEALED IN:

"The SECRET WORLD of JONATHAN KENT!"

6-3334-

WRITER: *CARY BATES* • PENCILLER: *CURT SWAN* • INKER: *FRANK CHIARAMONTE*
LETTERER: *BEN ODA* • COLORIST: *GENE D'ANGELO* • EDITOR: *JULIUS SCHWARTZ*

...AND ONCE EVERY WEEK SINCE SHE PASSED AWAY...I'VE BEEN COMING HERE TO THE CEMETERY TO PUT FRESH FLOWERS ON YOUR MOTHER'S GRAVE...

MARTHA CLARK KENT BORN ... DIED ...

...AND IN ALL THESE YEARS, SON, I HAVEN'T MISSED A SINGLE VISIT!

CHOKE IT PAINS ME SOMETHING FIERCE TO KEEP UP THIS PRETENSE IN FRONT OF CLARK...BUT I HAVE NO CHOICE!

MARTHA CLARK KENT

THE GROUND RULES FOR THIS INCREDIBLE VISIT WERE SPELLED OUT FOR ME IN NO UNCERTAIN TERMS!

I AM FORBIDDEN TO LET CLARK KNOW THE TRUTH ABOUT MY VISIT...ABOUT HOW AND WHY I'M HERE!

MYSTIFIED, READER? YOU'VE BEEN TOLD THAT JONATHAN KENT PASSED AWAY YEARS AGO...ONLY DAYS AFTER THE DEATH OF MARTHA KENT...

THEN HOW HAS HE SEEMINGLY DEFIED HIS OWN DEATH? WHY IS THERE NO TRACE OF HIS GRAVE ALONGSIDE HIS WIFE'S? AND WHAT ABOUT HIS ADVANCED AGE--AS IF JONATHAN KENT WERE STILL ALIVE AND GROWING OLDER WHILE HIS SUPER-SON HAD BEEN GROWING UP!

ALL OF THEM MIND-SHATTERING IMPOSSIBILITIES--AND YET...

...THERE IS A RATIONAL EXPLANATION--AS YOU WILL SOON FIND OUT!

AND THANKS AGAIN FOR SHOWING ME THAT FORTRESS OF SOLITUDE OF YOURS THIS MORNING! BUT IT'S AWFULLY BIG FOR JUST ONE PERSON, DON'T YOU THINK?

SPIT IT OUT, DAD! WEREN'T WE ALWAYS ABLE TO LEVEL WITH EACH OTHER?

WELL, IT'S JUST-- YOU KNOW...WITH ALL THAT ROOM...DOESN'T IT GET A TOUCH LONELY AFTER AWHILE...WITHOUT SOMEONE ELSE TO SHARE IT WITH?

SO THAT IS WHAT'S ON YOUR MIND!

2

NEXT STOP--*METROPOLIS*--AND CLARK KENT'S *APARTMENT* AT 344 CLINTON STREET, WHERE A FIGURE OF *RED* AND *BLUE* ZOOMS TOWARD A THIRD-FLOOR WINDOW...

TO TELL THE TRUTH, SON -- BY *NOW* I WOULD'VE EXPECTED YOU AND *LANA LANG* TO HAVE...

344 CLINTON

...WELL... *YOU KNOW* WHAT I MEAN! BACK IN YOUR *HIGH SCHOOL* DAYS, YOU TWO WERE PRACTICALLY *INSEPARABLE!*

THAT WAS *SMALLVILLE,* DAD! I'M NOT THE *SAME PERSON* I WAS BACK THEN... AND NEITHER IS *LANA!*

WE'RE *GOOD FRIENDS* NOW-- BUT THAT'S *ALL* WE ARE!

DING DONG

MR. KENT! MR. KENT!

WHY DON'T *YOU* ANSWER IT, PA!

GOT IT! SO YOU CAN MAKE A *SUPER-SPEED* WARDROBE CHANGE, RIGHT?

WELL, WHADYA KNOW! *TWINS*-- AND A FETCHING PAIR OF *BEAUTIES* AT THAT!

OH, MY GOODNESS! LOOK HOW *OLD* HE IS!

IT'S *IMPOSSIBLE* FOR HIM TO BE *HERE!*

ER... *DAD*... THESE ARE TWO OF MY NEIGHBORS, THE *MARIGOLD* TWINS, *APRIL* AND *MAY!*

GIRLS, THIS IS MY *DAD*-- HE'S IN FROM *SMALLVILLE* FOR A VISIT!

WHAT DID YOU MEAN, CHILD-- ABOUT IT BEING *IMPOSSIBLE* FOR ME TO BE *HERE?*

YOU TWO *HAVEN'T HEARD* YET? *WHERE* HAVE YOU BEEN? IT'S BEEN GETTING FULL COVERAGE ON *TV* AND *RADIO!* LISTEN--

... AND THOUGH SOME OF THE COUNTRY'S FINEST *SCIENTIFIC MINDS* ARE HERE AT OUR LOCAL *S.T.A.R. LABORATORIES*...

③

LOOK AT THAT, SON -- IT'S *LANA!*

SHH, PA -- SHE MUST BE *FILLING IN* FOR *JEB ROLLAND,* THE VETERAN *WGBS* MORNING NEWSCASTER!

...NONE OF THE *YOUNGER* RESIDENT GENIUSES WHO ARE *LEFT* CAN OFFER ANY PLAUSIBLE *EXPLANATION* FOR WHAT'S *HAPPENED* IN *METROPOLIS!*

AS FAR-FETCHED AS IT SOUNDS...

...EVERY ABLE-BODIED PERSON *OVER 30 YEARS OF AGE* HAS LEFT *METROPOLIS!*

YOU SEE WHAT I MEAN, MR. KENT?

ARE YOU ALL RIGHT, SIR? DO YOU ... ER ... FEEL ANY *URGE* TO LEAVE?

NEVER FELT *BETTER* --!

APRIL AND I ARE GOING TO *CHECK OUT* THE OTHER *TENANTS...*

KEEP YOUR DOOR *LOCKED,* MR. KENT! MAYBE YOU WON'T BE *ABLE* TO LEAVE ... EVEN IF YOU *WANT* TO!

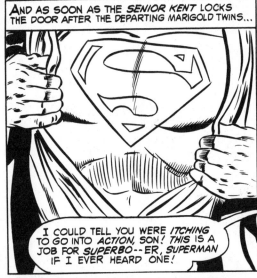

AND AS SOON AS THE *SENIOR KENT* LOCKS THE DOOR AFTER THE DEPARTING MARIGOLD TWINS...

I COULD TELL YOU WERE *ITCHING* TO GO INTO *ACTION,* SON! THIS IS A JOB FOR *SUPERBO* -- ER, *SUPERMAN* IF I EVER HEARD ONE!

IF THIS *OVER-30 EXODUS* IS *TRUE* -- WE'LL HAVE TO DETERMINE WHY *YOU* WEREN'T AFFECTED!

I AGREE, SON! PERHAPS MY *IMMUNITY* MAY PROVIDE A *CLUE* FOR DEALING WITH THIS CRISIS!

THERE'S ONLY *ONE REASON* POSSIBLE WHY I'M *IMMUNE* TO WHATEVER STRANGE FORCE HAS GRIPPED THE OTHERS!

BUT I COULDN'T *DARE* MENTION IT TO CLARK! I GAVE MY *WORD!*

WITHIN SECONDS, A RAPID SCAN OF *TELESCOPIC VISION* SWEEPS ACROSS THE CITY...

I SEE... I BELIEVE... BUT I DON'T UNDERSTAND!

WITH THE EXCEPTION OF *BED-RIDDEN* OVER-30 PATIENTS LAID UP IN HOSPITALS--

--METROPOLIS HAS BEEN COMPLETELY *ROBBED* OF ITS "OLDER" GENERATION!

AND AFTER A SPLIT-SECOND FLIGHT OUTSIDE THE *CITY LIMITS*...

THERE THEY ARE... *THOUSANDS* UPON *THOUSANDS*...!

THEY LOOK LIKE *LOST SOULS*... WITH NOWHERE TO GO!

WELCOME TO METROPOLIS CITY LIMITS

PERRY WHITE... MORGAN EDGE... STEVE LOMBARD! I *KNEW* I'D FIND SOME *FAMILIAR* FACES IN THIS CONFUSION!

AT LAST, *SUPERMAN!* I TOLD EVERYONE YOU'D SHOW UP HERE!

IT'S TIME YOU PUT A *STOP* TO THIS *NONSENSE!*

YOU'VE GOT THE *BALL* NOW, *SUPES*-- WIN ONE FOR *GALAXY!*

BUT THE *ANSWERS* THE *ACTION ACE* RECEIVES ARE EVEN MORE *PUZZLING* THAN THE *QUESTIONS*...

...AND THAT'S THE WAY IT HAPPENED! ONE MINUTE WE WERE ALL GOING ABOUT OUR DAILY ROUTINES--

--AND THE *NEXT MINUTE,* WE FOUND OURSELVES OUTSIDE METROPOLIS-- *OFF-LIMITS!*

AND AS HARD AS WE TRY TO *GO BACK*-- SOMETHING *STOPS* US COLD AT THE *CITY-LINE!*

IT COULD BE A *FORCE-FIELD* HOLDING YOU BACK--

OH, IT'S *BETTER* THAN A *FORCE-FIELD,* SUPERMAN--

5

... MUCH BETTER! I CALL IT "PLEASE-POWER"!

GREAT CAESAR'S GHOST! A VOICE OUT OF THIN AIR!

I KNOW THAT VOICE...!

UHH... WHAT'S THAT STRANGE TUG I FEEL--?

THE NEXT ASTOUNDING INSTANT...

THE METROPOLIS SEWER-SYSTEM?! HOW DID I GET HERE--?

BY PLEASE-POWER, OF COURSE! I WANTED TO SHOW YOU I'VE GOT A SUPER-POWER YOU DON'T HAVE!

STARSHINE! I'VE BEEN LOOKING FORWARD TO MEETING YOU AGAIN!

SO YOU COULD GET EVEN FOR WHAT I DID TO YOU WHEN WE FIRST MET*--?

* This encounter took place last issue! --Julie

THAT WILL COME LATER! FIRST-- ARE YOU RESPONSIBLE FOR THE OVER-30 EXODUS OUT OF METROPOLIS?

HEYYY-- HANDS OFF THE THREADS! LET'S HAVE A LITTLE RESPECT HERE!

NO-- MAKE THAT A LOT OF RESPECT...

...OOO PLEASE!

SOMETHING FORCING ME TO LET GO OF HIM!

YOU'RE ABOUT TO BE GROUNDED, SUPERMAN! BETTER CUT YOURSELF SOME SLACK!

THERE! THAT *DEMO* SHOULD PROVE *YOU'RE* AS *HELPLESS* AGAINST MY *PLEASE-POWER* AS THE *REST* OF THE WORLD!

I HATE TO *ADMIT* IT... BUT THIS *"STARSHINE"* ISN'T JUST TALKING THROUGH HIS *PONCHO!*

SOMEHOW HE'S GAINED THE POWER TO ENFORCE HIS *WILL* ON ANYONE--

--MERELY BY SAYING THE WORD *PLEASE!*

THIS MUST BE HIS IDEA OF *"RESPECT"*: COMPELLING ME TO *BOW DOWN* AT HIS FEET!

AT THAT VERY MOMENT--AS A WISTFUL *ELDERLY MAN* GAZES FROM THE WINDOW OF HIS *SUPER-SON'S* APARTMENT...

JONATHAN KENT! IT IS *VITAL* FOR US TO *COMMUNICATE* WITH YOU AT ONCE!

GREAT JEHOSHAPHAT! NOT *THEM*-- NOT *NOW!* IT'S WAY TOO *SOON* FOR THEM TO BE HERE!

NOT ONLY IS PA KENT *UNIMPRESSED* BY HIS *EERIE, UNEARTHLY* VISITORS -- HE SEEMS DOWNRIGHT *ANNOYED!*

YOU *PROMISED* ME A FULL *30 HOURS* IN THIS TIME-PERIOD -- THAT MEANS I'VE GOT TILL 6 O'CLOCK *TONIGHT!*

WE SHALL NOT GO BACK ON OUR *PROMISE* TO YOU, JONATHAN!

WE ARE HERE TO *ALERT* YOU TO A POSSIBLE *CATASTROPHE* ...AND TO *WARN* YOU NOT TO *INTERFERE!*

AS JONATHAN KENT HEEDS THE *TELEPATHIC VOICE* BEAMING INTO HIS HEAD -- HE CANNOT HELP BUT RECALL HIS *FIRST ENCOUNTER* WITH THE ALIENS STANDING BEFORE HIM ...

...A MEETING WHICH TOOK PLACE IN *SMALLVILLE* MANY YEARS *BEFORE*, WHEN HIS SON WAS A TEEN-AGED *SUPERBOY!*

FOR *HELPING* US AND COMING TO OUR *AID*, EARTHMAN, WE ARE GOING TO *FULFILL* YOUR *FONDEST* DESIRE--

--A *SUBCONSCIOUS* DESIRE YOU ARE NOT EVEN *AWARE* OF!

*As revealed in *SUPERBOY #5*-- MAY, 1980.--*Julie*

7

TO MAKE THIS DEEP *DESIRE* A *REALITY* WOULD BE DEEMED UTTERLY *IMPOSSIBLE* BY YOUR MOST BRILLIANT *SCIENTISTS*-- BUT *NOT* BY US!

ONE DAY SOON, WE SHALL *RETURN* TO *EARTH* TO CARRY OUT OUR *PROMISE!*

AND THE FACT THAT I'M *HERE*-- IN THIS YEAR OF *1980*-- PROVES IT! BUT WHAT'S THIS ABOUT A *CATASTROPHE?*

IF YOU WILL RECALL, JONATHAN ...

"...YOU *MATERIALIZED* IN *METROPOLIS* IN AN *ISOLATED* AREA CHOSEN BY *US* THAT WOULD BE FREE OF TROUBLESOME *WITNESSES!*"

"BUT EVEN *WE* COULD NOT FORESEE EVERY *CONTINGENCY!*"

THAT'LL TEACH YOU TO BEG FOR *HANDOUTS*, YOU NO-GOOD *HIPPIE!*

OOOOFF!

HOW WAS I SUPPOSED TO KNOW THAT DUDE WAS A *MUGGER?* BESIDES, I SAID *PLEASE!*

I CAN STILL REMEMBER MOM TELLING ME OVER AND OVER THAT *PLEASE* WAS A *"MAGIC WORD"* ... THAT I'D GET *WHATEVER* I WANTED JUST BY SAYING *PLEASE!*

SO FAR IT HASN'T WORKED...

I'LL GIVE IT JUST *ONE MORE CHANCE*--

SNIFF WHAT'S *THIS* I'VE WALKED INTO HERE-- A CLOUD OF *ORANGE SMOG?* FAR OUT!

⑧

"OUR *REGA-MISTS* -- WHICH WOULD BE DEEMED A *'MAGIC CLOUD'* BY YOUR PRIMITIVE TECHNOLOGY -- REMAINED *POTENT* FOR A BRIEF TIME *AFTER* YOU *EMERGED,* JONATHAN!"

"LAND O' GOSHEN! ARE YOU TELLING ME THAT... JUST AS THE *REGA-MISTS* MADE IT POSSIBLE FOR MY SECRET DESIRE TO BE GRANTED--"

--*PRECISELY!* THE MISTS ALSO PERFORMED THE SAME FUNCTION FOR THE ERRANT *YOUTH!*

SIMPLY BY *RECITING* A PARTICULAR *WORD* IN YOUR LANGUAGE -- HE CAN VIRTUALLY CAUSE *ANYTHING* TO HAPPEN... TO *ANYONE*--

--*INCLUDING* YOUR *SUPER-SON!*

BUT YOUR TECHNOLOGY IS SO *ADVANCED* YOU CAN PERFORM *MIRACLES* THAT SEEM LIKE SHEER *MAGIC!* SURELY YOU CAN DO *SOMETHING*...

NOTHING -- ANY MORE THAN WE COULD *TERMINATE* YOUR *VISIT* BEFORE IT RUNS ITS *COURSE!*

ONCE SET IN MOTION, *REGA-MIST* EPISODES ARE *IRREVERSIBLE!*

344

BECAUSE YOU BOTH SHARE THE BENEFITS OF THE MISTS, YOU ALONE ARE *IMMUNE* TO THE YOUTH'S NEW-FOUND *POWER!*

BUT SHOULD YOU ATTEMPT *DIRECT CONTACT* WITH HIM TO *ASSIST* YOUR *SON*--

--*BOTH* YOUR *DESIRES* WILL INSTANTLY *CANCEL* EACH OTHER OUT!

AND AS THE SOMBER *SPACE-BENEFACTORS* SHIMMER AND FADE AWAY...

YES... I SHALL *ABIDE* BY YOUR *WARNING*... BUT I NEED TO KNOW THE *SITUATION!*

A *REASONABLE* REQUEST!

GRANT ME THE POWER TO *SEE* MY SON IN ACTION--

CLOSE YOUR EYES AND *CONCENTRATE* ON *SUPERMAN!*

YOU WILL SEE HIM IN YOUR *MIND'S EYE*... YOU WILL EVEN KNOW HIS *THOUGHTS!*

YES! I SEE HIM FROM AFAR...

BUT SOMETHING'S *WRONG!* HE'S *INJURED!*... BADLY *HURTING!*

9

"I DON'T UNDERSTAND -- HOW COULD ANYTHING OR ANYONE *BRUISE* MY *INVULNERABLE* SON? HE'S GROGGY... BARELY *CONSCIOUS!*"

"I'M READING HIS *THOUGHTS!* 'I WAS *HOPING* TO MAKE IT BACK TO MY APART- MENT... BUT I *CAN'T!* TOO WEAK!"

"'FALLING... JUST HAVE ENOUGH ENERGY LEFT TO REACH *LOIS'S* PLACE...'"

LOIS'S PLACE? WHERE'S *THAT?*

WAIT-- I RECALL SOMETHING-- AS THOUGH CLARK *REALLY HAD* BEEN WRITING TO ME ALL THESE YEARS!

YES... *LOIS LANE!*

TWENTY MINUTES *LATER,* AFTER A HURRIED TRIP TO AN APARTMENT BUILDING AT *922 OAK HILL...*

BZZZZ

YES... WHO IS IT?

L. LANE

JONATHAN KENT! I MUST *SPEAK* WITH YOU!

YES... YOU'RE CLARK KENT'S *FATHER* FROM *SMALLVILLE!* I *RECOGNIZE* YOU FROM PHOTOGRAPHS CLARK'S SHOWN ME!

IT'S NICE TO *MEET* YOU, MR. KENT, BUT--

I *KNOW*-- RIGHT NOW YOU'RE *BUSY* TAKING CARE OF A *SICK* FRIEND!

?!? WHY, THAT'S *RIGHT!* BUT *HOW* DID YOU--

NEVER MIND! I'VE GOT TO BE WITH HIM!

10

HAS HE SAID *WHO DID THIS* TO HIM--?

UHHH...

N-NO...HE'S BEEN TOO *DELIRIOUS!* I DON'T THINK HE EVEN KNOWS WE'RE *HERE!*

BUT I *DO* THINK *YOU* HAVE SOME *EXPLAINING* TO DO, MR. KENT!

HUSH, CHILD! HE'S COMING AROUND...

UHHH... *STARSHINE!* HIS POWERS MUST BE *MAGICAL*...OR *SUPER-ADVANCED* EVEN BY *MY* STANDARDS!

ONLY EXPLANATIONS I CAN THINK OF...

"...TO *RATIONALIZE* WHAT *HAPPENED* TO ME!

ALL MY LIFE... STARTING WITH MY *OLD LADY*...I'VE GOTTEN NOTHING BUT *HASSLES* FROM THE *OLDER GENERATION!*

THAT'S WHY I USED MY *PLEASE-POWER* TO MAKE *ALL* OF 'EM *BLOW* THIS TOWN, TAKING THEIR ESTABLISH-MENT *HANG-UPS* WITH 'EM!

SINCE YOU'RE NOT *OVER 30* YET, *SUPES-BABY,* YOU CAN STILL BE *ONE OF US* ...*IF* YOU GET SOME *SMARTS* AND LEARN TO *MELLOW-OUT* LIKE THE REST OF US!

BUT JUST TO MAKE *SURE* YOU GET MY DRIFT *LOUD* AND *CLEAR*... ONE LAST *SPECIAL REQUEST!*

YOU'RE GOING TO TEACH *YOURSELF* A *LESSON,* MAN OF KRYPTON!

I WANT YOU TO *TAKE OFF* AND *THINK* ABOUT WHAT I SAID...WHILE YOU'RE *PUNCHING YOURSELF* TILL YOU'RE *BLACK* AND *BLUE!*

PLEASE!

11

"FIRST HE HAD COMPELLED ME TO HUG MYSELF AS IF I WERE WEARING AN INVISIBLE STRAITJACKET -- AND THE NEXT THING I KNEW..."

¡OFFF!¡ ¡UHHH!¡ EVEN I'M NOT INVULNERABLE TO THE FORCE OF MY OWN SUPER-PUNCHES!

CAN ALREADY FEEL THE BRUISES...

DON'T WORRY ABOUT THE INJURIES, SON! REMEMBER YOUR SUPER-RECUPERATIVE POWERS! ALL YOUR BRUISES WILL HEAL THEMSELVES IN A FEW MORE MINUTES!

WHAT ARE YOU DOING HERE ...IN LOIS'S APARTMENT? YOU WOULDN'T RISK TALKING TO ME THAT WAY UNLESS SHE WERE GONE...!

ON THE CONTRARY, SON -- LOIS IS RIGHT HERE!

GREAT KRYPTON!

Y-YOU CALLED HIM SON... TWICE! BUT IF- IF YOU'RE HIS FATHER THAT CAN ONLY MEAN...

SUPERMAN IS --AND ALWAYS WAS--CLARK KENT!

THAT ABOUT SUMS IT UP, LOIS! HE MAY BE A MAN OF STEEL TO THE WORLD...BUT TO ME, HE'LL ALWAYS BE MY BOY!

WHY, PA? AFTER ALL THE TIMES YOU HELPED ME PROTECT MY SECRET IDENTITY...

...WHY??

CLARK...I DON'T EXPECT YOU TO UNDERSTAND WHAT I DID TODAY!

ALL I CAN ASK YOU TO DO IS NOT TO LOSE FAITH IN ME... AND TRUST ME!

BESIDES -- I'VE BEGUN TO REALIZE LOIS IS AN EXTRA-ORDINARY YOUNG LADY!

I SAW THE WAY SHE RUSHED TO YOUR SIDE AND TENDERLY CARED FOR YOU WHEN YOU COLLAPSED!

YOU SAW?! BUT YOU WEREN'T HERE WHEN THAT HAPPENED!

HOW COULD YOU KNOW...UNLESS YOU HAVE SUPER-VISION, TOO?

12

BECAUSE OF MY *BLUNDER*, YOU TWO FEEL AWKWARD AND UNEASY AROUND EACH OTHER RIGHT NOW... BUT THAT'LL SOON *PASS!*

I MAY BE AN *OLD MAN*, BUT I'M STILL *SHARP* ENOUGH TO SEE THERE'S A LOT *MORE* BETWEEN YOU TWO THAN MEETS THE *EYE!*

IT'S NOT THAT I DON'T *TRUST* YOU, LOIS... BUT THIS IS ALL SO *SUDDEN!* I'M GOING TO NEED *TIME* TO SORT THINGS OUT!

I UNDERSTAND, CLAR--ER...*SUPERMAN!* I'M KIND OF *OFF-BALANCE* MYSELF RIGHT NOW!

I'VE STILL GOT A JOB TO DO--A *MENACE* TO DEAL WITH... AND A WHOLE *CITY* THAT HAS TO BE RETURNED TO *NORMAL!*

WE'LL TALK *LATER*, LOIS!

BE *CAREFUL*, DARLING...

...AND *GOOD LUCK*, SON!

AND AFTER THE *WHOOSH* OF THE DEPARTING *ACTION ACE* FADES AWAY...

I THINK HE'S REALLY *PEEVED*, MR. KENT! HE DELIBERATELY *SNUBBED* YOU ON HIS WAY OUT!

ALL IN ALL, YOU TOOK THE *REVELATION* VERY WELL, LOIS! YOU'RE A LOT LIKE MY *MARTHA* WAS-- *UNFLAPPABLE!*

YOU'RE SWEET, MR. KENT! BUT *THINK* ABOUT IT--

--FOR ALL *YOU* KNOW, MAYBE I HAD *ALREADY* FIGURED OUT FOR *MYSELF* THAT CLARK WAS *SUPERMAN...*

...AND I'VE JUST BEEN *SMART* ENOUGH NOT TO *LET ON!*

WELL, I'LL BE SWITCHED! BEAUTY *AND* BRAINS-- WITH AN *OUTSTANDING* SENSE OF HUMOR TO BOOT!

ER...YOU *WERE* ONLY *JOSHING*... RIGHT?

NOW THAT WOULD BE *TELLING*, WOULDN'T IT? ANYWAY-- I'M SO *GLAD* I FINALLY *MET* YOU!

SAME HERE! OKAY, BE MYSTERIOUS IF YOU LIKE! SOMEDAY YOU AND MY BOY WILL MAKE A *PERFECT MATCH!*

13

AT THAT MOMENT, ON A GRASSY KNOLL IN *METROPOLIS PARK*...

HIDEHO, *SUPES!* HOPE THERE'S NO *HARD FEELINGS* ABOUT OUR LITTLE *RUN-IN!* LET'S BE *BUDDIES*-- WHADDYA SAY?

YOU TOOK THE WORDS RIGHT OUT OF MY MOUTH *STARSHINE!*

I EVEN BROUGHT YOU A *PRESENT* AS A *PEACE-OFFERING!*

HEY, I WASN'T *EXPECTING* ANYTHING LIKE THIS! YOU'RE SURE FULLA *SURPRISES!*

I SUPPOSE YOU *COULD* SAY THAT...

...BUT FOR YOU, SAYING *ANYTHING'S* GOING TO BE *IMPOSSIBLE*--

...ONCE MY REMOTE-CONTROL *MUZZLE* LOCKS INTO PLACE!

MMMFFF! UNNNG!

STOP MUMBLING, STARSHINE! I CAN'T UNDERSTAND A WORD YOU'RE *TRYING* TO SAY!

NOW LISTEN TO *ME:* ONLY MY *SUPER-STRENGTH* CAN *BREAK* THOSE MUZZLE-STRAPS FOR YOU!

BUT *FIRST*-- YOU AND I MUST COME TO AN *UNDERSTANDING!* CAN YOU *DIG* WHERE I'M *COMING FROM*, MAN?

MMMFFF! UNNN!

14

HHHNNN! HHHNNN!

I GATHER THAT'S A *YES!* I HAD A FEELING YOU'D START *SEEING* THINGS IN A DIFFERENT PERSPECTIVE!

OOOOMM!

THERE! NOW THAT YOU'VE GOT A NEW *SLANT* ON EVERYTHING--ONE LAST ORDER OF BUSINESS AND YOUR *REHABILITATION* WILL BE COMPLETE!

YOUR *PEACE MEDALLION* SHOULD BE JUST WHAT I NEED TO FINISH THE JOB!

I'M SUBJECTING YOU TO *SUPER-HYPNOTISM,* STARSHINE!

OBJECT: TO *COMPEL* YOU TO *OBEY* ME!

WHEN I REMOVE THE MUZZLE, YOU WILL SHOUT A *FINAL "PLEASE"*-- TO INSTANTLY *RETURN* ALL THE *OVER-30* CITIZENS BACK TO THEIR RIGHTFUL PLACES IN *METROPOLIS!*

AND AFTER YOU'VE UNDONE ALL THE *DAMAGE* YOU CAUSED... YOU'LL VOW *NEVER* TO USE *PLEASE-POWER* AGAIN!

CLOSE YOUR EYES ONCE IF YOU *UNDERSTAND* AND *OBEY!*

15

STILL UP TO YOUR *LAST-MINUTE* APPEARANCES, CLARK--? ONE OF THESE DAYS IT'S *REALLY* GOING TO BE A *NO-SHOW!*

SORRY ABOUT THAT, LANA! I'VE BEEN TERRIBLY *BUSY* THIS AFTERNOON!

CAN'T TELL HER I SPENT HOURS SEARCHING *METROPOLIS* WITHOUT FINDING A TRACE OF *PA KENT!*

YOU'RE NOT THE *ONLY* ONE WHO'S BEEN *BUSY!* WHEN YOU READ YOUR *SCRIPT,* YOU'LL FIND OUT *SUPERMAN* DEFEATED *STARSHINE* AND THAT EVERYONE OVER THIRTY IS *BACK HOME!*

WISH I COULD SAY THE SAME FOR *DAD!*

OH, BEFORE I *FORGET*-- YOUR *FATHER* STOPPED BY THIS AFTERNOON AND LEFT THIS *NOTE* FOR YOU! HE SAID HE WAS *SORRY* HE COULDN'T STAY *LONGER!*

GREAT SCOTT! I NEVER THOUGHT OF LOOKING FOR HIM *HERE!*

"*DEAR SON*-- HOPE YOU'RE NOT STILL PEEVED AT ME FOR TELLING YOUR *SECRET* TO LOIS! VERY SOON IT MAY NOT *MATTER* AS MUCH AS YOU *THINK!*"

"ANYWAY, I'LL BE BACK IN *SMALLVILLE* BY THE TIME YOU READ THIS! WHY DON'T YOU *DROP* IN FOR A *RETURN VISIT* AFTER YOUR NEWSCAST?"

"ALL MY LOVE --*PA.*"

GOOD EVENING! THIS IS *LANA LANG* KICKING OFF THE WGBS 6 O'CLOCK REPORT FOR THIS *MARCH 6TH,* 1980!

LANA HAS HER *DATES* CROSSED MARCH 6TH WAS *YESTERDAY*-- TODAY IS THE *7TH!*

OUR *TOP STORY* TONIGHT IS THE *KILLER TYPHOON* WHICH RAGED THROUGH THE *SEA OF JAPAN...*

WHAT'S *GOING ON* HERE? THE *KILLER TYPHOON* WAS *YESTERDAY'S* TOP NEWS! *WHY* ISN'T LANA DELIVERING TODAY'S STORY ABOUT *STARSHINE?*

NOW *WHAT?!* PA KENT'S *NOTE* IS *DISAPPEARING* RIGHT BEFORE MY EYES!

EVERYTHING'S SUDDENLY GETTING *HAZY...* MY MIND GOING *BLANK...*

16

AT THAT VERY INSTANT -- HIGH IN THE SKY ABOVE...

REST ASSURED, JONATHAN KENT! AS WE ORIGINALLY PROMISED, NO ONE ON EARTH WILL RECALL ANY OF THE EVENTS OF THE PAST 30 HOURS-- INCLUDING YOUR SUPER-SON!

AS FAR AS EARTH IS CONCERNED-- YOUR "DAY" IN METROPOLIS NEVER HAPPENED!

IN EFFECT WE "FROZE TIME".. IN ORDER TO FULFILL YOUR FONDEST DESIRE WITHOUT UPSETTING THE BALANCE OF THE SPACE-TIME CONTINUUM!

YES... YOU MORE THAN SATISFIED IT-- BY GIVING ME A GLIMPSE OF SOMETHING I THOUGHT WOULD BE IMPOSSIBLE TO SEE--

-- MY SON'S FUTURE AS AN ADULT!

NOW I KNOW HE'S BECOME EVERY BIT THE SUPERMAN MARTHA AND I HOPED HE'D BE! THANK YOU, MY FRIENDS!

AS YOU EARTHLINGS SAY--IT WAS OUR PLEASURE!

AND A FEW MOMENTS AFTER THE WRAP-UP OF THE 6 O'CLOCK REPORT FOR MARCH 6TH...

STUDIO B

I'M MEETING LOIS FOR DINNER AT MARCEL'S... BUT WE COULD MAKE IT A TABLE FOR THREE! CARE TO JOIN US, LUV?

ER... SORRY, LANA! I HAVE A PREVIOUS APPOINTMENT!

ONLY I CAN'T REMEMBER WHAT IT IS!

STUDIO C

HEY, MAN-- CAN YOU DO A GUY A FAVOR AND SPARE SOME CHANGE... PLEASE?

GREAT KRYPTON... IT'S COMING BACK TO ME .... MY "APPOINTMENT"--

A SUPER-SWIFT FLIGHT TO SMALLVILLE AND A CEMETERY...

ODD... I DON'T KNOW WHY I HAD THIS SUDDEN URGE TO VISIT MY FOSTER-PARENTS ... BUT SOMEHOW I FEEL CLOSER TO THEM THAN I'VE FELT IN YEARS...

...ESPECIALLY PA!

JONATHAN KENT

BORN FEB 17 1904

DIED MAY 11 1977

THE END. 17